The Economic Decline of the West

"It's not personal Sonny. It's strictly business."
—Michael Corleone, in The Godfather, 1972

Wim Naudé

The Economic Decline of the West

Guns, Oil and Oligarchs

Wim Naudé
RWTH TIM Institute
RWTH Aachen University
Aachen, Germany

ISBN 978-3-031-82298-8   ISBN 978-3-031-82299-5   (eBook)
https://doi.org/10.1007/978-3-031-82299-5

© The Editor(s) (if applicable) and The Author(s), under exclusive license to Springer Nature Switzerland AG 2025

This work is subject to copyright. All rights are solely and exclusively licensed by the Publisher, whether the whole or part of the material is concerned, specifically the rights of translation, reprinting, reuse of illustrations, recitation, broadcasting, reproduction on microfilms or in any other physical way, and transmission or information storage and retrieval, electronic adaptation, computer software, or by similar or dissimilar methodology now known or hereafter developed.

The use of general descriptive names, registered names, trademarks, service marks, etc. in this publication does not imply, even in the absence of a specific statement, that such names are exempt from the relevant protective laws and regulations and therefore free for general use.
The publisher, the authors and the editors are safe to assume that the advice and information in this book are believed to be true and accurate at the date of publication. Neither the publisher nor the authors or the editors give a warranty, expressed or implied, with respect to the material contained herein or for any errors or omissions that may have been made. The publisher remains neutral with regard to jurisdictional claims in published maps and institutional affiliations.

This Palgrave Macmillan imprint is published by the registered company Springer Nature Switzerland AG.
The registered company address is: Gewerbestrasse 11, 6330 Cham, Switzerland

If disposing of this product, please recycle the paper.

Preface

> Does history have any meaning or purpose? It's full of sound and fury, but signifies nothing. Does the human past have any lessons for our future? Fewer and fewer, if it ever had any to begin with. —Alex Rosenberg, 2012: 3

We humans have a fascination with endings. This is perhaps because we think in terms of narratives—stories. Stories have a beginning, a middle, and an end. Much in life and the universe thus seems to us to conform to this pattern. As individuals, we all have a beginning (our births), mid-life, and death. Firms are started, grow, and eventually dissolve. Empires have a beginning, a middle age, and a period of decline and fall, as many historical examples illustrate. As far as we can tell, even the universe started with a Big Bang birth and will eventually end in a Heat Death. The fascination with endings reflects the need for a satisfactory story—things will hang in the balance without an ending. So, endings are necessary for a good narrative structure. However, endings are also fascinating because they may hint at new beginnings—reflecting that there has always been the idea in human philosophies and religions that there is some cyclical rhythm to nature and reality. Perhaps if we die, we will be resurrected, regenerated, or reincarnated. Perhaps the fall of one Empire will open up space for another, better one, to raise Phoenix-like from its ashes. Perhaps the universe will re-bounce after a great crunch at the end of time.

For various reasons, we have come to live in a time where a preoccupation with endings, specifically with civilizational collapse, has become an increasingly vocal industry. Hardly a day goes by without some prediction or warning that civilization will collapse soon, or that humanity's existential threats have never been more significant. Almost anything nowadays that is unpleasant to stomach has been argued by someone to signal that the end of civilization as we know it is near. For some, the collapse of civilization may spell the end of humanity altogether, an extinction event. For others, civilization collapse will be dramatic, but not extinction. Some, for instance, view the collapse of the Empire of the United States (the West) as inevitable—but not necessarily an overall bad event or catastrophe for all humanity. Others see the global order collapsing with bad outcomes for most of humanity except the West. Still, others seem to invite Armageddon, welcoming the end times in a violent catastrophe and preparing actively for it.

While reading about all the ways the world may end makes for dismal and depressing reading, one may take some solace—or not—from the fact that humans have always been very wrong as far as predicting the end of the world or the collapse of civilization is concerned. For one, we are not extinct. On the contrary, more humans than ever live, on average, longer lives. Trying to make predictions from history or extrapolate from the past is notoriously difficult—if not impossible—and has a bad record. Hence the quote at the top of this page.

This book is, therefore, not about the collapse of civilization or even the collapse of the West, at least not as it is typically approached by drawing historical parallels. The book is about the economic decline of the West (a concept defined in the first chapter), where economic decline is a particular and measurable outcome, which has been extensively documented and even given a label—the Great Stagnation. This book warns that this decline could, if left unchecked, lead to the eventual collapse of the West and even considers how such a collapse may play out from an economic perspective. However, as is emphasized, the collapse of the West per se is not inevitable. Instead, what the book suggests will collapse—and need to collapse if the eventual collapse of the West is to be avoided—is the economic system known as neoliberal capitalism. Over the past 500 years, this system has gradually come to dominate the West—and the Rest. Herein is, however, also a conundrum: failed predictions of the end of capitalism are as frequent as failed predictions of the end of civilization. Perhaps such predictions of capitalism's collapse, at least going back to Karl Marx, just require more time for capitalism to run its course. The problem is that the world is running out of time. Earth Systems' failures, due to the ecological overshoot caused by the dependence of neoliberalism on continued economic growth, are not waiting patiently. The questions that this book ultimately aims to answer are these: *Why is neoliberal capitalism so resilient? Why is this resilience being paid for at an ever-higher price? How can neoliberalism be brought to a faster collapse?*

The short—and simple—answer to these questions is that it is due to the effects of what can be called a Guns, Oil, and Oligarchs nexus. These elements reinforce each other's roles and damage; they are consequences of the Great Stagnation, and in turn, they deepen the Great Stagnation. The simple answer to help reverse or slow down the decline of the West is to break the grip of the oligarchs.

Maastricht, The Netherlands Wim Naudé
October 2024

Acknowledgements

This book grew out of a short monograph that the editors of Foundations and Trends® in Entrepreneurship asked me to write at the end of 2023 about the Great Stagnation and its relationship with entrepreneurship. The monograph was published as *The End of the Empire that Entrepreneurship Built: How Seven Sources of Rot will Undo the West*, *Foundations and Trends® in Entrepreneurship*: Vol. 20: No. 5, pp 481–573. https://doi.org/10.1561/0300000126.

This book also quotes from, and builds on, my *Palgrave Pivot* title published in 2024 and entitled *Economic Growth and Societal Collapse: Beyond Green Growth and Degrowth Fairy Tales*, Palgrave Macmillan Cham. https://doi.org/10.1007/978-3-031-45582-7

As they were very helpful during the writing and publication of this book, I wish to acknowledge the support from Wyndham Hacket Pain, Senior Editor at Palgrave Macmillan and his team. This was my second book with Wyndham as Editor, and his guidance and efficiency are much appreciated. Finally, I am grateful to anonymous referees who read the initial manuscript for their helpful comments and suggestions. The usual disclaimer applies.

Contents

1. **Introduction** — 1
   - 1.1 *Introduction* — 1
   - 1.2 *Concepts and Definitions* — 4
     - 1.2.1 Western Empire — 4
     - 1.2.2 Neoliberal Capitalism and Entrepreneurship — 6
     - 1.2.3 Decline and Collapse — 7
     - 1.2.4 Oligarchy — 8
     - 1.2.5 Military-Industrial Complex and War Economy — 9
   - 1.3 *Is the West Reaching the Limits to Economic Growth?* — 9
     - 1.3.1 The Great Take-Off and the Great Divergence — 10
     - 1.3.2 The Great Acceleration — 11
     - 1.3.3 The Great Stagnation — 12
   - 1.4 *The Future of Growth* — 14
   - 1.5 *Does the Fate of the Soviet Union Await the West?* — 16
   - 1.6 *Drivers and Symptoms of Western Economic Decline* — 17
     - 1.6.1 The Growth Trap — 17
     - 1.6.2 Oligarchs — 18
     - 1.6.3 Oil — 18
     - 1.6.4 Guns — 18
   - 1.7 *The End?* — 19

2. **The Economic Growth Trap** — 21
   - 2.1 *Introduction* — 21
   - 2.2 *The Myth of Perpetual Economic Growth* — 23

		2.2.1	The Grow-or-Die Golden Rule: Economic Growth as an Imperative	25
		2.2.2	Escaping from Its Own Exhaust: The Firm Growth Imperative	28
	2.3	The Dangers of the Perpetual Growth Myth		30
		2.3.1	Dismantling the Welfare State	31
		2.3.2	Undermining Economic Stability	33
		2.3.3	The Problem of Bigness: Enter the Oligarchs	33
		2.3.4	A Ghastly Future: Ecological Overshoot	34
		2.3.5	Achilles' Lance: The Myth of Sustainable Business and Entrepreneurship	37
		2.3.6	A Nation of Mammon: Erosion of the Social Fabric	39
		2.3.7	Triggering a Global Polycrisis?	42
	2.4	The Great Stagnation		43
		2.4.1	Outline of the Ossified Economy	43
		2.4.2	Let the Zero-Sum Games Begin	45
		2.4.3	The Great Enshittification	47
	2.5	Anthropocene Traps		50
	2.6	Concluding Remarks		53
3	**Oligarchs**			55
	3.1	Introduction		55
	3.2	The Rise and Nature of the Oligarchy		56
		3.2.1	Definition of Oligarchy	56
		3.2.2	Who Is the Oligarchy?	58
		3.2.3	Rise of the Oligarchy	62
		3.2.4	Tenets of Neoliberal Ideology	64
		3.2.5	The Financial Elites: The Banker's Takeover	66
		3.2.6	The Rise and Financialization of Industrial Agriculture	71
		3.2.7	The Tech Bro's and Digital Dystopias	72
	3.3	How the Oligarchy Wields Influence and Control		73
	3.4	The Oligarchy and Declining Innovation		77
	3.5	The Oligarchy and the Decline of Science		87
	3.6	The Oligarchy and Decentralized, Democratic Decision-Making		91
	3.7	Concluding Remarks		95

4 Oil   97
- 4.1 Introduction   97
- 4.2 The Energy-Economy Nexus   99
  - 4.2.1 The Nature of Fossil Fuels   99
  - 4.2.2 Energy Blindness and the Tooth Fairy Syndrome   100
  - 4.2.3 The Hydrocarbon Age and Its End   101
- 4.3 The Energy-Environment Nexus   108
  - 4.3.1 The Driver of Climate Change   108
  - 4.3.2 A Ghastly Future   111
  - 4.3.3 Energy Cannibalism and the Complexities of the Energy Transition   114
  - 4.3.4 The Fossil Fuel Oligarchy   115
- 4.4 The Energy-Conflict Nexus   119
  - 4.4.1 The Future Tinderbox   119
  - 4.4.2 How Oil Fuels War   120
- 4.5 Concluding Remarks   123

5 Guns   125
- 5.1 Introduction: The Road to Barbarism   125
- 5.2 From the Business Plot to Bombenomics   127
  - 5.2.1 Gangsters of Capitalism   127
  - 5.2.2 War Is a Racket   128
  - 5.2.3 The War on Terror   130
  - 5.2.4 The Militarization of Africa   131
  - 5.2.5 The Expansion of NATO and the War in Ukraine   135
  - 5.2.6 Reshaping the Middle East   142
  - 5.2.7 The Grand Chess Board: Containing China   146
  - 5.2.8 Bombenomics   148
- 5.3 The Rise and Rise of the Military-Industrial Complex   150
  - 5.3.1 Diplomacy by Armed Force Alone   150
  - 5.3.2 The Military-Industrial Complex as an Oligarchy   153
  - 5.3.3 Europe as Cash-Cow for the Military-Industrial Complex   154
- 5.4 Silicon Valley's Pivot to the Military-Industrial Complex   156
  - 5.4.1 Silicon Valley Hawks   156
  - 5.4.2 A Seat at the Table of the Permanent War Economy   157
  - 5.4.3 Counting the Spoils of War   158
  - 5.4.4 Murder on an Industrial Scale   160
- 5.5 Economic Warfare with a Third of the World   162

	5.6	How the War Economy Contributes to the Decline of the West	165
	5.7	Concluding Remarks: A Dangerous and Delusional Hegemon?	170
6	**The End**		173
	6.1	Introduction	173
	6.2	Broad Narratives of Collapse	175
		6.2.1 Defining Collapse	175
		6.2.2 From Spengler to the Eventual Todd	176
		6.2.3 Through the Kübler-Ross Grief Cycle	179
		6.2.4 Over the Seneca Cliff	179
	6.3	War and Global Warming for the Rest of Us	180
		6.3.1 Environmental Collapse	181
		6.3.2 Economic Collapse	183
		6.3.3 Political Collapse	188
		6.3.4 Population and Collapse	192
	6.4	Declinists vs. Optimists	195
	6.5	Concluding Remarks: Ars Moriendi	197
7	**Beyond the Growth Trap**		199
	7.1	Introduction	199
	7.2	The Nature of a Post-growth Society	201
	7.3	Achieving Post-Growth via Degrowth	203
	7.4	Business, Entrepreneurship, and Degrowth: Compatible?	204
	7.5	Dismantling the Entrepreneurial Ecosystem	206
		7.5.1 Free from Innovation	207
		7.5.2 Free from Finance	207
		7.5.3 Free from Profits	208
		7.5.4 Free from Globalization	208
		7.5.5 Free from Material Pursuits	209
	7.6	Holding Business Firms Fully Accountable	209
	7.7	Will Rosa Luxemburg Have the Last Word?	210
	7.8	Conclusion: Damned If You Do, Damned If You Don't	212

References 215

Index 261

About the Author

Wim Naudé, PhD is a development economist and a graduate of the University of Warwick (UK). His academic journey has seen him serve as a lecturer and research officer at the University of Oxford (UK), Senior Research Fellow at the World Institute for Development Economics Research (WIDER) at the United Nations University (Finland) and Professor of Business and Entrepreneurship at Maastricht University (the Netherlands).

He is a Fellow of the African Studies Centre, University of Leiden (the Netherlands), Visiting Professor of Technology and Development at the TIM institute at RWTH Aachen University (Germany), and Distinguished Visiting Professor of Economics at the University of Johannesburg (South Africa). In 2022–2023, he was a top-ten candidate for the Dutch Green Left Party (GroenLinks) in the country's provincial parliamentary elections.

Wim's early career took a unique turn when he became a member of the liberation movement in South Africa. He served for five years as an elected councillor for the African National Congress (ANC) in the first democratic local government in the country (2000–2006).

His scholarly work deals with the relationships between technological innovation, entrepreneurship, trade, and economic growth and development. This work has been published widely in peer-reviewed scientific journals, and he has been editor, co-editor, and author of several academic books published by, amongst others, Palgrave Macmillan, Oxford University Press, Routledge, Springer, and Cambridge University Press.

He is the author of *Economic Growth and Societal Collapse: Beyond Green Growth and Degrowth Fairy Tales,* which was published by Palgrave Macmillan in 2023.

According to Stanford University and Elsevier's Global Ranking of Scientists (2022, 2023, 2024), Wim is among the top 2% of scientists worldwide.

He lives in Maastricht, the Netherlands.

Abbreviations

ABCD	Archer Daniels Midland (ADM), Bunge, Cargill, and Louis Dreyfus
AI	Artificial Intelligence
ARPA	Advanced Research Projects Agency
AU	African Union
BRICS+	Brazil, Russia, India, China, and South Africa, plus new members.
CBO	Congressional Budget Office
CDOs	Collateralized Debt Obligations
CSCE	Conference on Security and Cooperation in Europe
DARPA	Defense Advanced Research Projects Agency
DHS	Department of Homeland Security
ECS	Equilibrium Climate Sensitivity
EES	Entrepreneurial Ecosystems
ENSO	El Niño-Southern Oscillation
EROI	Energy Return on Energy Invested
ESG	Environmental, Social and Governance
EU	European Union
GDP	Gross Domestic Product
GFC	Global Financial Crisis
GHG	Greenhouse Gas
GIS	Greenland Ice Sheet
GJ	Gigajoules
GMST	Global Mean Surface Temperature
GPS	Global Positioning System
GWP	Global World Production
HGFs	High-Growth Firms
ICC	International Criminal Court
ICJ	International Court of Justice

ICT	Information and Communication Technology
IEP	Institute for Economics and Peace
IMF	International Monetary Fund
IPCC	Intergovernmental Panel on Climate Change
ISM	Indian Summer Monsoon
km^3	Cubic kilometres
LCS	Local Currency Settlements
LtG	Limits to Growth (study)
MF	Material Footprint
MIC	Military Industrial Complex
ML	Machine Learning
Mt/y	Million tonnes per year
NASA	National Aeronautics and Space Administration
NATO	North Atlantic Treaty Organization
NHS	National Health Service
NWF	National Wealth Fund
ODA	Official Development Assistance
OECD	Organisation for Economic Cooperation and Development
PMC	Private Military Companies
R&D	Research and Development
REAIM	Responsible AI in the Military Domain
RSF	Rapid Support Force (Sudan)
SDGs	Sustainable Development Goals
SIPRI	Stockholm International Peace Research Institute
SMEs	Small and Medium Enterprises
TBTF	Too Big to Fail
THC	Atlantic Thermohaline Circulation
TNI	Transnational Institute
UK	United Kingdom
UN	United Nations
U.S. or US	United States of America
US-AFRICOM	United States Africa Command
UAE	United Arab Emirates
WAIS	West Antarctic Ice Sheet
WAM	Sahara/Sahel and West African Monsoon
WEF	World Economic Forum
WMD	Weapons of Mass Destruction
WMO	World Meteorological Organization
WW2/WWII	World War Two

List of Figures

Fig. 1.1	GDP per capita, West and the Rest, 1820–2018. (Source: Author's compilation based on data from Our World in Data)	11
Fig. 1.2	Capitalism is failing to maintain economic growth: % growth in advanced economies, 5-yr MA, 1978–2023. (Source: Author's compilation based on data from the World Bank Development Indicators Online)	13
Fig. 2.1	World Material Footprint (t) and Real GDP (US$), 1970–2019. (Source: Author, based on data from UNEP's Global Material Flows Database)	36
Fig. 2.2	World GDP and Greenhouse Gas Emissions, 1990–2022. (Source: Author, based on data from the World Bank's World Development Indicators Online)	36
Fig. 2.3	Share of Top 10% in pre-tax national income, selected countries, 1910–2022. (Source: Our World in Data.org/economic-inequality CC BY, using World Income Inequality Database WID.world 2024 as source)	40
Fig. 3.1	Share of top 1% in pre-tax national income, US, 1913–2022. (Source: Author, based on data from the World Income Inequality Database, https://wid.world)	58
Fig. 3.2	The Zero-Sum Games have Begun: GDP per Capita growth per Decade in Western Europe, 1820s to 2010s. (Source: Naudé, 2023a: 111, which is based on data from the Maddison Project Database)	81
Fig. 3.3	The decline in hourly labour productivity growth in the UK, 1760–2016, 10-yr MA (Source: Author's Compilation on Bank of England Data "An A millennium of macroeconomic data")	82

Fig. 4.1	World GDP and fossil fuel consumption, 1820–2018. (Source: Naudé, 2023a: 50)	102
Fig. 4.2	Rising oil prices dampens economic growth: World GDP growth and oil prices, 1955–2021. (Source: Author's compilation based on data from the World Bank Development Indicators Online and Our World in Data)	103
Fig. 4.3	Peak Oil: Hubbert's prediction for the US. (Source: Naudé, 2023a: 53, which is adapted from Fix [2020b, Fig. 2])	105
Fig. 4.4	Relative energy consumption per capita, the West and China, 1965–2022. (Source: Author's compilation based on data from BP's Energy Institute Statistical Review of World Energy)	107
Fig. 4.5	Carbon emissions and global warming, 1850–2022. (Source: Author's compilation based on data from Our World in Data: https://github.com/owid/co2-data)	109
Fig. 5.1	Oil Revenue and a War Chest: Russia's Imports, Exports, and Foreign Exchange Reserves, 2000–2023 (Source: Author's compilation based on data from the World Bank Development Indicators Online and Yermakov, 2024, p. 3)	137
Fig. 5.2	Militarization of the USA and Europe, Relative to the World (Source: Author's calculations based on SIPRI Military Expenditure Database)	151
Fig. 5.3	Economic Warfare by the West, Active US Sanctions, April 2024 (Source: Author's compilation based on data from Stein & Cocco, 2024a, 2024b)	163
Fig. 6.1	The Seneca Cliff (Source: Naudé, 2023a:131, based on Bardi, 2020)	180

List of Tables

Table 1.1	The Great Acceleration in numbers, 1950–2015	12
Table 2.1	Anthropocene traps	51
Table 4.1	Top 21 fossil-fuel companies in the world	117
Table 5.1	US Arms Sales to African Countries, 2009–2021, US$ millions	132

CHAPTER 1

Introduction

1.1 Introduction

Over the centuries, various empires rose and fell in the far western peninsula of Asia now known as Western Europe—from the Greek Republics to the Roman Empire in antiquity to the post-Renaissance Portuguese, Spanish, Dutch, and British empires. More recently, following the Industrial Revolution that started in the late eighteenth century, Western Europe and its "Western offshoots"—the United States (US) primarily—have evolved into a global empire. After World War II, and under the hegemony of the US, the notion of the "West" as a modern-day empire was formed.

The rise of the West since the Industrial Revolution has significantly shaped the modern global economy and political systems, much as empires did in the past, but on a much larger scale. This is reflected in the global impact of humanity not only on the complex and interdependent global economic system but in its impact on Earth Systems—to the extent that the last 70 years have been argued to be heralding an entirely new geological epoch, the Anthropocene.

For example, from around 1820, Global World Production (GWP) grew exponentially. Today, the average citizen has an income around 5600% higher than it was roughly 11,000 years ago and uses around ten times as much energy as the average citizen back then (Syvitski et al.,

2020). This remarkable transformation of human society from largely Neolithic-type farmers and feudal serfs into the modern West with its globe-spanning business empires has been termed the *Great Take-Off* (Landes et al., 2010; Mokyr, 2016).

The Great Take-Off has generated a large literature explaining why and how it happened, and asking whether it can be sustained, and, if not, when this empire will decline and even collapse. As Gordon (2012: 1) remarked, "There was virtually no economic growth before 1750, suggesting that the rapid progress made over the past 250 years could well be a unique episode in human history rather than a guarantee of endless future advance at the same rate."

In 1973 the Club of Rome's Limits to Growth (LtG) study's business-as-usual scenario warned of collapse setting in around the 2030s, give or take (Meadows et al., 1971). A recent update of the LtG model found that the world is closely tracking the business-as-usual scenario (Turner, 2014). Various scholars have in recent years built on the pioneering work of Olson (1982) and Tainter (1988) on civilizational collapse or degrading, including Bardi (2020), Bostrom (2013), Diamond (2005), Gowdy (2020), Kotkin (2020), Odum and Odum (2001), Ord (2020), Turchin (2023), Naudé (2023b), and, to an extent, Varoufakis (2023). This list of authors writing on decline and collapse grows almost daily.

This book argues that the Western, US-led Empire is in economic decline and makes the case by invoking a terrible threesome of interrelated causes and symptoms: Guns, Oil, and Oligarchy. The *Guns-Oil-Oligarchy* nexus refers to how the West has gradually, over time, been caught in a Growth Trap, facing a gradual *Great Stagnation* in economic fortunes, increasingly reverted to Guns (a Permanent War Economy), saw its economy become ever more concentrated and dominated by a class of billionaire oligarchs, and remained deeply dependent on oil, which, however, is driving catastrophic climate change through the carbon emissions associated with its use, and which is inevitably declining in terms of access and affordability.

The economic decline of the West that is explained with reference to this *Guns-Oil-Oligarchy* nexus may end in its collapse. This is not necessary, however; hence, this book is not primarily about predicting or explaining the collapse of the West or "civilization." To emphasize, rather than dwell on collapse, this book explains how, with the backdrop of the Great Stagnation, climate change and the decline in affordable and easily accessible energy—and hence Peak Oil—the West is inflicting on itself further, and completely avoidable damage, through the perpetuation of oligarchies and war. Although it is unlikely that the West will reverse its relative decline as an economic power, much damage, death, and destruction can be avoided if the West can jettison the oligarchy and the Permanent War Economy and manage the slow and painful end of fossil fuels smoothly.

The economics of how these lead to decline is rather simple, hence the subtitle of this book. Taking the simplifying view by explaining the West's decline through the lenses of the *Guns-Oil-Oligarchy* provides a sobering counter-narrative to the current fashion to *complexify* and complicate the grand global challenges that humanity is said to confront, often with dramatic and newly minted labels such as "poly-crisis" or "meta-crisis." For instance, Bradshaw et al. (2021: 1) claim that threats to humanity are now so great that "is difficult to grasp for even well-informed experts." Although climate science, biology, and complex systems thinking are indeed complicated, and economics often seems complex due to being presented in unnecessarily intricate math (economists try to ape physicists), this book shows that one does not need to be an expert in these to understand the basic drivers and symptoms of the decline of the West, which manifest itself in many, if not most, of the broad pathologies the world is currently suffering from. One does not need to understand the workings of the internal combustion engine to understand that a speeding car rushing towards the cliff without functioning breaks is courting disaster.

While the focus is on economic decline and not so much on collapse, the implication is that economic decline can eventually trigger a collapse. Suppose this book somehow makes a subtle case for a *welcome* collapse. In that case, it implies that what needs to collapse is not the West, or its constituent countries as such, but the system of neoliberal global capitalism that has come to mark the West and is entrenching its Growth Trap. Mitigating further climate change, adapting to a world that wreaks less havoc on Earth Systems, phasing out the use of greenhouse gas (GHG) emitting fossil fuels, and pulling the world back from the brink of a nuclear war necessitate the collapse of the system of neoliberalism capitalism whose slash and burn doctrine is not only hastening the economic decline of the West but moreover ultimately does threaten the prospects of the Earth as habitable planet.

Herein is, however, also a conundrum: failed predictions of the end of capitalism are as frequent as failed predictions of the end of civilization.

Perhaps such predictions of capitalism's collapse, at least going back to Karl Marx, just require more time for capitalism to run its course. The problem is that the world is running out of time. Earth Systems' failures, due to the ecological overshoot caused by the dependence of neoliberalism on continued economic growth, are not waiting patiently. The questions that this book ultimately aims to answer are: *Why is neoliberal capitalism so resilient? Why is this resilience being paid for at an ever-higher price? How can neoliberalism be brought to a faster collapse?*

Thus, in a sense, this book *is* about the collapse, not only of the West but of civilization, as the unchecked and out-of-control system of neoliberal capitalism is turning the world into a slaughterhouse. Hence, this book extends and prefaces the current literature on collapse. It also complements the literature on imminent threats and crises, such as Roubini (2022), which focuses on the imminent occurrence of disasters ("megathreats") that could trigger collapse. In contrast to imminent threats, this book discusses three core and slow-burning issues that weaken the West subtly over a span of time (Guns, Oil, and Oligarchs), which is precisely why they are eventually more destructive.

The rest of this introductory chapter will set out the key concepts and definitions in Section 1.2 and then provide background for the chapters, then follow by presenting the economic rise of the West in Section 1.3, noting that from a *Great Take-Off*, the West is now in a *Great Stagnation*. Section 1.4 explores the future of growth, providing background for Chap. 2. Then, Section 1.5 asks whether the West will suffer the same fate as the Soviet Union, which suffered a long and gradual economic ossification followed by a sudden collapse. Section 1.6 sets out and provides broad explanations of the terrible threesome—Guns, Oil, and Oligarchs—that are advanced as drivers of economic decline in the West, pointing to some, at least superficial, resemblances with the Soviet Union, where militarization and centralized political and economic authority are widely amongst the reasons for its decline and eventual collapse. Section 1.7 concludes.

1.2 Concepts and Definitions

1.2.1 Western Empire

Empire can be defined as "the implementation of an economic, social, and cognitive order historically birthed through violent colonial subjugation by Western European powers, and subsequently constituted and defended by multinational corporations, multilateral trading and military arrangements, global financial and trade institutions, among others" (Almeida et al., 2023: 2).

Thus, for purposes of this book, Empire will refer to the West—mainly the US, Europe, and the so-called Western offshoots such as Australia and New Zealand. This is the most recent and wealthiest of "Western empires," evolving from many smaller, prototypical empires such as the Venetian, Portuguese, Spanish, Dutch, French, and British "empires." These emerged roughly a thousand years after the collapse of the Roman Empire—a collapse which arguably made possible the rise of new empires in Western Europe, which then spread through offshoots (Greer, 2005). Karl Marx (1867) saw these prototypical empires arising in the fifteenth and sixteenth centuries as heralding the beginnings of modern "capitalism."

Mokyr (2007: 85) argues that it was the rot that had set into the ruling elites of the Middle Ages that allowed the modern West to start emerging after the Middle Ages since "by the beginning of the sixteenth century, the system has rotted away, so badly that it becomes impossible for the powers representing the status quo to suppress new ideas and innovation. Not so much because they are becoming more receptive to new ideas, but because they just cannot get their act together."

Roughly by 1950 the "West" emerged as a reasonably coherent empire led by the US (although it avoids the label empire). The half-century after 1950s has been its peak. It is a period that, as will be explained below, has been described as the *Great Acceleration* and as the start of the Anthropocene, a proposed new geological epoch[1] (Steffen et al., 2015b; Head et al., 2021).

There is a vast and continually expanding literature that tries to explain the rise of the West, also in relation to non-Western empires, over a very long period of history. See, for example, Morris (2010), who ascribes it to geography, and Jared Diamond (1997), who memorably pointed to the West's advantages in "Guns, Germs, and Steel." It is not the purpose of this book to review or add to this, at times, Eurocentric and controversial literature, but rather to take the West as defined here and examine sources of rot contributing to its economic decline. As such, this book is not

---

[1] In early 2024 the International Union of Geological Sciences rejected the formal adoption of the term Anthropocene as a new geological epoch (Witze, 2024).

concerned about Western civilization, which has been argued to be an ideological construct[2] (Morris, 2010).

1.2.2 Neoliberal Capitalism and Entrepreneurship

Because Western economies have been based on neoliberal capitalism, increasingly since the fifteenth century but most substantially after World War II, this book will focus particularly on this system and its notions and hero-worship of entrepreneurship. Chapter 2 explains this in detail.

Neoliberal capitalism, which is "capitalism on steroids" (Monbiot & Hutchison, 2024, p. 9), can be described as

> an economic system founded on colonial looting. It operates on a constantly shifting and self-consuming frontier, on which both state and powerful private interests use their laws, backed by the threat of violence, to turn shared resources into exclusive property, and to transform natural wealth, labor and money into commodities that can be accumulated. (Monbiot & Hutchison, 2024: 8)

Within this system, entrepreneurs are the individuals who create, finance, and grow firms and often manage them. They spot opportunities for profitable business, and as Chap. 2 explains in more detail, the need for profits is built into neoliberal capitalism and necessitates economic growth. Today, most of the top 1% of individuals at the top of the income distribution, the billionaire elite, are entrepreneurs (Brüggemann, 2021; Smith et al., 2019). They make up the oligarchy.

The extant literature has somewhat neglected a neoliberal capitalism/entrepreneurship lens on collapse, but not wholly so. The work of Karl Marx and, more recently, Mancur Olson and Thomas Piketty has already implied, even if somewhat indirectly, that capitalism with entrepreneurship may be a special feature during only a transient stage in history.

Marx (1867), for instance, argued that capitalism would evolve into communism, thus concluding the age of private entrepreneurship and property as it has been known. Olson (1982) put forward a theoretical model in which a long period of social stability sees the rise of special interest groups (such as labour unions) and social rigidities (such as regulatory creep) that eventually stifle innovative policies and entrepreneurship.

---

[2] And, as Mohandas Gandhi famously quipped when asked what he thought about Western civilization, "I think it may be a very good idea" (Lal, 2009: 281).

Piketty (2014) provided a model that implies that productive entrepreneurship would be feasible only when the rate of economic growth (g) exceeds the rate of return on assets (r)—when it does not when $r>g$—which he argues has been the case for most of history.[3] If so, the wealthy would live from the returns to savings, inequality would rise, new start-ups would face growing financing constraints, and entrepreneurship-driven growth would decline. According to Marx and Piketty, neoliberal capitalism undermines itself by fostering ever-higher levels of inequality due to the Growth Trap (see Chap. 2).

Similarly, in Olson's (1982) analysis, the pursuit of special interests gives rise to "distributional coalitions," which, although improving the position of the coalition members, reduces overall prosperity, leading to "institutional sclerosis."

The threats to the West—and the rest of the planet—that are outlined in this book, while not presented as a formal theory of social change as Marx, Olson and Piketty did, are, however, consistent with their overall narratives and provide, a set of case studies of how the Empire of the West undermines itself.

1.2.3 Decline and Collapse

The economic *decline* of the West meant the absolute and relative deterioration of the economic development level of the West. Absolute economic decline is reflected in declining economic and productivity growth rates, worsening income and wealth distributions, decreasing life spans and health outcomes, increases in addictions and "deaths of despair," a "crisis of early deaths," and a deterioration in the ecological systems supporting the economy. The relative decline is reflected in the deterioration of the West's control over global resources, for instance, in its smaller share of global GDP or energy use over time. It spells the end of Western hegemony.

Thus, decline is different from collapse. As indicated, the West's economic decline does not have to entail its collapse, although, as this book explains, it makes it more likely.

---

[3] Krugman (2014) summarizes Piketty's (2014) core arguments, explaining that "historically, r has almost always exceeded g [...] the kind of society we consider normal, in which high incomes reflect personal achievement rather than inherited wealth, is in fact an aberration driven by this exceptional period."

What is collapse? Tainter (1988) defined collapse as "a phase transition that leads to a state of reduced complexity, typically being rapid and abrupt." Important to note is that *the collapse* of the West does not have to imply the extinction of humanity. Collapse does not require an existential risk (*x-risk*), nor does it imply one.[4] If collapse entails reduced complexity, as in Tainter's (1988) definition, then it may make humanity more vulnerable to existential risks (Aschenbrenner, 2020).

Distinguishing collapse from extinction leaves the possibility open for a successive empire to arise, just as the modern West eventually arose from the ashes of the collapsed Roman Empire (Greer, 2005). In this sense, as will also be discussed in Chap. 6, collapse may not necessarily be all negative.

1.2.4 Oligarchy

Chapter 3 of this book discusses the rise of an oligarchy in the West in depth, and Chap. 5 describes how a military-industrial oligarchy emerged.

Curtis (2024) describes oligarchy as a system "where a small number of people exert control over the state," often operating under *the guise of democratic institutions.* An oligarchy is thus a system where a small, elite, and wealthy group wields significant economic and, consequently, political power, often at the expense of the broader population. Winters and Page (2009: 752) define oligarchy as "a specific kind of minority power that is fundamentally material in character," where "the wealthiest citizens deploy unique and concentrated power resources to defend their unique minority interests."

The oligarchy forms a "Power Elite" as described in 1956 by Mills (1956), who argued that a small group of individuals already back then controlled the most significant institutions in American society, namely the military, corporate, and political spheres, and that the ordinary citizen has limited influence over the decisions that shape their lives.

Oligarchs' political power can turn a democratic country into a *Plutocracy*, a term used to refer to a society ruled by an oligarchy, that is, individuals who have political influence or power primarily due to their wealth. One of the first warnings about a US Plutocracy was founded in

---

[4] Bostrom (2002) defines existential risk and provides a typology. An existential risk is "where an adverse outcome would either annihilate Earth-originating intelligent life or permanently and drastically curtail its potential" (Bostrom, 2002: 2).

1895 by Howard (1895). More recently, Chomsky (2017), Formisano (2015), Kuhner (2015), Mahbubani (2022), and Winters and Page (2009) are amongst those who have argued that the US is an oligarchy/plutocracy rather than a democracy.[5] According to Sachs (2018), as a result of becoming a plutocracy, *"American politics has become a game of, by, and for corporate interests, with tax cuts for the rich, deregulation for polluters, and war and global warming for the rest of us."*

1.2.5 Military-Industrial Complex and War Economy

The term "military-industrial complex" is often ascribed to US President Dwight D. Eisenhower, who, in his farewell address in 1961, described—and warned against—the close relationship between the military and the defence industry that supplies it with weapons, equipment, and services (Dunne & Sköns, 2009; Turley, 2014; Newlove-Eriksson & Eriksson, 2023).

Generally, the term refers to "the groups within society that benefit from military spending and its growth" (Dunne & Sköns, 2009: 2). More formally, it can be defined as "a coalition of interests and actors among defence firms and the military establishment" that "could shape policy, specifically that it could motivate the nation to start unwarranted wars." Moreover, "participants in the military-industrial complex share interest in high military expenditures, and a persistence of arms races" (Newlove-Eriksson & Eriksson, 2023: 562).

Oakes (1944) defined a War Economy to exist "whenever the government's expenditures for war (or 'national defense') become a legitimate and significant end-purpose of economic activity."

The definition of the MIC suggests that the perpetuation of a war economy becomes an objective.

1.3 Is the West Reaching the Limits to Economic Growth?

The introduction (Section 1.1) mentioned that the Western Empire arose out of the Industrial Revolution from around 1800 and experienced a subsequent two centuries of exponential economic growth, resulting in an unprecedented level of economic activity, wealth and income in the world.

---

[5] Winters and Page (2009) argue that a plutocracy can easily co-exist with a democracy.

This has been labelled the *Great Take-Off* (and a *Great Acceleration* since the 1950s), which also resulted in a Great Divergence between the West and the Rest, defining the global economic dominance and establishment of the "Western Empire."

By the end of the twentieth century, however, for various complex reasons, not all of which are entirely understood but which likely include declining population growth and the decline in the affordability of oil (see Chap. 4), the West has been experiencing a Great Stagnation, marked by declining economic and productivity growth and a decline in innovativeness. The Great Take-Off, Great Acceleration, and Great Stagnation are briefly outlined in this section to provide the necessary background for the discussion in Chap. 2 on the Growth Trap.

1.3.1 The Great Take-Off and the Great Divergence

One measure that perhaps most clearly summarizes the unique historical achievement and predicament of the West's empire is the explosion in economic growth since around 1800. This is depicted in Fig. 1.1, which shows Gross Domestic Product (GDP) per capita (in 2011 international $) from 1820 to 2018.

Figure 1.1 shows the hockey-stick shapes of GDP per capita in the West—in Western Europe and in the Western Offshoots of the US, Canada, Australia, and New Zealand. It also shows how the West has progressively moved away from the rest—the world average—in terms of economic size. By 2018, average incomes in the West were four to five times that of the world average. This has been called the Great Divergence (Pomeranz, 2021).

The 1820s were, of course, when the Industrial Revolution was in full swing in Europe, where it had started in Britain, due to a confluence, perhaps a lucky coincidence, of circumstances, including access to cheap coal, access to Enlightenment science, access to the transatlantic trade and hence the natural resources of North America, and institutions and policies that facilitated entrepreneurship, such as property rights, the rule of law, and the "mother of all industrial policies" (Robinson, 2009). The essence of these circumstances was, as Mokyr (2003) called it, that "useful knowledge" was generated—knowledge that could be, in a word, commercialized, and which commercialization often generated further helpful knowledge.

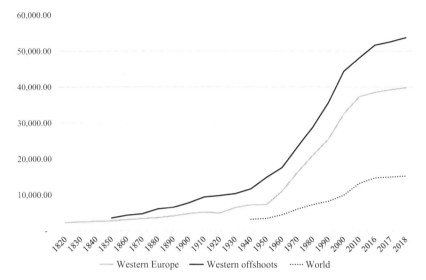

Fig. 1.1 GDP per capita, West and the Rest, 1820–2018. (Source: Author's compilation based on data from Our World in Data)

1.3.2 The Great Acceleration

The most rapid increase in income and wealth in the West occurred after 1950. Figure 1.1 shows how the slope of the lines swivels up after 1950. Table 1.1 summarizes the Great Acceleration.

Table 1.1 shows that global GDP increased by 1487% between 1950 and 2015. As noted by Naudé (2023a: 29), the "impact of this increase in the scale of human economic activity has been a tremendous uptake of material resources, for instance, as reflected in the 414% increase in energy consumption, 3115% increase in cement production and 765% increase in iron and steel production, amongst others."

The *Great Take-Off* and the *Great Acceleration* created unprecedented-sized economies and wealth. It also saw reductions in global poverty: For instance, in the hour that it will take to read this chapter, another 10,000 people will have escaped from absolute poverty.[6] Many other measures of

---

[6] One can track the drop in global poverty using the World Poverty Clock https://worldpoverty.io/headline).

Table 1.1 The Great Acceleration in numbers, 1950–2015

Measure	1950	2015	% Change since 1950
World population (millions)	2499	7349	194
Global energy consumption (EJ/y)	100	514	414
Global GDP (billions 1990 international $)	4656	73,902	1487
Global reservoir capacity (km^3)	705	15,534	2103
Number of dams	7361	50,346	584
Plastic production (Mt/y)	2	381	18,950
Cement production (Mt/y)	130	4180	3115
Ammonia (NH$_3$) production (Mt/y)	2	175	8650
Copper production (Mt/y)	2.38	19.10	703
Iron and steel production (Mt/y)	134	1160	765
Aluminium production (Mt/y)	2	58	2800

(Source: Naudé, 2023a: 29, who based it on Table 1.1 in Head et al., 2021: 5)

human development are showing similar improvements, as Pinker (2018) and Ridley (2011) document.

But not all is well: the Great Take-Off and Great Acceleration were accompanied by growing disparities and a growing ecological footprint—even an overshoot—in terms of its material demands (Table 1.1). Its sustainability is not at all guaranteed. As Gordon (2012: 1) remarked, "There was virtually no economic growth before 1750, suggesting that the rapid progress made over the past 250 years could well be a unique episode in human history rather than a guarantee of endless future advance at the same rate."

1.3.3 *The Great Stagnation*

The reality is that the West is experiencing a *Great Stagnation*—a secular decline in productivity and economic growth that started in the 1970s (Naudé, 2022a, 2022b; Cowen, 2010; Gordon, 2012). Figure 1.2 depicts the decline in economic growth in advanced economies.

The consequence of this gradual, but inexorable, decline in economic growth is that the West increasingly resembles a Zero-Sum Economy: One firm, or one country, can generally only make itself better off at the expense of another (Bris, 2023). Instead of production, redistribution becomes the economy's basis (Naudé, 2023c).

Fig. 1.2 Capitalism is failing to maintain economic growth: % growth in advanced economies, 5-yr MA, 1978–2023. (Source: Author's compilation based on data from the World Bank Development Indicators Online)

This zero-sum logic characterizes much of the digital economy, wherein Artificial Intelligence (AI) is but one product touted by a handful of dominating tech and digital platform firms, mainly US and Chinese firms and platforms.[7] These firms, knowing the economy is stagnating and that growth is declining, know that to maintain and grow profits, which they must do least they collapse given the nature of global capitalism (see Binswanger, 2013), they have to deter competitors out and extract as much profits as they can from existing markets. This they do by spending hundreds of millions of dollars lobbying policymakers for subsidies (Roeder, 2024), for trade protection (hence the US trade and tech war with China—see, e.g. Fetzer and Schwarz (2021) and Wang et al. (2023)), and for government contracts—most concernedly in recent times, contracts from the military-industrial complex (González, 2024). Chapters 2 and 5 explain these adverse coping strategies in greater detail.

---

[7] See, for instance, the Global Digital Platform Power Index 2023, which details the extent of domination of US and Chinese platforms.

They also try hard to prevent consumers from getting saturated by creating hype, hysteria, relentless advertising, and regularly making tweaks to their products to create the illusion of continuing novelty—which is one reason why there have been no less than 46 iPhone versions since 2007.[8] Moreover, of course, to squeeze all profits from a limited market, they offer poor quality, low-paying jobs—"bullshit jobs" (Graeber, 2019). It is, therefore, no surprise that since the rise of digital platform firms, there has been a sharp increase in indicators of corporate dominance and industry concentration and a decline in the share of labour in output (Autor et al., 2017a, 2017b; Covarrubias et al., 2019).

1.4 The Future of Growth

Economic growth has its place. This book is not anti-growth. Indeed, Goal 8 of the UN's 17 Sustainable Development Goals (SDGs), adopted in September 2015, is to "Promote sustained, inclusive and sustainable economic growth, full and productive employment and decent work for all." It contains a sub-goal (target) of at least 7% per annum GDP per capita growth for the least developed countries. The reason is simple: due to economic growth over the past two centuries, the world is better off on virtually all human development indicators (Pinker, 2018). Economic growth has enabled social progress. As recently as two centuries ago, human society routinely enslaved people, subjugated women as a matter of course to the patriarchy and considered autocratic states run by kleptocratic rulers God-given, amongst other horrors. The growing wealth, progressive values, scientific rationality, and tolerance that distinguish current human civilizations from those pre-growth can be seen as being dependent on a growing economy (Kish & Quilley, 2017).

Even the literature exploring the notion of a post-growth society and the literature on degrowth, a path towards the post-growth society (see Chap. 7 for more details), clearly states that economic growth is necessary for development. This is why the Degrowth movement calls for the wealthy West to degrow but not the Global South—to create space for catch-up growth in the Global South. Likewise, the notion of a post-growth society accepts the fact that growth is first required before post-growth can be entertained (Spash, 2015).

---

[8] See https://theapplewiki.com/wiki/List_of_iPhones.

The problem is not so much finite growth per se, as building an economy and society on the belief or assumption, the myth, that economic growth can continue forever or that the benefits of economic growth will always exceed the costs thereof. Chapter 2 describes the dangers of such beliefs. Moreover, it is worth pointing out that not only can the costs of economic growth come over time to exceed the costs, but eventually, economic growth, even sustainable growth, however green and sustainable one can imagine it to be, cannot last forever. Fundamentally, the myth of perpetual growth is irreconcilable with physics and the biophysical reality of the planet and economy. There are two aspects of this irreconcilable nature.

The first is that if, as tech optimists assume, one can just continue to innovate to reduce the negative consequences of economic growth, then ultimately, the extent of innovation needs to be so rapid and significant that it stretches the imagination to the limits to imagine how this could be done. Bettencourt and West (2010) point out that sustained growth will require breakthrough innovations to occur faster and faster, which seems impossible.

The second aspect is that there are fundamental physical limits to growth. Even if the hopes of tech optimists are realized through mind-boggling technological innovations that increase energy efficiency and decouple growth from physical resources, energy will remain necessary. Suppose such technological revolutions maintain the growth of energy use at roughly historical rates of 2,3%. In that case, energy use on the planet will grow from its 2019 level of 18 Terawatt (TW) to 100 TW in 2100 and 1000 TW in 2200. According to Murphy et al. (2022), at such a rate, the economy would use up all the solar power that reaches the Earth in 400 years and all the energy of the sun in 1700 years. Moreover, using so much energy would generate tremendous waste heat that would eventually be so hot as to boil the surface of the Earth in about 400 years (Murphy, 2022).

Given the impossibility of infinite growth on a finite planet, the dependence on an economic system—neoliberal capitalism—for such infinite growth does not seem like a good idea.

1.5 Does the Fate of the Soviet Union Await the West?

When the Soviet Union collapsed at the end of 1991, many in the West saw this as the validation of the superiority of neoliberal capitalism—the "market and liberal institutions" (Kotkin, 2008). The sentiment was, as voiced by Fukayama (1992), that the end of history had arrived. Thirty years later, a growing number of scholars, commentators, and social movements have rejected the end-of-history narrative and questioned the sustainability of (democratic) capitalism (Livingstone, 2024). A 2019 opinion survey found that in former Soviet Republics, such as Russia, Bulgaria, and Ukraine, a majority of respondents felt that they were better off under the Soviet Union.[9] And, with more than 50% of the world's population taking part in a democratic election in 2024, *The Economist* magazine, a staunch supporter of capitalism, reflected that "in theory, it should be a triumphant year for democracy. In practice it will be the opposite," amongst the reasons citing a disillusionment of citizens and a growing preference for illiberal leaders, also in Europe[10] and the US (Beddoes, 2023).

The fear that 2024 will not be a good year for democracy may make Klimm's (2022) prediction come closer. He modelled the evolution of political regimes between 1800 and 2018 and forecasts "*an increase of autocracies for the next 50 years […]. This indicates that the currently observed democratic backsliding might be a harbinger of further incline of partial democracies becoming autocracies.*"

A careful examination shows that the West today suffers from the same broad pathologies that precipitated the collapse of the Soviet Union. This raises the question: *Does the Fate of the Soviet Union ultimately await the West?*

Chan (2015a) categorized five sources of rot that ended the Soviet Union. According to Chan (2015a), the Soviet Union collapsed due to increasing militarization, the ideological undermining of science, the disincentivizing of innovation, "technological conservatism," and a centralizing hierarchy that obstructed the horizontal flow of information.

---

[9] See: https://www.pewresearch.org/global/2019/10/15/european-public-opinion-three-decades-after-the-fall-of-communism/

[10] See: https://ecfr.eu/publication/a-sharp-right-turn-a-forecast-for-the-2024-european-parliament-elections/

In the discussion in this book, it will become clear that all of these pathologies are currently present—and becoming more pronounced over time—in the West. These pathologies reflect the threats of *guns* (militarization), *oil* (the decline of the hydrocarbon age and financialization), and *oligarchs* (the disincentivizing of innovation and the decline in science, sensemaking, and information interpretation).

1.6　Drivers and Symptoms of Western Economic Decline

This section provides a snapshot of the rest of the book and describes the structure/outline of the following chapters.

1.6.1　*The Growth Trap*

Chapter 2 introduces the Guns-Oil-Oligarchy nexus as a cause and symptom of the economic decline of the West. It is argued that the multifaceted relationship between militarization, the need and decline of fossil fuels, and the growing concentration of economic power underpins and accentuates a "grow-or-die" rule in the global economy. Firms and the economy need to grow, or else it will collapse in on itself. However, this has caused Ecological Overshoot, resulting in climate change, biodiversity loss, and resource depletion. It also shows that this *Growth Trap* has fostered socio-political instability, rising inequality, and job insecurity and eroded the social fabric. The chapter also introduces the notion of the Great Stagnation, which, since the 1970s, has been slowly ending the Great Take-Off and Great Acceleration described in Chap. 1. While over the longer run the Great Stagnation could reduce the ecological impact of economic activity, the increasingly zero-sum economy that it is resulting in brings its own hazards. More specifically, as this book shows, under the pressure of the Growth Trap, the Great Stagnation will accentuate the dangers of the decline in oil, the rise of the oligarchy and the Permanent War Economy. It creates a dilemma of "damned if you do, damned if you don't" as far as economic growth is concerned.

1.6.2 Oligarchs

After describing who the oligarchs are and how they expand and consolidate their power and influence, this chapter studies how the Oligarchy in the West stifles innovation, undermines democratic processes, hinders responses to climate change and contributes to militarization and conflict. The chapter identifies powerful oligarchies in the oil industry (*Big Oil*), in finance (*The Bankers*), in industrial agriculture (*The Food Barons*), the tech industry (*The Technofeudalists*), and the mainstream media (*The Media Moguls*). It discusses the role of oligarchs in the 2008 financial crisis, the increasingly fragile global food system, and the digital economy. This prepares the reader for a deeper analysis of the role of the oligarchs in the oil and military industries, which is done in subsequent chapters.

1.6.3 Oil

Chapter 4 explains how Oil has been essential for the economic rise of the West and how it will feature in its decline. The Energy Trap, characterized by declining energy availability, more expensive energy and a complicated energy transition, is explained. Its role in fostering a cost of living crisis, lower living standards, and geopolitical instability is discussed. The relation between energy and conflict is also explored.

1.6.4 Guns

Chapter 5 explores the rise and influence of the West's military-industrial complex (MIC) and shows how its pursuit of a Permanent War Economy ultimately contributes to the West's decline. The chapter traces the historical development of the MIC, starting with early-twentieth-century interventions and the post–World War II economic boom, to the post–Cold War "projects" of the War on Terror, the militarization of Africa, NATO expansion, the reshaping of the Middle East and the containment of China. It explains how the MIC, through lobbying, campaign contributions, and control of media narratives, has secured its position and influence. While providing short-term economic gains, the West's militarization has significant negative consequences, including misallocated resources, the illusion of job creation, the distortion of market forces, and perpetuating a cycle of conflict. It also undermines the West's moral standing.

1.7 The End?

The final two chapters are Chaps. 6 and 7. These chapters consider how the arguments in Chaps. 2–5 resonate with the current literature on the decline and collapse of the West and how they shed additional light on this burgeoning literature.

Chapter 6 explores how the confluence of the military-industrial complex, the rise of the oligarchy, and the central, but declining, role of fossil fuels are reflected in the growing number of articles, books, and blogs that have, in recent years, announced the unavoidable collapse of the West. Such a collapse is a possibility if its economic decline, driven by the Guns-Oil-Oligarchy nexus, deepens. Definitions of collapse are explored, and the main arguments in the literature from scholars like Spengler, Turchin, Tainter, and others are explored. From this, four primary areas of concern, or "waves," that may characterize the potential collapse of the West are described: environmental, economic, political, and population collapses. The chapter concludes by pointing out that the debate about the potential collapse of the West is not one-sided. There are not only "declinists" who believe Western collapse is inevitable but also "optimists." The latter believes the West possesses the resources and adaptability to overcome challenges and avoid collapse. Some even posit that the West is stronger than ever.

Finally, with Guns, Oil, and Oligarchs driving and reflecting the economic decline of the West, and giving the potential of this economic decline to tip over and cause a broad collapse of the West's "empire"—which would be a more catastrophic event than a slow but steady economic decline—Chap. 7 examines whether a post-growth society is possible, how it may look like, and what it would imply for the current growth-dependent model of capitalism. The need to do this, to consider the outlines of a post-growth society, stems from the meta-problem outlined in Chap. 2—the Growth Trap. Cutting away the rot—the embeddedness of the Growth Spiral—will diffuse the cancerous spread of the MIC and the oligarchy and perhaps make the energy transition somewhat more manageable. This final chapter only provides an introductory exploration of the post-growth economy—economics and business studies have severely neglected this topic, which may be hoped will attract more research and policy interest in the future.

CHAPTER 2

The Economic Growth Trap

2.1 Introduction

This chapter serves as an essential background for the three core chapters of the book that deal respectively with Oligarchs, Oil, and Guns. It explains the essential nature of global capitalism—its growth obsession. Oligarchs, oil, and guns are profoundly shaped and interrelated due to their relationship with economic growth—how they drive economic growth and depend on economic growth. The nature of these relationships and dependencies is such that the global economy has been subjected to a grow-or-die rule: it can only continue to grow; otherwise, it will collapse. There is no in-between.

The danger in the third decade of the twentieth century is that economic growth rates and related metrics such as productivity growth and entrepreneurship start-up rates have, despite the efforts of the oligarchy and political elites, including efforts to access more energy and build the Permanent War Economy, been slowly declining in the West at least since the 1970s (Gordon, 2012; Cowen, 2010). The neoliberal narrative of the "entrepreneurial economy" is increasingly exposed as a fantasy, a reality resembling an Ossified Economy (Naudé, 2022a, 2022b). A post-growth economy is unavoidable despite the system's obsession with growth. The West is hardly ready for it, and dangerously, the oligarchs will likely go to exceptional lengths to maintain growth that benefits their business empires as long as possible, even if this results in a dystopian, Mad Max type of zero-sum global economy.

Ever since the Limits to Growth (LtG) study was published in the early 1970s (Meadows et al., 1971), a growing scholarship—and social activism—has raised concerns about the consequences of the obsession with growth that has defined global capitalism. It is worth stressing that the LtG study concluded that warned that "If the present growth trends in world population, industrialization, pollution, food production, and resource depletion continue unchanged, the limits to growth on this planet will be reached sometime within the next one hundred years" (Meadows et al., 1971: 23).

Despite the "grow-or-die" rule, the LtG predications, and the inexorable decline in economic growth in the West, the disproportionate beneficiaries of neoliberal capitalism—the oligarchs—continue business as usual, perhaps believing that they can escape the dire consequences of a growth and ecological collapse, and trying their best to influence the narrative that the neoliberal capitalist order they preside over is the best that is possible and that whatever negative consequences it has, can be addressed through suitable policies—of course policies that are "organized around the greater prosperity for those who already enjoy most of it." For instance, a generation of especially business school and entrepreneurship students and policymakers have been indoctrinated to believe that sustainable entrepreneurship, eco-entrepreneurship, social enterprise, impact investment, ESG compliance, and sustainable finance are in new growth opportunities—a "new paradigm" of a "knowledge economy," which acts like an "Achilles' Lance." This is the belief that economic growth would, like the mythical lance of Achilles, "heal the wounds that it inflicts" (Barry, 2020: 123).

This chapter starts by noting (in section 2.2) the West's obsession with entrepreneurship and firm growth and the view that firm growth is a driver of economic growth. It then explains the "grow-or-die" rule and how this results in a growth imperative, or Growth Trap. Section 2.3 then discusses the dangers of the quest for perpetual growth.

Section 2.4 describes the Great Stagnation that had affected the West since roughly the 1970s, when structurally, amongst others, the price of oil increased. The Great Stagnation heralds a slow end to the Great Take-Off, and Great Accelerations described in Chap. 1. However, while over the longer run, the declining growth of the West will reduce its ecological impact, the increasingly zero-sum economy that is resulting brings its own hazards. More specifically, as this book shows, under the pressure of the Growth Trap, the Great Stagnation will accentuate the dangers of the decline in oil, the rise of the Oligarchy and the Permanent War Economy.

Section 2.5 locates the Growth Trap in the context of what has been termed Anthropocene Traps. Anthropocene traps refer to phenomena occurring globally, where one or more human practices, initially beneficial, become maladaptive due to their adverse impacts on human well-being. Guns, Oil, and Oligarchs all, to some extent, fit this bill. Countries need arms to defend themselves, and international law is clear. As explained in Chap. 1, the commercialization and the use of oil were a significant driver of the Great Take-off. Moreover, a robust entrepreneurial class that can scale up their businesses can be beneficial if the resulting power is not abused and misused. Thus, as section 2.5 indicates, this book broadly argues that Guns, Oil, and Oligarchs have become maladaptive and that this is pushing the West towards decline, possibly collapse.

2.2 The Myth of Perpetual Economic Growth

> Growth! Growth of gross domestic product! That is a goal on which the world's nations all agree. This imperative is taken for granted, and no further explanation is needed. Everything else seems to follow from its achievement.—(Binswanger, 2013: 1)

Most billionaires and oligarchs are entrepreneurs. The West has become besotted with the notion of entrepreneurs-as-heroes. It believes that most of the world's problems can be fixed if only more entrepreneurs could establish firms and corporations that could grow fast. And the faster they grow, the better. These ideal firms, to be emulated as much as possible and supported as much as possible by governments, are known as high-growth firms (HGFs). These HGFs are widely advocated and taught to generations of starry-eyed students as being the key to high economic growth, job creation, social mobility, and development and peace. The stark truth that entrepreneurship and the pursuit of HGFS for the sake of economic growth do not necessarily translate into job creation, social mobility, and peace, and that instead the contrary has been marking the West, is mostly swept under the carpet of the belief system of neoliberalism capitalism. Moreover, the high growth that these HGFs will generate may be very bad news over time for the planet and has been turned into another opportunity to be pursued for profits and growth—the so-called green growth belief.

The obsession in the West with entrepreneurship and HGFs as the driver of economic growth reflects the broader societal acceptance of economic growth as an *institution* and as an i*deology* (Haapanen & Tapio, 2016). As an institution, economic growth is embedded in a Growth Spiral—as will be explained in section 2.1.

As an ideology, economic growth is a core tenet of neoliberalism, "capitalism on steroids" (Monbiot & Hutchison, 2024: 9), of which Hayek (1944, 1960) was an intellectual founder. Neoliberalism's beliefs, premised on a view of human society characterized by competition, perpetuate a false narrative that the wealthy are deserving because they became rich through their efforts and hard work. Consequently, it subscribes to and implies the perverse view that the poor and marginalized have only themselves to blame—that they are failures and losers. It supports the twisted belief that the entrepreneur is an inevitable hero who deserves the super-wealth as a reward for their remarkable efforts and ingenuity.

Monbiot (2016) explains how this entrepreneur-as-deserving hero ideology of neoliberalism has motivated public policies and corporate decision-making, which has played a significant role in a remarkable variety of crises, from the Global Financial Crisis (GFC) in 2007 to the climate crisis and beyond. Frequently beaten by these crises, ordinary citizens in many Western countries reject neoliberalism and protest. This, however, has resulted in a backlash from the oligarchs, who have intensified their assault on democracy. At the time of writing, neoliberalism had, to such an extent, degraded the political institutions of the West that it—and some client states—is facing what Monbiot and Hutchinson (2024: 91) describe as the "Attack of the Killer Clowns." The Killer Clowns refers to the rise of "maverick" politicians—such as Donald Trump, Boris Johnson, Jair Bolsanaro, Viktor Orbán, Benjamin Netanyahu, and Geert Wilders. They are "deeply flawed human beings with oversized egos and pathological insecurities" who are "distinguished by buffoonery, shamelessness, and a flaunting disregard for justice, due process and political standards. They come to power by stoking outrage" (Monbiot and Hutchinson, 2024: 91–92).

In light of the Great Stagnation (described in section 2.4) and the consequences of the Guns-Oil-Oligarchy nexus, there is much in the West and the Rest to be outraged about. But the attraction to the Killer Clowns politicians represents an adverse coping strategy and, at best, a distracting sideshow obscuring the deeper neoliberal agenda.

Thus, a destructive ideology that idolizes economic growth has become deeply entrenched because it convinces society that entrepreneurs are heroes and that economic growth is the outcome and just reward of their hard work.

2.2.1 The Grow-or-Die Golden Rule: Economic Growth as an Imperative

There's a saying, popularized by Fredric Jameson, that it's easier to imagine the end of the world than to imagine the end of capitalism.—Chiang (2017)

The question that arises is, why has economic growth become an institution and an ideology? According to Binswanger (2013), the answer is that the modern global economy has come to resemble not a circular flow of income and goods—as typically depicted in introductory economics textbooks—but an upward-moving Growth Spiral. This reflects that the system has a built-in growth imperative: it is either growing or shrinking, but there is nothing in between; no stagnation or zero-growth situation is possible. In light of the eventual consequences, this is a "doomed-if-we-do, doomed-if-we-don't situation" (Douthwaite, 1992: 3).

Businesses created and run by entrepreneurs and managers are central to this Growth Spiral. As Binswanger (2013) explains, a business firm needs to borrow money to purchase the inputs for producing consumer goods or services. The entrepreneur of such a business has to convince the financier that their investment is worthwhile. The Growth Spiral thus starts with entrepreneurial narratives that are needed to attract capital to start production—never mind that these narratives are often not rooted in reality: in fact, according to Janeway's (2018) First Law of Venture Capital, "All entrepreneurs lie."

Once the entrepreneur has convinced, by hook or by crook, the financier to invest by borrowing this money from the financial system, the financial system creates money—essentially out of nothing, given modern fiat banking. Because of the risk that the bank faces, given that the success of the business in selling to consumers is uncertain, lending requires that interest be paid on the loan. Hence, businesses are required to earn a profit—a surplus—at least covering their interest obligations—which will require future growth. The belief is that a firm with an expected growth rate of zero or negative will go bust (Gordon & Rosenthal, 2003). Note also that the need for borrowing before production can start requires the existence of banks. Once the economy gets going, the banks will have a vested interest in economic growth because of the claim on future goods and energy that debt creates (Hagens, 2020).

The investments that all entrepreneurs—in aggregate—make using the money borrowed from the financial system provide a means by which the economy, in the next period, allows for sufficient sales to attain the required profit. This creates a need for growth so that firms can pay the interest that becomes due. The growth imperative is amplified by capital-earning households (e.g. wealthy entrepreneurs) who invest their surplus in speculating on asset prices) and individuals who engage in higher consumption of positional goods. These are goods that society sees as desirable and signal high status, whether necessary for survival or not. According to Hirsch (1977), this triggers a spiral where "enough is never enough. Growth creates differences that cause further growth in the attempts to remove those differences" (Paech, 2017: 483).

Note that entrepreneurs who borrow money to pay for capital investments and other inputs expect to make a profit in the future by selling to consumers. Economic growth is required to ensure that enough consumers with disposable income absorb the production of the previous periods. Because entrepreneurs-owners will invest in labour-saving technology to raise their profits, labour income in total may decline, thus reducing the potential consumption by households (Jackson & Victor, 2015). Therefore, potential obstacles to perpetual growth are consumers becoming satiated and their income share declining. To address these potential demand constraints, businesses have resorted to actions like marketing, innovations to keep customers buying and loyal, agitating for lower taxes, and expanding globally when a local market becomes saturated (Trincado, 2010).

In the latter regard, firms' international expansion was remarked upon by Karl Marx and analysed by Rosa Luxemburg. According to the Luxemburg thesis, capitalist corporations depend on perpetual growth, and when they, at some point, inevitably start to run into domestic demand constraints, they need to become imperialistic. This results in the rise of global corporate giants that predate on and subjugate non-capitalist entities, such as foreign governments and their peoples (Luxemburg, 1913). This is why, as Darwin (2007: 399) describes, Vladimir Lenin "proclaimed in his famous wartime manifesto *Imperialism: The Highest Stage of Capitalism* (1916) that colonial freedom was the crucial first step towards destroying capitalism in its European heartlands."

The Luxemburg thesis implies that capitalism would collapse if this "rapacious" Growth Spiral were to be stopped (Monbiot & Hutchison, 2024: 13). Given that the system has, in effect, been globalized after centuries of colonialism and imperialism, the only way to prevent a collapse is to keep expanding into new territories. Hence, it is to be expected that growth-dependent corporates would be as they do now, turn to tokenize all of nature, mine the ocean floor, and plan to mine asteroids—as these are amongst the few extraction zones still available (Koetsier, 2021; Monbiot & Hutchison, 2024). In Chap. 5, it is also argued the artificial intelligence (AI) is a last extraction zone in the digital economy, grew out of the creation of the internet and the personal computer and which offered much hope in the early 1990s, which was subsequently dashed by its capture and takeover by the corporate oligarchy.

Alexander and Gleeson (2019) explain several reasons for modern capitalism's imperative for growth, which they describe as a "grow-or-die golden rule." These include the mechanism of debt creation, as per Binswanger's (2013) Growth Spiral, and the need to secure sufficient profits to compete against rivals not to be excluded from access to finance. The further reasons they add include the vested interests of capitalists and states. The latter have become dependent on economic growth for tax revenue as well as for geopolitical security because countries' relative geopolitical status depends on their economic and military might (Alexander & Gleeson, 2019).

Another, and partly related reason for the growth imperative is the desire of societies to avoid costly and violent zero-sum games and maintain peace amongst groups and nations. As discussed in section 2.4, one of the concerns about a post-growth society and degrowth as a way to get there is the zero-sum economy and the resulting conflicts it can generate—see also Naudé (2023b). Perret (2017: 291) argues that economic growth is a good "peacemaker" with reference to the stability and peace that the post–World War II integration has brought to Europe. Not only is economic growth a good peacemaker but also the age of exponential growth in the world economy, roughly between 1850 and 2000, has seen a significant decline in poverty and improvements in social and health outcomes (Pinker, 2018). China, where hundreds of millions of people escaped from poverty since the 1980s via high economic growth (generated in part by the global growth of Western corporations for which their own markets had become too small to sustain growth), has provided an example that many countries are trying to emulate.

2.2.2 Escaping from Its Own Exhaust: The Firm Growth Imperative

Having explained the grow-or-die rule in the previous sub-section, this sub-section focuses on the level of the firm or the corporation, to explain how and why firms have become caught in a Growth Trap. As was mentioned, the West has become besotted with entrepreneurship and the HGFs that they create, and the pursuit of such high-growth firms has become an ideal. Entrepreneurship scholars and policymakers are seemingly obsessed with and addicted to firm growth. Such HGFs are also referred to as "gazelles," "high-impact firms," or "scale-ups[1]." According to Coad et al. (2024: 1), "Scale-ups have received an almost mythical status." Such is the addition that even high growth seems to be in risk of becoming passé, the newest fad being "blitzscalers"—firms that prioritize their fast growth over efficiency (Belitski et al., 2023).

Why is firm growth so interesting that it has become addictive? In this subsection, it is argued that firm growth is believed to be essential for earning profits and, thus, firm survival and that high-growth firms and scale-ups drive economic growth and, hence, job creation and well-being in an economy. In the following section (2.3), it is argued that these beliefs have adverse consequences.

As far as the belief that firm growth is a requirement for firm performance and survival is concerned, De Souza and Seifert (2018: 333) state that firm growth is the "ultimate goal for any modern organization" and that firm growth reflects the firm's "administrative efficiency." Typical for the literature, the ultimate goal of growth is not questioned, and a firm's growth is a badge of administrative efficiency. If entrepreneurs, or managers, want to show that they are efficient, they should have a "growth aspiration" (Wiklund & Shepherd, 2003).

As far as the belief in a link between entrepreneurship and economic growth is concerned, Urbano et al. (2019: 30,22) declare that it "is one of the key factors that enhance economic growth," and Acs (2006) explains how "entrepreneurship is good for economic growth." Entrepreneurs who create HGFs and accelerate their firms' growth are especially important drivers of economic growth and job creation (Belitski et al., 2023; Coad & Binder, 2014).

---

[1] Scale-ups can be defined as "high-growth firms at an intermediate stage of organizational development [...] which pursue strategies that prioritize the attainment of economies of scale" (Piaskowska et al., 2021: 1).

Historically, the era of the appearance of big business in the US (the late nineteenth century) was one of high economic growth. Thus, the association between firm growth that results in large enterprises and economic growth that creates jobs and tax revenues was made. At that time, economic theory had no explanation for firm growth. The eventual explanation given was that it is due to entrepreneurs who leveraged new technologies to scale their firms. At the end of the nineteenth century, transportation and electricity were the key technologies. The entrepreneurs who grew their businesses into behemoths were hailed as the "captains of industry" (High, 2011).

Today, for many, the heroes of the entrepreneurship literature and practice are its new captains of industry, many of them Silicon Valley billionaires who have built their fortunes and influence on data and digital technologies, and who live and work by the dictum "move fast and break things" (Taplin, 2017). There is even a "Silicon Valley Mindset" that has become de rigueur for any aspiring entrepreneur (Rushkoff, 2023). This mindset is based on a myth closely related to the addition to growth, the myth of the supremacy of competition. This myth has seeped into Western conceptions of what entrepreneurship and corporations are, from the ideology of neoliberalism (Hayek, 1944, 1960). It values competition over cooperation (Perret, 2017: 288). Hence, according to the Silicon Valley Mindset, the entrepreneurial attitude should be that the world is a game they (the entrepreneurs) are playing where "winning means earning enough money to insulate themselves from the damage they are creating by earning money in that way. It is as if they want to build a car that goes fast enough to escape from its own exhaust" (Rushkoff, 2023: 10).

Idealizing high-growth-promoting entrepreneurs and belief in the entrepreneur as a hero underpin the American Dream. There was a time when this was useful, but it seems now has become maladaptive. The entrepreneur as the hero has become a dangerous myth. How the entrepreneur as hero myth jars with reality has been strikingly described by Cooke (2019: 1), who uses the example of the TV show *The Apprentice*, which made Donald Trump (more) famous in the US, which he concludes acts as something of a comfort to viewers brought up on the mythology of

> the American Dream of untold wealth in exchange for hard work and a bit of luck. For the stubborn reality is, for most, just that, a piece of mythology, which is little compensation for a hard-scrabble existence on less than two or

even three living wages per head of household, deindustrialized neighborhoods and the prospect of opiate-addiction or worse as the only way out.

As this quote from Cooke (2019) indicates, in contrast to the myths of the HGF that turn the entrepreneur into a hero who realizes the American Dream, the "stubborn reality" is that most firms do not grow, and most entrepreneurs are not heroes; in fact, most entrepreneurs are increasingly battling for survival in a stagnating, deindustrializing, and crisis-prone world. This is because only a small number of entrepreneurs, who constitute the Oligarchy, are the "winners" of the neoliberal game. As such, the obsession with firm growth, and firm growth as a means to perpetual economic growth, poses several dangers for the West. These will be discussed in the following section.

2.3 The Dangers of the Perpetual Growth Myth

Growth is, as Smil (2019, p.vii) eloquently explains, "an omnipresent protean reality of our lives." He is here referring to growth as a basic feature of nature—from the growth of microorganisms to the growth of megacities, and even "terraforming growth" which is the growth in the physical landscape of Earth caused by geotectonic forces. The growth of the world's economy is but an example of this general tendency to grow. Living and dynamic systems, also non-living, are all fundamentally characterized by cycles of change, of which growth during a part of the cycle, is a manifestation. Growth is in many ways "a sign of progress" (Smil, 2019: ix).

Economic growth per se is, therefore, not an aberration. Neither are entrepreneurs who create value and who contribute to an expanding economy. Growth and the contribution of entrepreneurs have indeed been an essential channel for material and cultural progress in the past, even as it had been accompanied by costs. As shown in Chap. 7, even those who most actively agitate for a post-growth and degrowth society recognize the importance of growth to provide a satisfactory quality of life for everyone. However, it is nevertheless so that the increasing risks or costs of economic growth over time must be recognized. It can become maladaptive—an Anthropocene Trap. The costs of a Growth Spiral that aims to maintain growth into perpetuity can come to overwhelm the benefits. It has been claimed that the world may be approaching this point, if it is not already in it. Spash (2015: 367), for instance, claims that many growing economies may be "in fact not growing at all, when assessed in terms of standard economic externality theory, due to the level of damages they create."

The solution is not, as many call for, to simply "stop growth." This could be extremely problematic, given the nature of the Growth Spiral described in the previous section. Before elaborating—in Chap. 7—on this "damned if you do, damned if you don't" predicament, it is first necessary to outline the major dangers of the striving for perpetual growth—on the firm and country levels—discussed. The first is the dismantling of the Welfare State.

2.3.1 Dismantling the Welfare State

A danger of the myth of firm growth is that the great majority of small and medium enterprises (SMEs) that are not high-growth firms are neglected. For perhaps most of these entrepreneurs, particularly those in family firms, growing their firms may not be attractive, even unwelcome. This could be because the control of their firm is central to what entrepreneurship means, or that the objective of growth conflicts with the other roles of the entrepreneur within the family, or that firm growth could cause stress, conflict and poor health (Naudé et al., 2014; De Souza & Seifert, 2018). Hence, it is unsurprising that, as Cyron and Zoellick (2018: 217) report, up to 40% of all owner-managers have no growth ambitions.

Neglect of the great majority of entrepreneurs and their firms is nevertheless what a central strand of not only the entrepreneurship literature by governments advocates. For instance, Shane (2009) has argued that policymakers should only be concerned with HGFs and that less specific policies that would support anyone are bad policies. Likewise, Schramm (2004: 105) criticized entrepreneurship policies favouring "cottage industries that add little to the economy in terms of productivity or growth." Moreover, Acs et al. (2016a, 2016b: 37) see such policies as wasting taxpayers' money. Audretsch and Thurik (2004: 1) have recommended that entrepreneurship policy should not be undertaken for "social and political reasons." This recommendation is consistent with the growth imperative of modern capitalism that proceeds on the basis of dismantling the welfare state for the sake of stimulating economic growth (Gordon & Rosenthal, 2003).

Consistent with the elimination of the welfare state and the shift of resources to support HFGs, government policies aiming at growth have come to be dominated by growth-dependent planning (Barry, 2020), which systematically has undone the welfare state. Most governments' economic planning documents are, according to Barry (2020: 122), riddled with growth ideology terms, such as "attracting foreign direct investment," "promoting free trade," "competitiveness," "increasing labour productivity," and "encouraging innovation." Growth-dependent planning culminates in governments' efforts to promote entrepreneurship as the ultimate driver of HGFs and economic growth through so-called entrepreneurial ecosystems (EES). Boland (2014) is critical of the often-excessive preoccupation of policymakers and EES builders with so-called competitiveness-enhancing policies, which he calls a virulent and dangerous obsession. Here, the obsession with firm growth and EES that can help catapult firm growth to create more gazelles and unicorns spills over into a fixation with ranking countries of regions as to how well their entrepreneurial ecosystems can generate high-growth firms (including unicorns) and high rates of GDP growth—see, for example, Leendertse et al. (2022).

The dismantling of the welfare state and the fixation of competition and rankings in the name of promoting HGFs not only have helped to drive ecological overshoot but can also be associated with declining levels of health and subjective well-being in the advanced economies where these policies are paramount. For example, in the US, relative and absolute life expectancy has been in consistent decline since the 1980s (Woolf, 2023) and the country is facing a crisis marked by sharply rising "deaths of despair"—deaths due to suicide, drug overdose, and alcoholism (Deaton & Case, 2021). It is also in a "crisis of early deaths" with the "number of working-age Americans who died [between 2019–2021] increased by 233,000—and nine in 10 of those deaths wouldn't have happened if the U.S. had mortality rates on par with its peers" (Yong, 2022).

Neoliberal capitalism with its high-growth entrepreneurial idolization carries a large portion of the blame because its addiction to growth has elevated capitalization, financialization, competition, and profits and driven rates in inequality higher and higher (Deaton & Case, 2021; Stiglitz, 2015). And is not only in the US. Entrepreneurs in high-growth firms and countries with more high-growth entrepreneurship, and generally more self-employment, are generally not happier (Blanchflower, 2004). Naudé et al. (2014) report evidence for an inverse U-shape relationship between opportunity entrepreneurship and national happiness indicators. This suggests that having more opportunities for entrepreneurship may make nations generally happier, but only up to a point. The West seems to have reached that point some time ago.

2.3.2 Undermining Economic Stability

Another danger of the addiction to and the myth of firm growth driven by entrepreneurs as heroes stems from the lack of policy usefulness of focusing on promoting high-growth firms to achieve desirable social outcomes. Léon (2022), for instance, used data on all formal firms in Senegal between 2006 and 2015 to find that growth rates of HGFs were negatively correlated across time, meaning that HGFs do not remain HGFs for long. In other words, high growth does not seem sustainable in their sample. Their findings also throw cold water on the belief that HGFs would always be better able to improve productivity—which is a basis for the belief that HGFs would boost economic growth. Coad and Binder (2014: 98–99) survey research on the persistence of HGFs, concluding that the bulk of research finds that high growth is not sustainable and tends to be random.

If HGFs cannot sustain high growth, and if most high-growth episodes are random occurrences in a firm's life, the obsession with HGFs is clearly misplaced (Grover Goswami et al., 2019). Coad and Binder (2014: 107) warn that the policy obsession with firm growth may not only be misguided but even be counter-productive, because this could lead to net job losses instead of job gains if support to HGFs are accompanied by greater firms exits overall.

Relatedly, Derbyshire (2012) argues that promoting HGFs may be counterproductive, but not from the perspective of increased firm churning, as Coad and Binder (2014) argue, but from the potential lack of churning that may result if policy focus shifts away from supporting a general entry of new firms into the market in favour of specific measures to support incumbent firms' growth faster.

2.3.3 The Problem of Bigness: Enter the Oligarchs

Despite the addition to growth and the fervent attempts by corporations and the entrepreneurs to grow as much and as long as is possible, the reality is that even the largest firm cannot continue to grow indefinitely. Even the most successful firms eventually run into diminishing growth rates and face stagnation. No firm lives forever. There is no infinite growth possible for any firm.

As firms scale up, their size has downsides. Lamoreaux (2019) and others describe this the problem of bigness. One of the most pervasive problems is the increase in firm concentration, and the oligarchies their dominance creates. In the US, concentration levels have increased by around 90% in recent decades, allowing firms to raise mark-ups to earn higher and higher profits (Covarrubias et al., 2019; Grullon et al., 2019). The extent of concentration is such that three firms, *BlackRock*, *Vanguard*, and *State Street*, control more than 40% of all public firms in the US (Fichtner et al., 2017).

Even if entrepreneurs and policymakers are chasing high firm growth and desire to build large firms that can dominate their markets and set high markups, earning high profits for further investments in scaling up, any benefits that they may obtain from this may ultimately be transient. The fact is, there is no perpetual growth—not of firms, and not of economies. As far as the limits of firm growth is concerned it can be noted that firm growth follows, as many other phenomena in nature, a S-curve trajectory over time—that is, a sigmoid function describes firm growth over time. West (2017) used data from almost 29,000 publicly traded firms in the US to find that after some point when maturity sets in, all firms stop growing. The half-life of a typical publicly traded company is roughly 10 years, and very few firms survive for even a century (Daepp et al., 2015; Naudé, 2022a, 2022b).

The firm growth myth is especially enticing because it is premised on the belief that entrepreneurship is the driver of economic growth and that perpetual economic growth is the normal state of affairs. The problem is that, without the myth of perpetual growth, the entire edifice of the West's attachment to entrepreneurship may collapse.

2.3.4 A Ghastly Future: Ecological Overshoot

Moving from the firm-level growth obsession to the country-level growth obsession, the first obvious danger is ecological overshoot. While there is little doubt that despite the unparalleled prosperity that economic growth has brought to many, it has also been hugely damaging to Earth's biophysical systems, increasingly threatening ecological collapse and multiple environmental crises, some have even claimed the world is facing a global polycrisis (Bradshaw et al., 2021; Lawrence et al., 2024).

As explained in Chap. 1, but worth repeating, starting around 250 years ago and boosted by the exploitation of fossil fuel energy since the mid-nineteenth century, the world's economy, energy use, and population grew exponentially (Hagens, 2020; Smil, 2019). Since the 1950s, these trends have manifested in a Great Acceleration, which reflects exponentially increasing impacts of economic activity on a broad range of socioeconomic, planetary boundaries and Earth Systems Steffen et al. (2015a, 2015b). For instance, global GDP increased by 1487% between 1950 and 2015, accompanied by a 414% increase in energy consumption, a 3115% increase in cement production and a 765% increase in iron and steel production, amongst others (Head et al., 2021). By 2020, world GDP per capita was, at an estimated US$5400, around 5600% higher than what it was around 10,000 years before (Syvitski et al., 2020).

The result of the Great Acceleration was an ecological overshoot. Ecological overshoot occurs when the economic system "generates flows larger than the carrying capacity" of the planet, which refers to "the maximum flow of energy that the system can maintain for a long time" (Bardi, 2020: 34). Climate change is but one of the many symptoms of ecological overshoot, which, as Rees (2021a, 2021b) points out, also includes "plunging biodiversity, plastic pollution of the oceans, landscape and soil degradation, and tropical deforestation." According to Hoekstra and Wiedmann (2014), the carrying capacity of the Earth system in terms of carbon, energy, land, material, and water has already been exceeded, and according to Rockström et al. (2023), seven of eight so-called Earth System Boundaries (ESB) have been exceeded. Bradshaw et al. (2021: 3) note that the global economy consumed 170% of the planet's regenerative capacity in 2016.

As discussed by Naudé (2023a), the breach of the planet's carrying capacity and planetary boundaries may cause the Earth system to tip into a state which would be detrimental to civilization and life—because of interdependencies and non-linearities, one ecosystem's collapse will feed into that of another (Rockström et al., 2009; Lenton et al., 2019; Ritchie et al., 2021). Several potential tipping points—also called "ecological doom-loops" (Dearing et al., 2023) are causing concern. For Rees (2021a, 2021b), ecological overshoot is an existential threat, and Bradshaw et al. (2021) warn that it will result in a "ghastly future" for humanity.

The extent of overshooting is increasing and shows no sign of diminishing, as measured by the Material Footprint (MF) indicator (Fanning et al., 2022; Giljum et al., 2015; Wiedmann et al., 2015). The MF of the world, as well as carbon emissions causing climate change, is strongly correlated with economic growth and the size of the global economy—as Figs. 2.1 and 2.2 show. Green growth, sustainable growth, and related concepts such as eco-entrepreneurship can ultimately never be disconnected or decoupled from a material footprint.

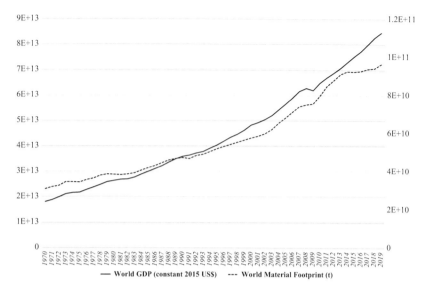

Fig. 2.1 World Material Footprint (t) and Real GDP (US$), 1970–2019. (Source: Author, based on data from UNEP's Global Material Flows Database)

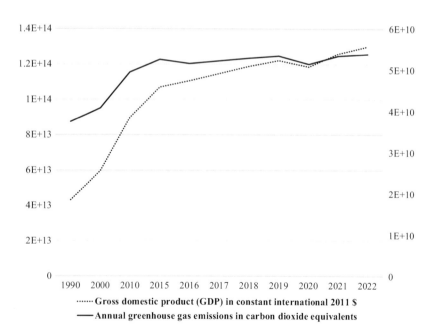

Fig. 2.2 World GDP and Greenhouse Gas Emissions, 1990–2022. (Source: Author, based on data from the World Bank's World Development Indicators Online)

In 2024, Earth Overshoot Day, "when humanity has used all the biological resources that the Earth regenerates during the entire year," fell on 1 August, whereas back in 1971, it fell on 25 December. Thus, the rate at which biological resources are consumed is speeding up as the world economy grows—despite all the attempts at green growth and sustainable entrepreneurship.

2.3.5 Achilles' Lance: The Myth of Sustainable Business and Entrepreneurship

Renewable energy technologies seem to be largely serving as a profitable investment for the wealthy, a way to funnel public money into private hands, and a distraction from the scale of the ecological problems we face (of which global warming is far from the worst) and the scale of solutions which are needed.—Wilbert (2022)

The obsession with economic and firm growth is such that when confronted with ecological overshoot as described in the previous section, entrepreneurs, corporations, and so-called green politicians have created the notion of green growth, sustainable business and entrepreneurship, including eco-entrepreneurship (Hart & Milstein, 1999; Shepherd & Patzelt, 2011; Muñoz & Cohen, 2018). These notions purports that firm and country growth does not have to be a problem and does not have to end—it can continue infinitely by becoming "green" or "sustainable."

The claim moreover is that not only can entrepreneurs grow their firms but they can do so without harming the planet. The claim becomes even more audacious in that it is fervently believed that socially and environmentally responsible firms will not only save the planet but, because they do so, grow faster. And on top of this miracle, purveyors of green growth and sustainable entrepreneurship often claim that social entrepreneurs will come along to wipe out inequality and exclusion. For example, in selling the idea of so-called sustainable entrepreneurial ecosystems, Theodoraki (2024: 3) advertises the concepts as ultimately being "conducive to economic growth." Thus, green growth and sustainable entrepreneurial are beliefs in the possibility to square the circle of sustainability and growth, not abandon the obsession with economic growth.

Green growth and sustainable entrepreneurship are instances of *reform environmentalism*, which is an environmentalism that considers technological and organizational innovations in production methods and markets as sufficient to avoid ecological overshoot and mitigate climate change, without abandoning economic growth.

It considers, as green entrepreneurship, the challenge of ecological overshoot and sustainable development a significant business opportunity (Anand et al., 2021). Hence, sustainable entrepreneurship is associated with a green growth industry that is furthering capitalism's expansion imperative by aiming to monetize, financialize, and commodify nature as far as possible. It includes the concept of environmental, social, and governance (ESG), which has evolved into a new engine of firm and economic growth (Diaye et al., 2022; Satyadini & Song, 2023), and which is increasingly associated with greenwashing (Johnson, 2023; Yu et al., 2020).

A new strategy to find ever more extraction zones for profit- and growth-seeking corporations is to "make biodiversity conservation profitable and scalable" (Michaelides, 2024). These include so-called innovations such as biodiversity banking, offsetting, green/blue bonds, species credits, extinction futures markets, and climate catastrophe bonds. It also includes "tokenizing the planet to save it," which is a growth and profit enabler. It uses blockchain technology to create "nature-backed financial instruments"—digital tokens. According to the entrepreneur behind a start-up in this field "nature is the new gold" (Koetsier, 2021). The proponents of these ideas seem to have a notion of the damages that the financialization of agricultural systems has wreaked on global food systems and may be more inspired by the super profits that the firms who dominate world food production and distribution are earning at the same time that world hunger is rising (Monbiot, 2022a, 2022b). Van Nieuwkoop (2019) estimates the costs/damages associated with the global food system to exceed US$6 trillion annually.

At the extreme, green growth and sustainable entrepreneurship could amount to deceptions: "What higher form of deception could you request than enlightened Green Capitalists doing favours for the proles while improving their personal bank balance and smoothing over the corporate image?" (Spash, 2015: 377). Even where the proponents green growth and sustainable entrepreneurship have no sinister attentions to profit from the ecological crisis, or to deceive via ESG strategies, the myth of economic growth is so ingrained that it has resulted in a pervasive belief that economic growth can like Achilles' mythical lance "heal the wounds that it inflicts" (Barry, 2020: 123).

The myth of green growth and sustainable entrepreneurship is partly due to the myth that economic growth can be decoupled from material resource use and emissions. In Chap. 1, it was shown that absolute decoupling of growth has not occurred. It is also not likely, fundamentally, due to the Jevons Paradox (or rebound effect), where higher productivity and efficiency in a more circular economy will result in more consumption and production, not less. An example is that the use of renewable energy has not lead to a decrease in the use of fossil fuels, but has amounted to an additional source of energy with which to fuel production and consumption (Galvin et al., 2021). A growing literature has noted the lack of absolute decoupling between economic growth and material use and economic growth and carbon emissions on a global level (Haberl et al., 2020; Hannesson, 2021; Jackson & Victor, 2019; Ward et al., 2016; Wiedmann et al., 2015).

Because economic growth cannot be decoupled from material throughput or emissions and pollution, sustainable growth is an oxymoron.

2.3.6 *A Nation of Mammon: Erosion of the Social Fabric*

The second broad risk associated with the perpetual Growth Spiral is that it is eroding the social fabric through growing inequality and marginalization of people and countries and reduced trust in each other and in governments, and facilitated the Attack of the Killer Clowns (Monbiot & Hutchison, 2024).

It was noted how the obsession with growth has caused ecological overshoot and driven Western colonialism and imperialism. This has resulted in a "Great Divergence" (Pomeranz, 2021) in wealth, reflected in high global inequality, exploitation and marginalization reflected in a divided world—a Global North-Global South dichotomy. The extent of these global disparities and the role of Western colonialism and imperialism in the aim for perpetual growth are well-known and are the topics of vast literature. A deeper discussion falls outside the scope of this book. The interested reader is referred to Patnaik and Patnaik (2021) for a pertinent recent account.

For present purposes, though, it is necessary to link the obsessions with firm growth and economic growth to the continued erosion of the social fabric between and within countries, including countries in the Global North.

A starting point is Fig. 2.3, which depicts the evolution of inequality—measured by the share of the top 10% of incomes in a sample of countries since 1910. It shows that between 1950 and the 1970s, inequality in

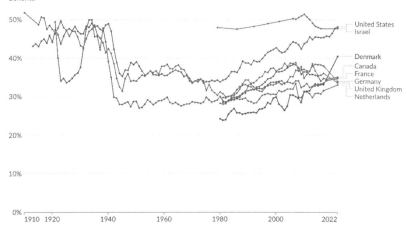

Fig. 2.3 Share of Top 10% in pre-tax national income, selected countries, 1910–2022. (Source: Our World in Data.org/economic-inequality CC BY, using World Income Inequality Database WID.world 2024 as source)

countries such as the US, the UK, and France declined slowly, only to pick up again in the 1970s. Since then, income inequality has steadily decreased in many countries since the 1970s, including in Israel, where the already very high inequality increased to the extent that the top 10% earned more than 50% of the income by 2010.

The 1970s are no coincidence as a turning point; it is the era following the ascendancy of Ronald Reagan and Margaret Thatcher, during and after which neoliberalism was intensively implemented in the Western world and imposed on the Global South, for instance, through the structural adjustment policies of the IMF/World Bank (the Washington Consensus)—for a concise description, see Monbiot and Hutchison (2024).

Overall, both economic growth theory and long-term data suggest a strong relationship between economic growth and inequality over time. In theory, economic growth models are consistent with the notion that periods of high economic growth will be accompanied by growing inequality. Finance and labour-saving technologies play a crucial role herein—as they do in setting the Growth Spiral mechanism explained above. Inequality even acts as a driver of economic growth in most growth models.

As far as the data is concerned, Chancel and Piketty (2021) document changes in global inequality between 1820 and 2020, finding that during the high period of Western colonialism, roughly 1820 to 1910, global inequality rose substantially and stabilized at a very high level since then, only starting to decline somewhat after the 1980s. Within countries, inequality declined between 1910 and 1980 (especially after WWII) but has risen since 1980. Monbiot and Hutchison (2024: 33, 45) report that since around 1989, the super-rich in the US have grown around US$ 21 trillion richer, whilst those with the lowest 50% of incomes have become US$900 billion poorer—and that the wealth of US billionaires increased 12-fold between 1990 and 2020. While a small exclusive club of entrepreneurs in the US gets richer and richer, the rest of the country is heading to be the world's "first former middle-class society" (Stiglitz, 2015). Chancel and Piketty (2021: 3025) note that inequality under neo-colonial capitalism at the start of the twenty-first century is similar to that under colonialism in the twentieth century. The persistence of inequality has according to *The Economist Magazine* (The Economist, 2014) heralded a new gilded age, headed by a class of entrepreneurs and crony capitalists who constitutes "new virtual nation of Mammon."

Thus, the Growth Spiral economy is marked by a *Matthew Effect*, that is, the rich get richer. The particular entrepreneurship dynamic underlying this effect is that a handful of successful HGFs and scale-ups dominate markets, gaining winner-take-all effects and engaging in defensive innovation strategies and the creation of "kill zones" (e.g. Kamepalli et al. (2020) to reduce the entry of new firms. Not surprising given the hero worship of high-growth firms in the literature, these firms have been labelled superstars.

Ever higher inequality and its associated pathologies are not unintended by-products of the Growth Spiral into which modern economies are locked or the obsession with high-growth entrepreneurship: it is a feature, not a bug, of the system. Inequality confers power on a small elite, and, as has been pointed out by Karl Marx and many others, growth-dependent capitalism is not designed to distribute wealth and incomes but to "capture and concentrate it" (Monbiot & Hutchison, 2024: 15). Isenberg (2014) is honest that the aspiration to capture and concentrate wealth is the defining feature of entrepreneurship when he admits that "successful entrepreneurship always exacerbates local inequality." The firms that lead in this are called superstars.

The obsession with growth obscures the recognition that it should be bizarre to laud a system that thrives on and promotes inequality. In effect, the obsession promotes acceptance of such corporate practices because these firms are believed to be the best drivers of economic growth (Banerjee et al., 2021). Hence, the growth ideology helps to avert punitive actions against corporate excesses.

It also obscures the underlying causes of rising social and military conflict in the world, which often reflects the continued attempts by growth-dependent Western countries and the corporate/ financial sectors to maintain their hegemony—even through promotion of a Permanent War Economy (Foster & McChesney, 2014). And it fuels the disillusionment with democracy, given that the growth imperative requires more technocratic and autocratic measures. Reitz et al. (2021) describe how these fuels the rise of far-right-wing parties who are often supported by rich entrepreneurs—the plutocracy. Larry Fink, the CEO of BlackRock, one of the largest and most influential global corporations, is reported[2] to have declared in a 2011 interview that "Markets don't like uncertainty. Markets like, actually, totalitarian governments […] Democracies are very messy."

In conclusion. Karl Polanyi in his 1944 book *The Great Transformation* argued that a fully self-regulating market economy is impossible in practice because it would ultimately lead to the destruction of society. He argued that treating labour, land, and money as commodities subject to pure market forces ("fictitious commodities") is unsustainable. He believed that subjecting these essential elements to the whims of the market would lead to social ills like poverty, violence, alcoholism, and exploitation of workers. Hence, Polanyi saw society resorting to certain defences against unbridled free markets, such as social welfare, collective bargaining, public control over land use, and central bank control over monetary policy (Polanyi, 1944; Milanović, 2024). The Oligarchy, however, has, as will be outlined in Chap. 3, considered to break down these defences.

2.3.7 Triggering a Global Polycrisis?

The interrelatedness of the Ecological Overshoot crisis and the social crises stemming from inequality and stagnation have given rise to what has been termed a "global polycrisis" (Tooze, 2022a, 2022b). According to

---

[2] As reported in Crypto News, 6 February 2024, available at: https://www.cryptonews.net/news/ analytics/28518066/

Tooze (2022a, 2022b), the world is experiencing a confluence of disparate shocks, such as pandemics, climate change-induced disasters, geopolitical instability, and economic volatility. Tooze (2022a, 2022b) points out the term "polycrisis" was borrowed from Edgar Morin, who used it in the 1990s when the dangers from growing ecological risks became clear.

The polycrisis has been defined as "the causal entanglement of crises in multiple global systems in ways that significantly degrade humanity's prospects" (Lawrence et al., 2024: 2). The entanglement of crises referred to is largely the outcome of the expansion of global capitalism. This has made the world much more vulnerable to risk. Because of hyper-connectivity and homogenization of economies, the impacts of an adverse event can spread faster and everywhere, and with everyone being homogeneous and thus similarly exposed, the consequences can be far deadlier overall (Lawrence et al., 2024).

Because a polycrisis is, per definition, a crisis of interconnections and feedback, the various dimensions of the polycrisis—environmental and social—must be addressed as a whole; they cannot be resolved individually (Lawrence et al., 2024). The simple common cause of much of these crises is the growth institution and ideology of modern capitalism and its relation with the Guns-Oil-Oligarchy nexus.

2.4 The Great Stagnation

There is a pervasive belief in the growth-obsessed West that it is living in a rapidly changing, highly innovative and technologically progressing world. The reality is that the West is deep in a Great Stagnation—a secular decline in productivity and economic growth in the West that started in the 1970s—and that has resulted in an "Ossified Economy" in the West (Naudé, 2022a, 2022b, 2023c; Cowen, 2010; Gordon, 2012).

2.4.1 Outline of the Ossified Economy

Based on Naudé (2022a), the outline of the Ossified Economy is described in this sub-section. Naudé (2022a, 2022b) argues that advanced economies are no longer experiencing the dynamic growth predicted in the 1990s, and instead are becoming "ossified" due to a decline in entrepreneurship. Naudé (2022a) discusses existing explanations for this decline such as excessive regulation and market concentration. Additionally, he proposes that increasing energy costs and negative scale effects from rising economic complexity are slowing down innovation and reducing returns to research and development.

Although Chap. 4 deals in depth with the role of energy in the rise and decline of the West, it is useful for the present narrative to highlight this and foreshadow what is to come in the following chapters.

The rise of the West, starting with the Industrial Revolution in the late eighteenth century, has been explained as the fortune confluence of innovation (e.g. the steam engine and the power loom) and entrepreneurship (under appropriate "institutions" such as property rights). In this, the role of energy is neglected. The fact is that the Industrial Revolution and the rise of the West relied heavily on the availability and low cost of fossil fuels. This era, as Chap. 4 details, has however reached its limits as energy demand keeps increasing while energy efficiency approaches its physical limits. For instance, Naudé (2022a) notes that energy prices in Britain in 2012 were 60% higher than in 1974. Higher energy prices divert household consumption and business investment towards energy, reducing discretionary spending power. This stifles demand and slows down economic growth. Higher energy costs also have a detrimental impact on entrepreneurship and innovation. These costs get integrated into the capital required for starting and running a business, discouraging individuals from taking entrepreneurial risks and hindering "experimental innovation." As new ventures often lead innovation, this exacerbates economic slowdown.

The world economy's complexity, made possible by cheap energy, has moreover generated more entropy in the form of pollution and waste. As the world grapples with the consequences of this entropy, economic and productivity growth is declining. As Bradford DeLong (2022: 431) concludes in his magisterial work on the economic history of the twentieth century, "*Energy diverted away from producing more and into producing cleaner would quickly show up in lower wage increases and profits*."

Thus, rising energy costs and complexity act as "brakes" on innovation and entrepreneurial activity, making it more difficult to launch and grow new businesses. The result is that capitalism is failing to maintain economic growth rates in the West—recall Fig. 2.2. According to a World Bank study, economic growth rates are continuing to decline, warning that "Today nearly all the economic forces that drove economic progress are in retreat" (Kose & Ohnsorge, 2024: xix).

Naudé (2022a, 2022b) describes the decline in entrepreneurship, innovation, and R&D that are the proximate causes for the decline in economic growth rates since the 1970s. For example, as far as entrepreneurship is concerned, in the US, the ratio of new firms to total firms has declined by about 50% from 1978 to 2011. Additionally, the share of entrepreneurs in the workforce decreased from 7.8% in 1985 to 3.9% in 2014. Similar trends are observed in other high-income countries like Belgium and the UK. It is not just that there are relatively fewer entrepreneurs, but the quality of entrepreneurship also seems to have declined—the percentage of young firms (less than 5 years old) in the US decreased from 47% in the late 1980s to 39% in 2006, and their share of employment has fallen by 30% since the 1980s. This is of concern as young firms tend to be the most innovative.

Hence, it is no surprise that a broad range of innovation indicators have also deteriorated over time. This includes research productivity, which in the US economy has decreased significantly since the 1930s, with the ratio of patents to GDP also declining. The cost of patenting has continuously increased, and the average age of inventors at the time of their first patent has risen, indicating a shift towards more complex and lengthy innovation processes. In addition, large firms in the US have reduced their involvement in scientific research, with the average number of scientific publications by these firms halving between 1980 and 2015. This withdrawal from fundamental research could be a factor explaining the slowdown in innovation (Naudé, 2022a, 2022b).

2.4.2 Let the Zero-Sum Games Begin

The consequence of this gradual but inexorable decline in economic growth described in the previous sub-section is that the West is increasingly resembling a zero-sum economy: One firm, or one country, can generally only make itself better off at the expensive of another (Bris, 2023). Redistribution, instead of production, becomes the basis of the economy (Naudé, 2023a).

Naudé describes how the West is resembling a zero-sum economy. In this zero-sum economy, firms try their best to keep out competitors and extract as much profits as they can from the dwindling economic cake. Accordingly, it is no surprise that all measures of corporate dominance and industry concentration have been increasing (Covarrubias et al., 2019), and that the share of labour in output have declined (Autor et al., 2017a, 2017b). As corporations struggle against each other for a declining market, they increasingly resort to lobbying, rent-seeking, and policy capture to obtain protection against competition and access to extraction zones. Accordingly it is no surprise that at the same time that economic growth has been declining, there has been a rise of industrial policy nationalism (Johnstone, 2023), a slowdown in globalization (Zeihan, 2022), and an eruption of trade wars (Fetzer & Schwarz, 2021).

In the zero-sum economy, not only are firms and corporations acting less innovatively to obtain a market share but also more defensively and dominating, but society more broadly is getting more risk averse. This reflects that people are loss-averse, preferring to try and hold on to what they have rather than risk it all for something more or different. The consequence is that, as Bhaskar (2021) notes, "society has become more hostile to radical innovation, risk-averse, fractious, short-termist." This risk-averse, short-termist focus renders the social fabric. A more risk-averse society has less tolerance towards migrants,[3] a greater distrust of government (public trust in government in the US has, for instance, fallen from 77% in 1964 to 17% in 2019),[4] more moral relativism (Boudry, 2021) and religious dogma (McPhetres & Zuckerman, 2018), and even more outright anti-science sentiment (Kuntz, 2012).

The policy capture and distrust of government that rises in a zero-sum economy contributes to undermining democracy, which could be one of the major casualties in such a context. Reitz et al. (2021) ascribe the economic decline in the West to a degradation of democracy, pointing out that there has been, however from the beginning, a tension between democracy and neoliberalism. As they put it, "while liberalism in many parts of the world has come under attack by right-wing populism, potentially even with neo-fascist tendencies, democracy has been seen to be devolving into a post-democratic, technocratic system ever since the high times of neoliberalism" (Reitz et al., 2021: 252).

As Reitz et al. (2021) discuss, the slow decline in economic growth in the West since the 1970s and the concomitant increase in corporate concentration, power, and policy capture—the rise of the Oligarchy (as documented in detail in Chap. 3)—has eroded the growth-based compromise that has been part of the social contract in the West in the post–World War II era. This "growth-based compromise" was a shared understanding that economic growth would lead to benefits for all members of society. Today,

---

[3] See https://news.gallup.com/poll/320678/world-grows-less-accepting-migrants.aspx
[4] See https://www.pewresearch.org/politics/2022/06/06/public-trust-in-government-1958-2022/

the growth-based compromise has been replaced by a zero-sum economy, which intensifies distributional conflicts between social classes and national or regional economies, and which places immense pressure on the existing systems of parliamentary representation and popular mass parties. This erosion of traditional political structures is, in their analysis, paving the way for more authoritarian forms of governance as anxieties about scarcity and competition for limited resources increase. Reitz et al. (2021) suggest that if this polarization continues unchecked, it could lead to a "refeudalized social order" characterized by extreme inequality and a breakdown of democratic norms.

2.4.3 The Great Enshittification

The zero-sum logic described in the previous sub-section characterizes also much of the digital economy, which had been a hoped-for escape from the Great Stagnation. Today, however, it is clear that the growth benefits of the digital revolution have been reaped, largely with moderate productivity and growth increases in the late 1990s. Over the past decade, it has become clear that the hoped-for-digital revolution had in effect been obstructed by the de factor take-over and dominance of digital technologies, including the Internet, by a handful of dominating tech and digital platform firms, mostly US and Chinese firms and platforms.[5]

These tech giants, knowing the economy is stagnating, and that growth is declining, know that to maintain and grow profits, which they must do least they collapse given the nature of global capitalism (see Binswanger, 2013), they have to keep competitors out and squeeze as much profit as possible from existing markets. This they do by spending hundreds of millions of dollars lobbying policy makers for subsidies (Roeder, 2024), trade protection (hence the US trade and tech war with China—see, e.g., Fetzer and Schwarz (2021) and Wang et al. (2023)) and government contracts—most concernedly in recent times, contracts from the military-industrial complex (González, 2024).

They also try hard to prevent consumers from getting saturated by creating hype, hysteria, relentless advertising, and regularly making tweaks to their products to create the illusion of continuing novelty—which is one

---

[5] See for instance the Global Digital Platform Power Index 2023 which details the extent of global domination of US and Chinese platforms

reason why there have been 46 iPhone versions since 2007.[6] And of course, to squeeze as much profits from a limited market, they offer poor quality, low-paying jobs—"Bullshit Jobs" (Graeber, 2019). It is therefore no surprise that since the rise of digital platform firms there has been a sharp increase in indicators of corporate dominance and industry concentration and a decline in the share of labour in output (Autor et al., 2017a, 2017b; Covarrubias et al., 2019).

The ICT/digital revolution failed to live up to its promise. The main reason is that the digital economy, as one of the last extraction zones available, has been a diminishing source of extraction. After all, the digital economy is at least three decades old—Tapscott (1995) was one of the first to use the term in the 1990s. By around 2009 however, the digital economy's low hanging fruits had been eaten—and it had even become to be seen as a potential cause of further economic stagnation (Frey, 2015).

The Internet, for instance, has been over-commercialized (Cheong & Shin, 2024) and marked by a decline in quality that always follows when oligopolistic firms have done their extraction—this has been called the "Enshittification" of the Internet (Verso Books, 2024). Enshittification is a term coined by Cory Doctorow[7] to describe the gradual decline in quality and functionality of online services over time. It entails a decrease of user control as internet services become more restrictive, limiting customization or access to features; increasing corporate control as companies exert more influence over content and user behaviour; growing commercialization as services become more focused on advertising and monetization; and shrinking innovation as service providers become less willing to experiment or take risks. Enshittification is a process where online services, once innovative and user-friendly, become increasingly degraded and corporate-controlled.

Around 2009 was also the time when modern machine learning (ML)-based artificial intelligence (AI) was pushed to the fore as the hoped-for saviour technology—to allow the big tech firms another instrument with which to extend their extraction of profits from the digital economy. The CEO of Google declared AI to be more important than fire or electricity, and countless pronouncements were made by industry analysts, tech aficionados and consultancy firms of the huge boosts to economic growth, productivity and ultimately that would result from AI. Perhaps the most

[6] See https://theapplewiki.com/wiki/List_of_iPhones
[7] See https://en.wikipedia.org/wiki/Enshittification

outrageous of these was the McKinsey declaration that AI could "increase corporate profits by $4.4 trillion a year" (Chui & Yee, 2023).

Even AI Doomerism—the belief that AI poses an imminent existential threat to humanity—was largely inspired by think tanks promoting Longtermism and funded by tech Oligarchs, amongst others, to elevate the importance of AI (and the need to colonize Mars) (Wong, 2023; McGoey, 2023). One of the most (in)famous of such think tanks was the Institute for the Future of Humanity (IFH) at Oxford University, which was, however, closed down by the university in 2023 and which has been described as leaving a "toxic and contested legacy" (Anthony, 2024; Robins-Early, 2024).

Despite this hype and hysteria around AI, the ability of AI as product and service to extend the extraction of profits from the digital economy by oligarchic firms faces fundamental limits. A reason is the energy problem that the broader economy is already grappling with. The use of fossil fuels has generated so much greenhouse gases (GHG) that, as explained in previous paragraphs, the world is facing potentially catastrophic climate change (Bradshaw et al., 2021). Moreover, fossil fuels are limited in supply, and as this supply declines—peak oil being imminent—prices will rise. As a result, the net energy, or Energy Return to Energy Invested (EROI) from fossil fuels, is declining since more and more energy is needed to extract energy (Murphy et al., 2022).

Imagine how world production would plummet if the 500 virtual workers toiling day and night is suddenly withdrawn, and image the potentially inflationary consequences—to be added to the inflationary consequences of continued money printing. Unfortunately, it is the case that, as The Honest Sorcerer (2024) recognizes, "Mainstream economists are just as clueless about our deteriorating energy situation as our leadership class." Yes, the demand for fossil fuels is declining and the supply of renewable energy is growing, but this is not nearly fast enough to replace fossil fuels substantially (Heinberg, 2024a). In Chap. 4 these arguments are elaborated in greater detail.

Both the Internet and AI were greeted with great optimism when they started to be commercially used in the 1990s and 2010, respectively. However, neither has fully lived up to its promise. This is not because the technology is inherently flawed but because of the capture of the digital economy by a few dominant firms that continue to build moats around their sphere of extraction, stifling competition and innovation and abusing their oligopolistic power. Varoufakis (2021) labels this Technofeudalism, pointing out that

Today, the global economy is powered by the constant generation of central bank money, not by private profit. Meanwhile, value extraction has increasingly shifted away from markets and onto digital platforms, like Facebook and Amazon, which no longer operate like oligopolistic firms, but rather like private fiefdoms or estates.

2.5 Anthropocene Traps

Sørgaard Jorgensen et al. (2023: 1) "Inspired by what some have called a polycrisis, recently explored whether the human trajectory of increasing complexity and influence on the Earth system could become a form of trap for humanity." They argue that the Anthropocene has created various "traps" for humanity. Anthropocene traps refer to phenomena occurring on a global scale, where one or more human practices, initially beneficial, become maladaptive due to their negative impacts on human well-being.

Søgaard Jørgensen et al. (2023) identify and describe 14 such global Anthropocene Traps and their interactions, which are categorized into three main groups, namely *Global Traps*, *Technology Traps*, and *Structural Traps*. Table 2.1 summarizes these 14 traps within their three broad categories.

With the help of Table 2.1, it can be seen how the three key drivers of the economic decline of the West, namely Guns, Oil, and Oligarchs relate to Anthropocene Traps, and how the economic Growth Trap is a central trap that connects these. Table 2.1 shows that Søgaard Jørgensen et al. (2023) explicitly highlight what they call the "growth-for-growth" trap as one element of the overarching global traps that the Anthropocene has set for humanity.

The growth-for-growth trap is described by Søgaard Jørgensen et al. (2023) as a scenario where societal structures become locked into pursuing economic growth, even at the cost of human well-being. The relentless pursuit of growth becomes an end in itself, rather than a means to improve quality of life, leading to potential negative consequences such as increased, inequality, environmental degradation, and diminished well-being. The earlier sections of this chapter detailed how the global economy has become enmeshed in this growth-for-growth trap through the Growth Spiral and growth obsession that marks global capitalism. To this can now be added the insights of Søgaard Jørgensen et al. (2023), who stress the interconnected nature of Anthropocene Traps. Hence, technology traps and structural traps interact with the growth-for-growth trap to result in even worse outcomes.

Table 2.1 Anthropocene traps

Category of trap	Trap	Description
Global traps	• Simplification	Specialization leading to simplified systems vulnerable to shocks.
	• Growth-for-growth	Prioritizing economic growth over well-being.
	• Overshoot	Exceeding ecological limits, causing resource scarcity and environmental damage.
	• Division	Instability of global cooperation leading to conflict.
	• Contagion	Increased interconnectedness accelerating the spread of negative events, like pandemics.
Technology traps	• Infrastructure lock-in	Dependence on existing, potentially harmful infrastructure, such as fossil fuels.
	• Chemical pollution	The creation of harmful and persistent chemical compounds
	• Existential technology	Development of technologies with the potential for human extinction, like nuclear weapons.
	• Technological autonomy	Risks associated with increasingly autonomous technologies not aligning with human goals.
	• Dis- and mis-information	Amplified spread of misleading or false information through digital platforms.
Structural traps	• Short-termism	Favouring short-term gains over long-term sustainability.
	• Overconsumption	Separation of production and consumption masking the true environmental costs.
	• Biosphere disconnect	Reduced exposure to nature leading to a diminished understanding of its importance.
	• Local social capital loss	Erosion of local communities and collective action due to digitalization.

(Source: Author's compilation based on Søgaard Jørgensen et al., 2023)

One interaction is with the infrastructural and institutional lock-ins that exist between the Growth Trap and oil (described in greater depth in Chap. 4) and the Growth Trap and institutional lock-in. The latter refers to the almost inability of global institution, such as the UN and the Bretton Woods institutions, to act decisively despite the clear knowledge that the global economy is unsustainable. Table 2.1 also shows that the growth-for-growth trap is further embedded in society through various structural traps, such as the short-term pressure for profits by firms who would otherwise collapse, which lead to decisions that prioritize short-term profits over the long-term health of the planet. Furthermore, the

Growth Trap is not always that visible, or understood as trap, due to structural factors such as overconsumption, biosphere disconnect, and scale mismatches. One pertinent example is that the globalized economy, pushed to further and further expand globalization by capitalist firms under the pressure to growth and seek out new zones of extraction, often obscures the link between economic activity in one location and its social and environmental consequences elsewhere. This disconnect makes it difficult to see and address the negative externalities of economic growth and trade.

As technology and structural traps lock-in the obsession with economic growth, and furthermore intensify the adverse outcomes in terms of ecological overshoot and social fragmentation and inequality, the potential for conflict increases, and moreover conflict becomes a potential source of extraction thus becoming itself embedded as an Anthropocene Trap—a trap of division as Søgaard Jørgensen et al. (2023) explains.

Conflict and division as traps, therefore, operate at various levels -from international relations and geopolitical struggles to individual behaviours and psychological biases—influencing the dynamics of these interconnected challenges. Søgaard Jørgensen et al. (2023), therefore, describe conflict as a "trapping mechanism" driving Anthropocene traps. The growth-for-growth trap, with its need for relentless economic expansion, exacerbates resource competition, fuelling social unrest and potentially leading to conflict. Disinformation and the erosion of trust can undermine cooperation, both within and between countries, making it harder to find common ground on critical issues like climate change or decolonialism.

To this, Søgaard Jørgensen et al. (2023) add an important insight, namely that global cooperation has become inherently unstable under capitalism. The authors describe how the diverging interests of large corporations and their states have subjected the planet to a "Tragedy of the Commons" scenario, where their pursuit of every remaining extraction zone contributes to the depletion of shared resources or the escalation of global problems, ultimately undermining collective well-being and laying the basis for conflict. The Tragedy of the Commons outcome and the propensity for conflict is heightened by the zero-sum state of the global economy as Western economies become increasingly ossified, as explained in the previous sections of this chapter. The instability—and largely ineffectiveness—of global cooperation suggests that new forms of global governance are needed if the world is to address the global polycrisis and halt the economic decline of the West.

In conclusion, Guns, Oil, and Oligarchs are Anthropocene Traps. Countries do need arms to defend themselves. The commercialization and use of oil were a major driver of the Great Take-off, as was explained in Chap. 1. And a strong entrepreneurial class that can scale up their businesses can be beneficial if the resulting power is not abused and misused. Thus, this book argues that Guns, Oil, and Oligarchs have become maladaptive and that this is pushing the West towards decline and possibly collapse.

2.6 Concluding Remarks

This chapter provided background for the rest of the book by providing context for the subsequent discussions on oligarchs, oil, and guns. This chapter argued that these three elements are intrinsically linked through their relationship with economic growth: they both propel and depend on it. It has been posited that this dynamic has created a "grow-or-die" rule (a Growth Trap) for the global economy, implying its dependence on perpetual growth for survival.

This chapter started in section 2.2 by establishing the prevailing obsession in entrepreneurship scholarship and policy with firm growth, arguing that it stems from the belief that firm growth drives economic growth. This has led to a fixation in policy and scholarship on high-growth firms (HGFs). In section 2.2, it was argued that this fixation on HGFs is misguided and that the foundation of this obsession, the idea of perpetual economic growth, is flawed. Moreover, it was pointed out that the fixation on growth is deeply rooted in neoliberalism. Neoliberalism promotes the narrative that the pursuit of economic growth is noble and that wealth is solely a product of hard work and merit. This helps justify the concentration of wealth in the hands of a select few, and lend support to policies that prioritize the interests of oligarchs.

In section 2.3, this chapter explored the mechanisms that perpetuate the growth imperative and its dangers. The modern economy operates as an upward "Growth Spiral" fuelled by debt. Entrepreneurs borrow money to start and grow their businesses, necessitating continuous growth in their business and, by implication, the broader economy, to repay the debt and interest.

For sustained business growth, firms must constantly expand into new markets, a phenomenon this chapter relates to Rosa Luxemburg's thesis on capitalist imperialism. As domestic markets become saturated, corporations seek new territories for extraction and expansion. This never-ending search for new zones of extraction explains current trends of modifying and financializing nature and attempts to address deep ocean and asteroid mining. Moreover, a danger of the obsession with growth is socio-political instability. This chapter argued that the pursuit of perpetual growth has fuelled rising inequality within and between countries. This concentration of wealth has eroded the social fabric and led to declining levels of well-being in many advanced economies.

Section 2.4 explained the Great Stagnation, characterized by declining productivity and economic growth rates in the West since the 1970s. The Great Stagnation results from rising energy costs, economic complexity and scale burden, and a decline in entrepreneurship and innovation. A danger of the Great Stagnation is that as economic growth slows, the economy becomes a zero-sum game where one actor's gain is another's loss. This chapter explained how this zero-sum dynamic strengthens the Oligarchy and deepens the West's dependence on military and economic conflict. The "Enshittification" of the Internet was provided as an example of how, in a zero-sum dynamic, the capture of the Internet has caused the big tech firms to prioritize profit extraction over innovation and user experience, leading to a decline in the overall value of the digital economy.

Section 2.5 concluded by introducing the concept of Anthropocene traps, defined as initially beneficial human practices that become maladaptive due to their negative long-term consequences. Fourteen global Anthropocene traps were discussed, categorized into Global Traps, Technology Traps, and Structural Traps, and linked to the Guns-Oil-Oligarchy nexus.

CHAPTER 3

Oligarchs

3.1 Introduction

[Who] wield unsurpassed influence over the political realm while promoting the notion that when the rules are organized around the greater prosperity for those who already enjoy most of it, everyone's the winner.— Goodman (2022)

This chapter critiques a key feature of neoliberal capitalism: the capture of the system by a narrow elite, the oligarchs, as defined in Chap. 1. It explains how this leads the system to collapse on itself. The central mechanisms of this are simple: neoliberal capitalism requires constant expansion and extraction to maintain rents and profits, which are facilitated by military force (guns) but which inevitably runs up against ecological constraints and the environmental damage that this causes and social resistance. Moreover, the use of military force becomes more than a mere tool of conquest—it becomes a source from which to extract further rents: the Permanent War Economy.

As such, this chapter details how the oligarchy contributes to the economic decline of the West. It illuminates how the oligarchy stifles innovation, undermines democratic processes, hinders effective responses to global challenges like climate change, and potentially contributes to militarization and conflict.

Section 3.2 describes the rise and nature of the oligarchy. The term "oligarchy" has been defined in Chap. 1 as a system where a small, elite, and wealthy group wields significant economic and, consequently, political power, often at the expense of the broader population (Monbiot, 2024). Their wealth translates into disproportionate political influence, which is then used to further enrich themselves. The various dimensions of this definition are explained and the rise of the oligarchy after World War II described.

Section 3.3 describes how the oligarchy wields influence and control. Sections 3.4 to 3.6 then dissect the oligarchy's impacts on innovation, science, and democracy, three pillars of Western prosperity.

Section 3.7 concludes this chapter.

3.2 The Rise and Nature of the Oligarchy

Just as we [the US] have the world's most advanced economy, military, and technology, we also have its most advanced oligarchy.—Johnson (2009)

3.2.1 Definition of Oligarchy

As mentioned in Chap. 1, the term oligarchy refers to a system where a small, elite, and wealthy group wields significant economic and, consequently, political power, often at the expense of the broader population. Winters and Page (2009: 752) define oligarchy as "a specific kind of minority power that is fundamentally material in character," where "the wealthiest citizens deploy unique and concentrated power resources to defend their unique minority interests." They argue that oligarchs are not merely elites, but individuals who command vast wealth, which they leverage for political gain.

Curtis (2024) similarly describes oligarchy as a system "where a small number of people exert control over the state," often operating under the guise of democratic institutions. He argues that while countries like the UK (and US) might have elections and a judiciary, the concentration of power in the hands of a few undermines genuine democratic accountability. This results in democracy becoming a plutocracy, where political power is most strongly wielded not by the ordinary citizens but by the oligarchy. This often empowers the military-industrial complex (MIC) and the War Economy; for instance, in the case of the UK, Curtis (2024) points out that *"British foreign policy-making is so centralised that it is akin to an authoritarian regime. A prime minister can send troops to war or bomb another country without even consulting parliament, as the UK has recently been doing in Yemen [...] Blair took the country into an illegal war in Iraq, killing hundreds of thousands, and has faced no prosecution. British ministers facilitated Saudi war crimes in Yemen for seven years during 2015–22—and rarely was anyone in authority even questioned about* it."

On 24 March 2022 the European Parliament[1] passed a resolution on the "fight against oligarch structures" noting that "*In the current EU political context, the term 'oligarchy' is used as a way of pointing out the influence of the wealthy and powerful in politics and government, and that of the economic, financial and industrial actors who can exercise influence that is typically used to benefit the few at the expense of the many; highlights that members of national governments and other holders of political positions are part of the oligarchy in some Member States and have actively sought to use EU funds to benefit themselves financially.*"

A defining feature of the Oligarchy is the translation of their wealth into political influence. They do this through lobbying efforts, campaign contributions, control over media narratives, and the "revolving door" phenomenon—where, for instance, government officials or political office bearers take up influential positions in the private sector following their term in government. Winters and Page (2009) constructed an *Individual Material Power Index* to measure, in the US, the extent of political power of the wealthiest Americans. They found that "each of the top 400 or so richest Americans had on average about 22,000 times the political power of the average member of the bottom 90 percent, and each of the top 100 or so had nearly 60,000 times as much" (Winter and Page, 2009: 737).

Third, oligarchy is close associated with the erosion of democracy and the rise of a plutocracy. Democracy is eroded by oligarchs directly shaping the agenda of politicians (e.g. through campaign contributions), through influencing the intellectual debate through think tanks, or influencing public opinion ("manufacturing consent") through their control of the mass media. In the process though, they undermine public trust in government, and erode democratic norms. Noam Chomsky (2017) described this as a vicious wealth-power circle, where wealth generates political power, and political power, in turn, generates further wealth.

---

[1] See: https://www.europarl.europa.eu/doceo/document/TA-9-2022-0100_EN.html

3.2.2 Who Is the Oligarchy?

Who is the Oligarchy—in the West—and what is its extent and power?

Oligarchs are typically billionaires. In the US, there are 813 individuals worth a combined $5.7 trillion—which is about a third of all billionaires in the world (Johnson, 2024; Zucman, 2024).

There are several ways to measure the extent and power of the oligarchy. One set of measures is the increasing share of GDP accruing to the top 1% of income earners, the declining relative share of labour in total GDP over time, and the growing extent of corporate concentration.

Regarding the share of GDP accruing to the top 1% of income earners, Fig. 3.1 shows the evolution of top 1% inequality in the US since 1913. It shows the "Great Compression" following the War and the post-War reconstruction, and then the resumption of "business-as-usual" with the rise of the oligarchs buoyed by neoliberalism since the 1970s. By 2022, the top 1% of income earners in the US were taking in 21% of pre-tax national incomes. This approaches the levels of the Gilded Age that preceded the Great Depression in the early 1930s.

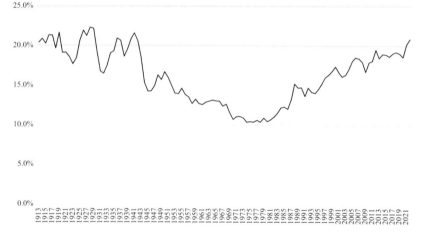

Fig. 3.1 Share of top 1% in pre-tax national income, US, 1913–2022. (Source: Author, based on data from the World Income Inequality Database, https://wid.world)

Monbiot and Hutchison (2024: 33, 45) report that since around 1989, the super-rich in the US has grown around US$ 21 trillion richer, whilst those with the lowest 50% of incomes have become US$900 billion poorer—and that the wealth of US billionaires increased 12-fold between 1990 and 2020. A study by Institute for Policy Studies examined the growing wealth of the US's 50 wealthiest families, which by 2020 held US$ 1.2 trillion in assets. This amount is equivalent to half the total wealth shared by the bottom 50% of all US households—an estimated 65 million families (Collins et al., 2021). The IPS report also found that the assets of the wealthiest 50 families have grown by 1007% between 1983 and 2020. This rate of growth outpaced the average American's wealth growth by a factor of 10 (Collins et al., 2021; Kohli, 2021).

The US's Congressional Budget Office (CBO) conducted a study on the trends in family wealth distribution in the US from 1989 to 2019 and found that the total wealth held by the top 1% increased from 27% to 34% over the same period and that families in the bottom 50% of the wealth distribution saw their share of total wealth decrease from 4% in 1989 to a mere 2% in 2019. The CBO study also highlighted significant racial disparities in wealth accumulation, for instance, White families' median wealth was 6.5 times that of Black families (Nichols, 2022). While a small exclusive club of entrepreneurs and wealthy families in the US gets richer and richer, the rest of the country is heading to be the world's "first former middle class society" (Stiglitz, 2015).

Elsewhere in the West, similar patterns of rising inequality reflect the power of the wealthy, especially in the old and fallen Empire that is the UK (Curtis, 2024; Monbiot, 2022a, 2022b; Hutton, 2024). As described by Hutton (2024) in the UK, "the gap between our richest and poorest 10% is now, the US excepted, the highest in the developed world. Accelerating since the financial crisis, wealth inequality casts a shadow over all our lives, affecting health, housing, education, productivity, enterprise, the media and even the vitality of our democracy." He notes that "the wealth gap between the top and bottom 10% grew from £7.5tn to £11tn between 2011" and warns that it is threatening the country's democracy and media:

> Wealth finances the capacity to lobby and generate knowledge and ideas that favour the rich rather than common interest outcomes. Very little of our

media is particularly profitable; it is much easier to recruit rich individuals from the pool of the wealthy prepared to underwrite an otherwise uncommercial media to make wealth defence arguments than it is to support a more liberal media. Media bias is not a law of nature, it is an outgrowth of wealth inequality. (Hutton, 2024)

Chancel and Piketty (2021: 3025) pointed out that inequality at the neocolonial twenty-first century is similar to that in the twentieth century. The persistence of inequality has, according to The Economist (2014), heralded a new gilded age headed by a class of entrepreneurs and crony capitalists who constitutes "new virtual nation of Mammon."

Various recent studies have documented the growing extent of corporate concentration in the US. Naudé (2022a, 2022b: 112–113) summarizes the recent literature, noting for instance that in the US "average increase in concentration levels has been around 90%" and that this has boosted the profits of the corporate sector, but not in a productive way, but "rather due to higher market power of incumbents allowing them to raise mark-ups." See Covarrubias et al. (2019) and Grullon et al. (2019) who provide empirical evidence for the rise in "bad" corporate concentration and how it has been driving profits through higher mark-ups. Kwon et al. (2024) describe the persistent increase in corporate concentration in the US over the past century. By 2018, the top 1% of US corporation's share of total assets reached 97%. They document a steady increase in corporate concentration for at least 100 years, regardless of whether it is measured by asset share, sales share, or net income share of top businesses (Kwon et al., 2024).

By 2017 only three firms, *BlackRock*, *Vanguard*, and *State Street*, controlled more than 40% of all public firms in the US (Fichtner et al., 2017). And four firms, the *ABCD* (Archer-Daniels-Midland Company, Bunge, Cargill, and Louis Dreyfus), control around 90% of the global grain trade (Harvey, 2022). They are the Food Barons.

With an oligarchy, the issue is that the wealthy individuals and corporations turn their material resources into political power. Having established the huge income and wealth inequalities in the US in the preceding paragraphs, the question is, what are the political consequences? Winters and Page (2009) constructed an *Individual Material Power Index* to measure, in the US, the extent of political power of the wealthiest Americans. They found that "each of the top 400 or so richest Americans had on average about 22,000 times the political power of the average member of the bottom 90 percent, and each of the top 100 or so had nearly 60,000 times as much" (Winter and Page, 2009: 737).

The wealthy not only turn their wealth into political power but also turn it disproportionately into GHG emissions. A study in *Nature Sustainability* found that "since 1990, the bottom 50% of the world population has been responsible for only 16% of all emissions growth, whereas the top 1% has been responsible for 23% of the total. While per-capita emissions of the global top 1% increased since 1990, emissions from low- and middle-income groups within rich countries declined" (Chancel, 2022).

Who are these individuals or families and which are the groups of spheres of influence to which they belong? Barak (2024), without being exhaustive, lists as famous individuals who are oligarchs people such as Jeff Bezos (Founder of Amazon), highlighted for his immense wealth and Elon Musk (Head of Tesla, X, SpaceX), as well as Donald Trump. Other sources would mention Mark Zuckerberg (Meta), and Peter Thiel as oligarchs. Typical US corporations that are mentioned as be oligarchic include Amazon.com, Inc.; BlackRock, Vanguard, and State Street; Koch Industries; Walmart; Starbucks; JPMorgan Chase, Wells Fargo, Citibank (and other major banks), American, Southwest, Delta, and United Airlines; Comcast, Disney, Warner Brothers and the major US Drug Companies. In addition to these are the tech giants Apple, Microsoft, IBM, Meta, Google, and the military-industrial complex corporations—the Guns Oligarchs (see Chap. 5 for detail).

Various categorizations of oligarchs have been made in the literature, such as corporate elites, financial elites, individuals, and families with inherited wealth, and donors and lobbyists. Corporate elites are CEOs and boards of directors with immense wealth and influence. Financial Elites are associated with powerful financial institutions and asset managers like Blackrock in shaping investment flows and influencing the economy. Inherited wealth also plays a role in perpetuating oligarchy. Individuals and families who have accumulated wealth over generations often wield significant economic and social power. Wealthy donors and lobbyists have significant influence on politicians, these include of course corporate and financial elites.

Hartmann (2021, 2023) distinguishes between business oligarchs and political oligarchs. Business oligarchs, for example, Elon Musk, obtain political power as a result of their business wealth. Political oligarchs, on other hand, are individuals who obtain political power first and then leverage that power to amass wealth. Vladimir Putin is an example.

Two key groups of oligarchies that feature in this book are the oligarchs that form the military industrial complex (MIC) (Chap. 5) and those that form Big Oil (Chap. 4). In section 3.2.3, three other groupings of oligarchs, who overlap with those of the MIC and Big Oil, are introduced: the financial oligarchy (The Bankers), the food oligarchy (The Food Barons), and the digital oligarchy (The Technofeudalists). All of these clusters of oligarchs project their influence through the mainstream mass media oligarchy. Before proceeding it is necessary to emphasize the growing role that the mainstream media owned by the Media Moguls plays to influence public opinion.

According to Nayak (2020)

> The essence of neoliberal capitalism and its affiliated media is to create domesticated and uncritical mass audience and destroy critical voices representing people. The idea is to create mass produce social, cultural and political values that accepts the dominance of illegitimate authority and power. It is the market monopoly that controls the media today. The market monopolies are controlled by oligarchs of mass media. There are six companies (Comcast, Disney, Time Warner, Fox, CBS and Viacom), which control almost all 90% media in USA and other parts of the world.

3.2.3 Rise of the Oligarchy

While the popular narrative describes the West as a collective of liberal democracies, and while Western countries are indeed—at least nominally—democratic, the West has nevertheless become a de facto oligarchy and plutocracy. Curtis (2024), Fishkin and Forbath (2024), Sachs (2018), and Winters and Page (2009) outline how the US and other Western societies, despite their democratic facades, are increasingly characterized by oligarchic tendencies, where a small elite exerts disproportionate control over political and economic systems. And Chomsky (2017), Formisano (2015), Kuhner (2015), and Mahbubani (2022) are amongst those who argue that the US is a plutocracy rather than a democracy.

Mahbubani (2022: 35) asks what is the evidence for claims that the US has become an oligarchy/plutocracy? He answers this question as follows:

It [the evidence for plutocracy] is massive. The wealthy have seized most of the new wealth [...] But the wealthy are not satisfied with seizing more wealth. They are also seizing political power. Two Princeton University political scientists, Gilens and Page, have documented in detail how political outcomes in America reflect the interests of the wealthy, not the mass voters. Hence, they sadly conclude 'in the United States, our findings indicate, the majority does not rule—at least not in the causal sense of actually determining policy outcomes.'

While the rise in the fortunes of the super-rich in the US, and in many other Western countries, has been dramatic since the 1970s and 1980s, the origin of the US oligarchy is, like that of the military industrial complex (MIC), much deeper historically. In 1895, Howard (1895: 7–15) already described the "rise of the oligarchy" in the US, relating it to the system of growth-obsessed capitalism that ignited a "mad rush for wealth" in which wake "the spirit of liberty took flight" to be superseded by "the spirit of gain and avarice."

Hartmann (2023) documents the historical development of the US oligarchy, which he traces back to the intensive adoption of the *cotton gin*[2] in the eighteenth century in the American South. The gin enabled the mass production of cotton, which increased the demand for enslaved labour and concentrated wealth in the hands of a small number of plantation owners (see also McMichael, 1991; Lakwete, 2003). This economic power translated into political power, creating a "police state" where these elite families held sway. Hartmann (2023) posits that the US Civil War was, in part, a fight against this oligarchic system. While this was partly the case, the Civil War "enthroned" corporations in the political landscape of the US. In this respect, Howard (1895: 8–9) quotes Abraham Lincoln, who warned after the end of the Civil War against the rise of the oligarchy. He describes that, in 1864 Abraham Lincoln "wrote these memorable words":

> Yes, we may congratulate ourselves that this cruel war is nearing its close. It has cost a vast amount of treasure and blood. The best blood of the flower

---

[2] A cotton gin is a tool that separates the seeds from cotton fibres. It is often states that this was invented by Eli Whitney in 1793/94 and subsequently revolutionized the cotton industry in the US—and contributed to the expansion of slavery in the South (McMichael, 1991; Oakes, 2016). Lakwete (2003) however argues that Whitney did not invent the cotton gin, but that it was invented centuries before in Asia and Africa.

of American youth has been freely offered upon our country's altar that the nation might live. It has been, indeed, a trying hour for the Republic; but I see in the near future a crisis approaching that unnerves me and causes me to tremble for the safety of my country. As a result of the war, corporations have been enthroned and an era of corruption in high places will follow, and the money power of the country will endeavor to prolong its reign by working upon the prejudices of the people, until all wealth is aggregated in a few hands and the Republic is destroyed.

According to Barak (2024) there is a parallel between this historical oligarchy and present day corporations like Amazon, which despite massive profits, have paid minimal taxes, while their owners have seen enormous increases in their personal wealth, echoing the earlier concentration of wealth in the hands of plantation owners and in corporations that arose during the Civil War.

Monbiot (2024) argues that the normal state of politics is one of oligarchy, and the period following World War II, often idealized as a time of shared prosperity and strong social safety nets in the West, was actually an anomaly in the long trajectory of wealth and power concentration. The War caused a "Great Compression" of wealth inequality through the wartime destruction of assets, high taxes, and the rise of labour movements. However, over time, the impact of these factors has faded, and oligarchic tendencies have reasserted themselves.

The reassertion of oligarchic tendencies has been facilitated by the rise of neoliberal ideology after the War. The pivotal moment was the economic crises of the 1970s that was set in motion by the oil price crises and which resulted in inflation and slow growth. These crises created an opening for neoliberal ideas to take hold, and resulted in the "Great Neoliberal Experiment" (Hartmann, 2024). This entailed the assumption of political power by political leaders such as Ronald Reagan and Margaret Thatcher who implemented neoliberal policies not only in the West but exported it to the Global South. According to Hartmann (2023) this resulted in a shift towards oligarchy in various countries, including Russia, Turkey, the Philippines, and South Africa.

3.2.4 *Tenets of Neoliberal Ideology*

Neoliberal ideology has three key tenets and consequences, which will become clear in the rest of this chapter and are summarized here. The first is its belief in laissez faire and minimum government intervention in the economy. Hence, neoliberal policies include policies such as privatization, reductions in tax and social welfare, limitations on trade union power. A second tenet of neoliberal ideology is the promotion of globalization and the freedom of mobility for international capital, for instance through reduction of tariffs and foreign exchange controls, and the facilitation of international investment. A third, implicit, tenet is the undermining of democracy by shifting political power to corporations.

Economic policies such as deregulation and privatization reduced the role of government in the economy for the poor; however, as will be seen, as far as spending to bail out wealthy bankers or fill the coffers of the military-industrial complex has been concerned, the government has remained a very active economic agent. Moreover, the corporate capture of institutions has seen greater control of key institutions of Western thinking, science, culture and sensemaking, including universities, regulatory bodies, and media outlets, undermining innovation and democracy.

Due to the belief in individual liberty—and free speech, the US Supreme Court made rulings in 1976 and 1978 that equated political campaign contributions with free speech, laying the groundwork for increased corporate and wealthy individual influence in elections. According to Hartmann (2023), this shift signalled to oligarchs that the political system was receptive to their influence.

There was—and still is—a coordinated and strategic push to spread neoliberal ideology (Monbiot & Hutchison, 2024). Influential think tanks, many funded by wealthy elites, have been instrumental in the widespread acceptance of neoliberal ideas. An early promoter was the Trilateral Commission, which was established in 1973 by David Rockefeller. In the 1960s, the commission argued that the US was facing a "crisis of democracy," arguing that the surge in democratic participation and demands for greater equality during the 1960s made it challenging to govern Western democracies effectively—as the more educated citizens are, the more they would question the government. This could be seen as the start of the oligarchy's problem with democracy. Today, the Trilateral Commission is seen as being widely influential in driving the corporatization of US universities (Jones, 2020).

More recently, the oil oligarchy (see also Chap. 4) captured the US Republican Party regarding its stance on climate change and the regulation of fossil fuels. As Faber (2023: 12) describes,

Fourteen years ago, many Republicans were in favor of measures to address climate change and protect the public from its deleterious effects […] Then the imperilled fossil fuel industry—led primarily by Charles and David Koch—threw its tentacles into the pockets of GOP members standing in opposition to climate change legislation, and stances flipped across the party. […] In the 116th Congress (2019–2021), some 150 Republican climate denialists accepted $68 million in donations from the fossil fuel industry, compared to $23.6 million in 2006.

The consequences of decades of intellectual capture of western thought on how economies should best be managed by neoliberal ideology have resulted in growing inequality, the establishment of an oligarchy, and increased environmental destruction, with the political power of the elite growing in tandem with the growing wealth, and hence a gradual but steady transformation of the US and other Western countries into plutocracies. Six groups of oligarchies can be discerned—*Big Oil, the mainstream media owners, the bankers, food industry oligarchs, the Technofeudalists, and the MIC (defence contractors)*. The Bankers, Food Oligarchs, and Technofeudalists will be discussed in the following sub-sections, while Chaps. 4 and 5 will pay more attention to Big Oil and the mainstream media owners.

3.2.5   *The Financial Elites: The Banker's Takeover*

By the 1970s, say General Electric could make more profit playing games with money than you could by producing in the United States. You have to remember that General Electric is substantially a financial institution today. It makes half its profits just by moving money around in complicated ways. It's very unclear that they're doing anything that of value to the economy.—Chomsky (2017)

When faced with crisis, policymakers have often called on entrepreneurs to rescue the day. *The Economist* magazine, in 2009 in the midst of the Global Financial Crisis (GFC, roughly 2008–2010), a special section on entrepreneurs as *Global Heroes*[3] (Naudé, 2016). The previous time when *The Economist* magazine published such an enthusiastic endorsement of entrepreneurship was during the 1970s recession. Its 25 December 1976

---

[3] See: http://www.economist.com/node/13216025

edition carried an article entitled, "The Coming Entrepreneurial Revolution: A Survey."[4] See also Naudé (2016).

On both occasions, entrepreneurship was resorted to because policy-makers and academics had run out of other policy options. And in both cases the articles and sections in *The Economist* turned out not as hoped for: the subsequent deregulation widely adopted in the 1980s and staunchly promoted by Margaret Thatcher and Ronald Reagan heralded in a period of unbridled growth in the incomes and wealth of the top 0.1% of the population in the US and Europe (Atkinson et al., 2011). There was no entrepreneurial revolution; rather, entrepreneurial talent was increasingly (mis)-allocated to the financial sector, which, following financial deregulation in the 1970s, led to the rapid financialization of the US and European economies. This *The Bankers'* "Takeover" stimulated the corporate greed and risk-taking that eventually caused the 2008–2009 Global Financial Crisis (Johnson & Kwak, 2011).

The Global Financial Crisis, as Gries and Naudé (2011: 2–3) describe its timeline and causes, was triggered by the collapse of the investment banking firm Lehman Brothers on 15 September 2008. At the time, Lehman Brothers had assets of US$639 billion, which made it back then largest bankruptcy in US history. Lehman's collapse was the first of many caused by what is labelled the "sub-prime mortgage" crisis. The sub-prime mortgage crisis itself was the outcome of the combination of the deregulation of the US's financial system which created a massive moral hazard for the banking sector, and incentivized unsustainable risk-taking. The deregulation led to the extension of mortgage finance—by 2006 exceeding US$1.3 trillion (Lin, 2008) to households with little prospects of repaying their loans—so-called Ninja-bonds (to households with no-income-no-jobs). The moral hazard was due to the fact that most of the banks considered themselves too big to fail (TBTF) thus assuming that if their risk taking goes bad, they will be bailed out. They were correct, and after the bailouts many of the largest banks became even bigger (Cho, 2009). The moral hazard was also strengthened by what banks perceived to be perpetually rising house prices, which meant that if households should default, the property could be resold at a higher value.

As Gries and Naudé (2011: 3) explain, the financial sector also tried to hide the risk by securitizing the expected income streams from these bad loans, packaging them in with other securities such as Collateralized Debt

[4] See http://normanmacrae.ning.com/forum/topics/entrepreneurial-revolution

Obligations (CDOs). The sales of these throughout the world was facilitated by another bad incentive structure, namely Credit Rating Agencies, who were clients of the financial sector, who provided these CDOs with AAA ratings (Ely, 2009; Barth, 2008).

Eventually the housing price bubble burst, mortgage defaults started to rise, as did short-term interest rates, making the servicing of mortgage debt more difficult. By 2007 it was clear that an economic and financial crisis was looming, and by mid-2008, almost 40% of sub-prime mortgage loans extended in 2006 were non-performing (Gries & Naudé, 2011: 3). With the collapse of Lehman Brothers in September 2008 the sub-prime crisis became systemic, and soon afterwards, global. Around US$25 trillion in wealth was wiped from global stock markets in the months following Lehman's collapse. In 2009 global trade collapsed by 11%, the largest decline since World War II. Deregulation, the financialization of the US and EU economies, greed, and moral hazards had caused the deepest global recession since the Great Depression of the 1930s.

It has been argued by many that the Global Financial Crisis (GFC) has only been papered over (with taxpayers' money, in the form of amongst other bailouts and quantitative easing) and that the underlying financial fragility, due to excessive financialization, remains a cause of concern. Research by the US Federal Reserve shows that financial instability is far from over, and that the share of firms in financial distress in the US have "reached a level that is higher than during most previous tightening episodes since the 1970s" (Perez-Orive & Timmer, 2023).

Summarizing the causes of the GFC, Minniti et al. (2023: 25) write that the GFC has resulted from

> Contracting problems by rationally bounded agents […] the core problem was mortgage contracts extended to households with no collateral and/or insufficient income to repay the mortgage. For as long as house prices kept on rising, banks could continue this practice. Moreover, they could contract with investors through sales of collateralised debt obligations (CDOs), thereby passing on the risk to the investors who, being boundedly rational, had neither the resources nor the ability to adequately evaluate the risk of investing in CDOs.

Additionally, banks knew that if they were eventually going to suffer losses as an extent of their excessive risk-taking, they were too-big-to-fail (TBTF) and would be bailed out. Banks had become TBTF as a result of regulatory capture: the successive deregulation of the financial sector was the result of decades of lobbying by the financial sector, and a cosy relationship—referred to as a "revolving door"—between the big banks and politicians in Washington, DC (Johnson & Kwak, 2011; Johnson, 2009; Stiglitz, 2009).

To understand how financialization happened and how it is undermining the fabric of innovative, productive entrepreneurship in the West, consider the case of Iceland and how the Bankers' Takeover led to the collapse of its economy during the Global Financial Crisis of 2008–2010.

Iceland was once hailed a miracle economy and an example of an entrepreneurial economy par excellence, compared in the latter aspect favourably with the bastion of entrepreneurship, the US: Iceland has been described as a European country with a US labour market (Keiser, 2008). But by 2008, Iceland's entrepreneurs had created a financial sector that was by 2008 ten times the size of its GDP. As the sub-prime mortgage crisis started to unfold, the country's bloated financial sector collapsed in October 2008. It was rapidly followed by the collapse of the country's government, in January 2009 (Naudé, 2016). What happened to the miracle entrepreneurial economy?

What happened was that entrepreneurs had captured the financial system and the policy-making process. Three entrepreneurial families, who made their fortunes in the shipping, brewing, and frozen food industries, took complete control of the country's banks, the Glitnir, Landsbanki, and Kaupthing (Mason, 2008). Emboldened by an ideology of free markets, financial deregulation, and financial engineering, they seemed to have convinced and lobbied policymakers of the soundness of their business model and that there were no conflicts of interest between them owning Iceland's banks and running many large businesses in other sectors of the Icelandic economy. As the *Special Investigative Committee* (SIC, 2010) [p. 10] report into the Icelandic crisis reported:

> The SIC thinks that the operations of the Icelandic banks were, in many ways, characterized by their maximizing the benefit of the bigger shareholders, who held the reins in the banks, rather than by running reliable banks with the interests of all shareholders in mind and showing due responsibility towards creditors. It appears that worries about conflict of interest between the operation of the banks and the operation of other companies owned by the same parties had vanished. (Naudé, 2016)

In the US, a similar dynamic as in Iceland had led to the regulatory capture of government by a financial oligarchy. This regulatory capture has been described as a "coup." Taibbi (2009), writing in *Rolling Stone Magazine*, pressed on the sore when he wrote:

> The reality is that the worldwide economic meltdown and the bailout that followed were together a kind of revolution, a coup d'état. They cemented and formalized a political trend that has been snowballing for decades: the gradual takeover of the government by a small class of connected insiders, who used money to control elections, buy influence and systematically weaken financial regulations.

Johnson (2009) and Taibbi (2009) have called the GFC a coup—a "quiet coup"—in which "elite business interests-financiers, in the case of the U.S.-played a central role [...] making ever-larger gambles, with the implicit backing of the government, until the inevitable collapse." Moreover, Johnson (2009) describes how the bankers used their political power to "prevent precisely the sorts of reforms that are needed" and that "the government seems helpless, or unwilling, to act against them." They got their political power over decades, through political funding and "cultural capital" or an ideology of the superiority of free markets. As Johnson (2009) puts it, "the American financial industry gained political power by amassing a kind of cultural capital-a belief system. Once, perhaps, what was good for General Motors was good for the country. Over the past decade, the attitude took hold that what was good for Wall Street was good for the country." It also helped that "the banking-and-securities industry has become one of the top contributors to political campaigns."

The regulatory capture of the state by the financial oligarchs in the US parallels the Soviet Union, or more accurately, post-Soviet Russia. Writing in 2009, Johnson (2009) describes the plight of a Russia, which had failed in its post-Soviet transition to a market economy, seeing its economy taken over by a powerful oligarchy. He also sounded a warning, stating that

> Boris Fyodorov, the late finance minister of Russia, struggled for much of the past 20 years against oligarchs, corruption, and abuse of authority in all its forms. He liked to say that confusion and chaos were very much in the interests of the powerful-letting them take things, legally and illegally, with impunity. When inflation is high, who can say what a piece of property is really worth? When the credit system is supported by byzantine government arrangements and backroom deals, how do you know that you aren't being

fleeced? Our future could be one in which continued tumult feeds the looting of the financial system, and we talk more and more about exactly how our oligarchs became bandits and how the economy just can't seem to get into gear.

What makes this prospect, of "continued tumult" feeding the "looting of the financial system" especially scary is that, as Johnson (2009) points out, in the case of the US, "just as we have the world's most advanced economy, military, and technology, we also have its most advanced oligarchy."

3.2.6 The Rise and Financialization of Industrial Agriculture

Like the financial system before the 2008 crisis, the global food system has experienced increasing consolidation, with a few powerful corporations dominating the market. These corporations are becoming increasingly interconnected through shared strategies, similar risk management practices, and a heavy reliance on a few key crops and production methods (Monbiot, 2022a, 2022b).

Only four corporations dominate the modern agri-food system—The Food Barons. They are known as the ABCD, standing for Archer Daniels Midland (ADM), Bunge, Cargill, and Louis Dreyfus. These corporations are major traders of grain globally and have shaped the global food system in several profound ways. The ABCD companies influence the regulatory environment through lobbying efforts, campaign contributions, and placing former employees in government positions. They advocate for policies that benefit their interests, such as trade liberalization and deregulation (Murphy & Burch, 2012).

By controlling the global grain trade, they have substantial leverage in setting prices and influencing what farmers grow. They are, however, not just traders but operate across the entire agri-food supply chain, from providing inputs to farmers to processing and transporting agricultural products. This includes the financialization of commodity markets by establishing financial services divisions that manage investments in agricultural derivatives. This has increased speculative investment in agricultural markets, which leads to price volatility. Furthermore, all four companies are involved in the biofuels sector, supplying inputs, producing biofuels, and investing in biofuel crops. This has raised concerns about the impact on food prices and land use, as it has increased demand for crops like maize and soybeans for fuel production rather than food (Murphy & Burch, 2012).

ABCD companies are also increasingly acquiring land, either directly or through subsidiaries. This has fuelled concerns about land grabbing and the displacement of smallholder farmers (Murphy & Burch, 2012).

Monbiot (2022a, 2022b) has warned that, just like the global financial system collapsed as a result of concentration, financialization and short-sighted strategies, the global agri-food system is at threat of collapse. He argues that the concentration of power within the global food system raises the risks of a collapse significantly because of a number of consequences of concentration, such as common risk management practices, the stripping away of redundancies and backup systems within the food system and the reliance on a few key nodes and chokepoints within the global food system. This all will amplify the impact of disruptions so that a problem in one area can cascade throughout the entire system, in a similar way as to how the failure of Lehman Brothers in 2008 triggered the Global Financial crisis. Similarly, the growing dominance of a few major crops in global agriculture, often grown in geographically concentrated areas using standardized farming techniques, makes the entire global food system susceptible to collapse in the face of an unexpected disaster (Monbiot, 2022a, 2022b).

3.2.7 *The Tech Bro's and Digital Dystopias*

Just as oligarchies dominate the financial and agricultural sectors, the digital economy is dominated by an oligarchy. In Silicon Valley speak, this oligarchy is referred to as The Technofeudalists—the Tech Bros (the billionaires leading the giant tech firms tend to be middle-aged white men). They consist of the GAFA—Google, Apple, Facebook (Meta), and Amazon. To these, one can add Microsoft.

Yanis Varoufakis argues that the Tech Bro oligarchy "killed capitalism" and heralded in a new stage of capitalism, which he calls Technofeudalism. According to Varoufakis (2024a, 2024b), this stage of capitalism is characterized by a shift from profit-driven capitalism to a system driven by rent extraction, much like the feudal systems of medieval Europe. Digital platforms like Amazon and Apple are, in essence, "digital fiefdoms" where their oligarchs are rentier capitalists extracting "cloud rents" from whoever is using their platform—precisely analogous to the feudal practice where farmers had to give up a share of their production to the Feudal

Lord for the privilege of farming the land. Apple, for instance, takes a 30% rentier commission on transactions on its App Store. Furthermore, users of digital platforms contribute to the "cloud" capital of these companies through their data and content creation. This free labour likened to the work of serfs on a feudal estate, is labelled by Varoufakis as "cloud serfs" (see also Meaker, 2023).

Technology is a primary tool for the oligarchy to consolidate power and influence, enabling surveillance, data collection, and algorithmic decision-making. This erodes privacy, limits individual freedoms, and enables new forms of social control (Tirole, 2021; Zuboff, 2015). It raises concerns about the future of democratic governance (Varoufakis, 2023).

It is not only in the West where oligarchs are availing themselves of technology to deepen and entrench power. Markus and Charnysh (2017) examine how oligarchs in post-Soviet states have leveraged technology, mainly through media ownership and control over communication networks, to shape public opinion, manipulate information flows, and consolidate their political power.

3.3 How the Oligarchy Wields Influence and Control

In her book *Vulture Capitalism*, Grace Blakeley describes how the oligarchy influences public policy and opinion through lobbying, control of the media, and also by threatening to relocate their businesses if they do not get what they want (Blakeley, 2024). She argues that capitalism should not be confused with "free markets." Instead, oligarchs, and not impersonal market forces (the invisible hand), wield control. Blakeley, 2024 uses the example of Boeing, a major player in the aerospace and defence industry (MIC), to illustrate the close relationship between corporations and the US government. Boeing benefits from billions of dollars in government contracts, particularly from the Department of Defense, along with various forms of so-called corporate welfare, such as subsidies and tax breaks (Blakeley (2024).

Monbiot (2024), like Blakeley (2024), contends that oligarchs threaten democracy by weakening regulatory bodies, suppressing dissent, undermining public services to justify privatization, and controlling media narratives. According to Monbiot (2024), oligarchs deliberately weaken public services to create a pretext for privatization—he cites the gradual deterioration in the National Health Service in the UK as an example. UK oligarchs, through, amongst others, their control of the media, are also argued to have helped suppress the anti-Brexit movement—because they were motivated to escape EU regulations and oversight.

Jones (2020) suggests that oligarchs have also reshaped the American educational landscape by helping to turn universities into corporate ventures where tuition is expensed and aimed at providing vocational training rather than a liberal arts education. Jones (2020) relates how this came about once oligarchs, like Lewis Powell Jr., feared the perceived radicalism of academics as a direct threat to the "American free enterprise system." As mentioned, The Trilateral Commission argued that the expansion of higher education endangered "democracy" and hence started advocating limiting the expansion of higher education and aligning it more closely with the needs of the economy (Jones, 2020).

In addition to weakening regulatory bodies, suppressing dissent, undermining public services and controlling the media, oligarchs donate royally to politicians, especially in the US (Harrington, 2024). For instance, in 2024, several prominent tech CEOs reversed their opposition to Donald Trump and came out actively endorsing and donating to his political campaigns. In turn, they expect future government policies to support their business interest. Hartmann (2023) discusses how the US Supreme Court has enabled oligarchs' influence through decisions that have effectively legalized political bribery by removing limits on campaign contributions.

An example of how government policies have been aligned to oligarchs' interests is provided by Winters and Page (2009), who present evidence of oligarchic influence on tax policy in the US, noting how loopholes and exemptions disproportionately benefit the wealthy, while monetary policy, such as the 2008–2009 global financial crisis bailouts, prioritized financial institutions over ordinary citizens. Indeed, oligarchs do not lobby only to influence regulations, obtain government contracts, and secure access to other resources via government actions. However, they lobby to reduce their tax liabilities, that is, to obtain "corporate welfare"—and they know how to exploit loopholes that often are explicitly created for them to be exploited. For instance, "in 2017 and 2018, Amazon paid no taxes" (Barak, 2024). In 2018, America's billionaires paid just 23% of their income in taxes. This marked the first time in US history that billionaires had a lower effective tax rate than working-class Americans (Zucman, 2024).

In 2023, *ProPublica*, a non-profit news organization, obtained confidential IRS data revealing how America's wealthiest oligarchs, including

Warren Buffet, Jeff Bezos, and Elon Musk, used various legal strategies, such as leveraging unrealized gains, taking out large loans, and engaging in stock buybacks, to pay less tax (Eisinger et al., 2021; Leopold, 2024). Concerning stock buybacks, Leopold (2024) discusses the example of Boeing, which has been laying off workers and cutting corners on safety, while its CEO received $30 million in stock incentives. More generally, the grow-or-die rule described in Chap. 2, seen in the light of the Great Stagnation, and the incentive to buy back their stocks have caused corporations to lay off workers and lobby for anti-union policies and the erosion of worker protections. Leopold (2024) notes that as a result, the percentage of private-sector workers in unions has declined drastically, from 35% in 1955 to just 6% in 2924.

According to Harrington (2024), oligarchs share a common mindset: They are above national laws and societal constraints and seek to operate without the constraints of democracy. At the same time, as Rushkoff (2022a, 2022b) discusses, the oligarchs are, instead of working to address societal problems, preparing for societal breakdown by investing in luxury bunkers and space travel projects (to escape any form of social control ultimately).

Johnstone (2023) explains that oligarchs use three primary tactics to maintain control. The first tactic is to control mainstream culture—through control over mass media, entertainment, and cultural narratives—to promote their agendas and maintain their grip on power. As she put it, the West has become a

> highly controlled society where mainstream culture is designed to serve the powerful. A society where the public's minds are continually being shaped by mass-scale psychological manipulation to ensure that they keep thinking, speaking, working, consuming and voting in ways which serve the rich and powerful.

For example, in the case of promoting the military industrial complex (MIC) and the Permanent War Economy (see also Chap. 4), this influence on mainstream culture can take the form of framing wars as battles between "good guys" and "bad guys," using celebrities and influencers to promote pro-war stances, and suppressing or discrediting dissenting voices. She uses the example of "The Simpson characters waving Ukrainian Flags" and of a General Dynamics-sponsored opera about a drone operator to illustrate how seemingly apolitical art forms can be co-opted to sanitize and normalize the military-industrial complex. This type of cultural production, she argues, serves to desensitize the public to the realities of war and make them more accepting of militaristic solutions to complex geopolitical problems (Johnstone, 2023).

Curtis (2024) discusses how the Media Moguls in the UK influence political outcomes, as demonstrated by the campaign against Jeremy Corbyn. Curtis (2024) also describes how the Guns Oligarchy has influenced UK foreign policy and how they are supported by the Media Moguls to promote the narrative of "enemy states" while downplaying the UK's militarism. Related, and in a non-Western context but where the West is embroiled in a devastating war, Markus and Charnysh (2017) examine how Ukrainian oligarchs use media ownership to advance their interests.

The second tactic used by oligarchs is to exploit noble causes. By co-opting the language of humanitarianism, social justice, or national security, oligarchs and the political elite can manipulate well-intentioned individuals into supporting systems and actions that might contradict their values (Johnstone, 2023). Humanitarian justifications for war often mask ulterior motives, such as securing access to resources or benefiting specific industries, like the military-industrial complex. The World Economic Forum (WEF), at the centre of many conspiracy theories, fulfils such a function for what has been called "Davos Man" (Goodman, 2022).

The third tactic is the suppression of dissent. Johnstone (2023) describes how by publicly condemning or punishing individuals who dare to challenge the official narrative, a "chilling effect" is created that helps maintain a self-censorship climate. One example is the suppression of climate activism in the West—which threatens the profits of oil companies. A report by Climate Rights International criticizes Western countries for clamping down on climate activism, while at the same time hypocritically champion the right to peaceful protest internationally. This suppression of climate activism is evident in that countries like the UK, Germany, and the US have imposed record prison terms for individuals involved in non-violent climate protests. Western authorities are also described as using preemptive arrests to detain individuals suspected of planning peaceful protests. Several countries are enacting new laws to criminalize various activities associated with peaceful protests (Taylor, 2024).

Climate Rights International has pointed out that authorities and the mainstream media are increasingly labelling climate activists as "hooligans, saboteurs, or eco-terrorists"—essentially framing them as criminals rather than citizens exercising their democratic rights (Taylor, 2024).

Finally, the manner in which the oligarchy controls society implies a lack of empathy. Research has documented the negative correlations between individual wealth and empathy and consideration. For instance, it has been found that wealth and privilege can generally make individuals more selfish, entitled, and narcissistic and that wealth can decrease compassion and empathy for those less fortunate. Wealthier individuals are less likely to stop for pedestrians, are less emotionally affected by the suffering of others, and donate a smaller proportion of their income to charity. This suggests that wealth can create a disconnect from the struggles of those with less. It has also been found that wealth can lead to a greater emphasis on efficiency over equality and a sense of entitlement and justification for inequality (Mechanic, 2021; Grewal, 2024).

Oligarchy-run societies are not compassionate societies. As Chap. 5 will explain, they may even have no qualms about pursuing war as a source of profits.

3.4 The Oligarchy and Declining Innovation

Hanson (2024a) compares the West to an old, tenured professor in academia who

> put in less effort, are less focused on doing big-win projects, and are less willing to change locations, research sub-fields, or classes taught. They publish less and change their minds less. But they are also more pompous in their speech; they complain more in public about outcomes for they and their local groups and are more willing to advocate radical changes in other parts of society.

It is indeed a metaphor for "how our civilization changes as it gets rich and old." In such an older, tenured-professor type of society, innovation is seen by many as an activity that needs to be closely controlled. The tenured professor that is the West, has become risk averse. Bhaskar (2021) describes how, in the West, "society has become more hostile to radical innovation, risk-averse, fractious, short-termist."

In this tenured-professor type of society, entrepreneurs need increasingly, to ask permission to innovate. And getting such permission is getting harder. Thierer (2016) describes how this has become a feature in the

West, arguing for a return to a more permissionless innovation[5] environment. But rather than permissionless, bottoms-up approaches to innovation, the West is even on its way to becoming a "stop-button" society (Naudé, 2023c).

How did this come to be, and how does this extend, support and maintain the hold of oligarchs over Western societies?

In October 1957, the West suffered the "shock of the century," as Dickson (2007) describes it, when the Soviet Union launched the first human-made satellite, Sputnik, into space. To the shock and horror of the West, it seemed to have taken a backseat to the Soviet Union in the technology race. Despite its impressive science and vast resources devoted to science and technology, the Soviet Union eventually lost the technology race to the West. What went wrong? Essentially, the Soviet Union's institutions entrenched incentives that were inimical to sustained innovation and commercialization (Kornai, 2013) and inimical to spreading innovations and opportunities through trade (Stone, 1995).

Kornai (2013) lists 111 radical innovations in the world since 1917 (the establishment of the Soviet Union) and asks why these did not originate in the Soviet Union despite the scientific basis being available. Stone (1995) asked, as far as trade was concerned, why "the Soviet policy of economic integration with Eastern Europe was such a conspicuous failure?" In both cases, the incentives in the system worked against initiative, risk-taking, experimentation, error-correction and learning that were prevalent in Western economies at the time.

Chan (2015a, 2015b: 5) sums up the essence of the incentive problem by noting that "the Soviet Union sought innovation in the same way that it pursued industrialization—that is, in a way that circumscribed innovation within a linear model in which x amount of factor input yields $c(x)$ amount of innovative output, where c is a positive constant. The same bureaucratic logic used to run the command-and-control economy was applied to scientific and technological development, largely ineffectually. Five-year plans were handed down from bureaucratic managers who

---

[5] Permissionless innovation "means that experimentation with new technologies and business models should generally be permitted by default. Unless a compelling case can be made that a new invention will bring serious harm to society, innovation should be allowed to continue unabated and problems, if they develop at all, can be addressed later" (Thierer, 2016: 3).

exercised central direction but lacked the technical know-how to make reasonable expectations and goals."

Five-year plans (The Plan) were, as Stone (1995: 12) describes, "the most important source of incentives constraining" managers and bureaucrats in the Soviet Union, as "determined everything from the number of ball bearings that went into a fighter aircraft to the topics of reports prepared by an elite research institute." Moreover, "Soviet officials exercised such domination over their subordinates, and had so little recourse to defend themselves from their superiors' whims" that "it was very difficult to make the kind of credible commitments to one's subordinates that would allow them to reveal compromising information or to take appropriate risks." Consequently, across the spectrum, from finding and utilizing new ideas to international trade, "risky projects were often eschewed for their uncertain upside rewards and huge downside risks" (Chan, 2015a, 2015b: 5).

The Soviet System's command-and-control directing of technological innovation (and production) was successful in enabling it to prevail in World War II and to launch the world's first satellite. However, it was not sustainable, it was not suited to the rapidly changing environment and context of the late twentieth century, and it came with unintended consequences, such as crowding out risk-taking. In the case of the West, these unintended consequences would include the surveillance state and surveillance capitalism, tech feudalism, loss of sensemaking, and lethal autonomous weapons systems.

Ironically, in its response to the Soviet's Sputnik success in 1957, the US adopted and steered towards elements of the Soviet logic. In 1958 the US established the Advanced Research Projects Agency (ARPA) and in 1961 US President John F. Kennedy, addressing Congress, announced the US's target "to land human beings on the Moon and bring them back safely" before the end of the decade (Dickson, 2007). This "Moonshot" required investment of around US 264 billion (in current prices) and mobilizing 400,000 workers. It culminated in 1969 with the Apollo 11 moon landing and Neil Armstrong's moonwalk (Ghosh, 2021).

The Moonshot depended on the military-industrial complex from the start. Indeed, all civilian space programs were removed from ARPA, who in 1972 became the Defense Advanced Research Projects Agency (DARPA) and has since pursued the goal of "the militarization of space, including global surveillance satellites, communications satellites, and strategic orbital weapons systems" (Foster & McChesney, 2014: 12). It has created the Military-Digital Complex on top of the military-industrial complex.

Moonshot / mission-oriented steering of innovation has, by anno 2024, thus been widely embraced in the West, not only the US, which took much of the logic from the Soviet Sputnik success, but also Europe. The latter has bought into the logical of steering innovation, through government's driving "Moonshots." Its flagship science investment program, the US$117 billion *Horizon Europe* programme, is explicit based on Moonshot/mission-oriented thinking, and, as discussed by Ghosh (2021) "targets five missions: adaptation to climate change; climate-neutral and smart cities; soil health and food systems; healthy oceans and other waters; and cancer."

The (modern) intellectual basis for this logic, and indeed for *Horizon Europe's* missions, has been put forward by Mazzucato (2011, 2021), who cites, as many others, the technological successes of from ARPA /DARPA and the NASA's original Moonshot. These technologies, many built on technologies developed during World War II (such as in computing, nuclear and rocket sciences), include the global positioning system (GPS), the Internet, (Bloom et al., 2019) and have catalysed the personal computer, lasers, Microsoft Windows, and Google's search algorithm (Lenderink et al., 2019; Geroski, 1990; Azoulay et al., 2018).

Concomitant with the rise of a dirigiste approach aimed at steering innovation into "desirable" directions, the West has entered a period of declining productivity growth, GDP growth, and business dynamism. Naudé (2022a, 2022b) described these declining trends in innovative entrepreneurship as signs of an "ossifying" economy. Innovative entrepreneurship has been declining according to a broad range of direct and indirect measures (Naudé, 2022a, 2022b). These declining trends in productivity, GDP growth, and business dynamism have been termed the *Great Stagnation* (Cowen, 2010). It can, for example, be seen clearly in the steady decline in decadal growth rates in Western Europe—Fig. 3.2.

It is also clear in the decline in labour productivity growth in the UK, where availability of data going back to the eighteenth century allows examination of the evolution of technological change and innovation, to the extent that productivity growth is an indirect measure of technological innovation. In the UK, labour productivity growth has declined from a high in the 1970s to its current rates, which are the lowest in 200 years (Tenreyro, 2018). Figure 3.3 depicts the UK's labour productivity growth.

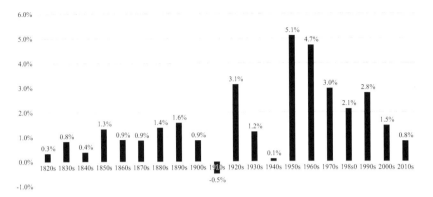

Fig. 3.2 The Zero-Sum Games have Begun: GDP per Capita growth per Decade in Western Europe, 1820s to 2010s. (Source: Naudé, 2023a: 111, which is based on data from the Maddison Project Database)

The sharply and consistent declining in UK labour productivity growth since around 1970s is reflected in the decline in business dynamism in the UK. In this respect, Hutton (2023) recently bemoaned the fact that the "British corporate sector is dying in front of our eyes [...] Britain has created no great companies in the past 20 years; instead, 50 firms that would have been in the FTSE 100 are now foreign owned." Hutton's (2023) conclusions are based on the findings of Tory (2023), who describes a declining UK corporate sector that is "at the tail-end of a self-reinforcing liquidation process."

Other European countries show similar declines in innovation and entrepreneurship. In Germany, as Naudé and Nagler (2022) document, economic growth dropped to an average of 2% between 1975 and 1990, and further declined to a paltry 1% between 1990 and 2010. According to Lang (2009: 1438), the rate of return of R&D in German manufacturing had "reached an all-time low spanning the last 45 years." Rammer and Schubert (2018) reported a sharp decline in the number of German firms engaged and Zabala-Iturriagagoitia et al. (2021), drawing on the 2019 European Innovation Scoreboard, concludes that the national innovation system in Germany has been getting less productive. Its consequent ossification is apparent in declining innovative entrepreneurship, as reflected in the fact that "in Germany's DAX 30 index of leading

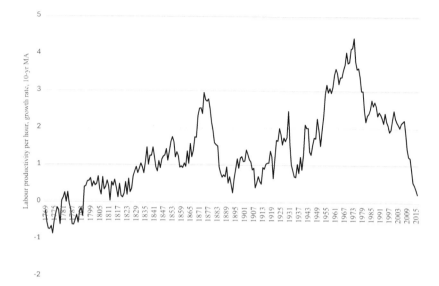

Fig. 3.3 The decline in hourly labour productivity growth in the UK, 1760–2016, 10-yr MA (Source: Author's Compilation on Bank of England Data "An A millennium of macroeconomic data")

companies, only two were founded after the 1970s" (Erixon & Weigl, 2016: 10–11).

Thus, the dirigiste approach to innovation and production enabled the Soviet Union to win World War II and to initially win the space race, as far as putting a satellite in orbit. But the approach was not sustainable and contributed to the eventual collapse of the Soviet Union. Similarly, the dirigiste approach to innovation, which arose out of the Moonshot response to the Sputnik shock enabled the West to win the Cold War, and the technology race, especially in the creation of the digital economy. But as in the case of the Soviet Union, this approach is not sustainable (as was argued, the military-industrial complex needs continual wars on the periphery and surveillance). In the Soviet Union, as Kornai (2013) has explained, one problem was that technical and organizational inventions could not be commercialized. In the US, this was not a problem, rather the problem was, just like the oligarchs in post-Soviet Russia appropriated the state's material assets, predominantly of natural resources such as gas and oil, in the US a class of Silicon Valley entrepreneurs in effect appropriated the advances in digital technology.

This de facto appropriation of Moonshot-induced digital technology in the US has led to what has been termed digital platform capitalism, Technofeudalism, and the Silicon Valley Mindset (see Naudé, 2023b; Rushkoff, 2023; Srnicek, 2016; Varoufakis, 2023)—all accompanied by a decline in entrepreneurship, and a rise in market concentration and dominance.

What are the evidence for the decline in entrepreneurship. The share of highly educated people starting new firms has been declining. In the US, entrepreneurs with higher education declined from 12% in 1985 to 5,3% in 2014 (Kozeniauskas, 2018). The share of young firms (those less than five years old) declined from 47% in the late 1980s to 39% in 2006 (Decker et al., 2014, 2017). At the same time, the share of "old" businesses, that is those older than 16 years, rose from 22% of all businesses in 1992 to 34% in 2011 (Goldschlag & Tabarrok, 2018). These declines in entrepreneurship have, since 2000, also been apparent in the high-tech sector (Haltiwanger, 2022).

The rise in corporate concentration in the US has been well-documented. Naudé (2022a, 2022b: 112–113) summarizes the recent literature noting for instance that in the US "average increase in concentration levels has been around 90%" and that this has boosted the profits of the corporate sector, but not in a productive way, but "rather due to higher market power of incumbents allowing them to raise mark-ups." See Covarrubias et al. (2019) and Grullon et al. (2019) who provides empirical evidence for the rise in "bad" corporate concentration and how it has been driving profits through higher mark-ups. Today three firms, *BlackRock*, *Vanguard*, and *State Street*, control more than 40% of all public firms in the US (Fichtner et al., 2017). The four firms, the *ABCD* (Archer-Daniels-Midland Company, Bunge, Cargill, and Louis Dreyfus), control around 90% of the global grain trade (Harvey, 2022).

Relatedly, Gutiérrez and Philippon (2020) found that in the US "that the contribution of the largest companies to productivity growth has declined" and Akcigit and Ates (2019a, 2019b) described how the more concentrated US corporate sector had shifted towards defensive innovation practices, such as patent thickets (the "use and abuse of patents") and the buying out of possible threatening new start-up firms. In the latter regard the emergence of start-up "kill zones," which is when the possibility that a large firm may buy out a start-up, reduces the value of investment in those start-ups by venture capitalists (Kamepalli et al., 2020: 1). The rise an entrenchment of corporate concentration is therefore a cause of these decline in entrepreneurship noted in the previous paragraph.

Hence, the conclusions to draw from the preceding paragraphs are that one, the dirigiste, mission-oriented approach to innovation has only been successful in narrow domains (weapons and digital tech), and has been accompanied by a long-term decline in innovation and research productivity in science, and the new technologies have to a large extent been appropriated by oligarchs. In this context entrepreneurship has been declining, almost on all indicators (Naudé, 2022a, 2022b).

The fact that ultimately the dirigiste approach is missing the mark, and increasingly so over time, is largely due to the approach being based, like that in the Soviet Union, of a faulty appraisal of the nature of innovation, and its relation to the macro context. Ridley (2020) argues that "innovation prefers fragmented governance" and not a top-down dirigiste approach, because it is a bottom-up, trial-and-error process. As put by Chan (2015a, 2015b: 5), innovation requires "learning-by-doing" which is characterized not by steering, but by an "evolutionary process in which progress comes in spurts that generate accelerating returns."

As discussed by Caverley (2023), one of the scholarly supports for the idea that the government should steer and fund innovation, long before the advocacy of Mazzucato (2011, 2021) and others, came from economist Kenneth Arrow. In his paper "Economic Welfare and the Allocation of Resources for Invention," Arrow (1962) set out to prove the theoretical case for government leadership in and funding of innovation. His essential argument was that without government intervention, even a perfectly competitive market would supply less innovation than what was "socially desirable"; in other words, the government must fund basic innovation because the private sector would not do enough of it (Arrow, 1962: 619). Arrow did this as he was "fearful that the launch of Sputnik meant that the Soviet Union was about to overtake the West in terms of technological capability" (Caverley, 2023).

Subsequent theoretical and empirical research has cast in doubt this belief, showing that private firms do engage in substantial basic scientific research to generate innovations and do this facing significant private incentives (e.g. Czarnitzki & Thorwarth, 2012), that the impact of government R&D on economic and productivity growth was not positive or low—in contrast to business R&D[6] (e.g. Baily, 2003; Sveikauskas, 2007), and that government funding of basic research (R&D) may significantly distort private innovation—even to extent of seeming to crowd-in[7] private R&D. Rosenberg (1990), for instance, starting out from the recognition that "in the United States, the federal government in the years since World War II has provided the vast majority of all funds devoted to basic research," found that:

> In 1984 about 30 percent of R&D expenditures by private industry was stimulated by the prospect of securing government procurement contracts (primarily defense) [...] a large share of private R&D may not be directed toward normal commercial markets where they might contribute directly to productivity growth and improved competitiveness in domestic or international markets: rather, they may be shaped by the desire to signal the capabilities of the firm as an attractive candidate for delivering weapons systems to the federal government," and that "the larger role of the military tends to reduce the importance of basic research spending within the federal budget.

Many start-ups in the ICT sector have one ambition only—to be purchased by the military and defence industry. The distortive effects of this on entrepreneurship and innovation can be significant.

Mazzucato (2011, 2021) and others regularly emphasize and use the examples mentioned earlier as successes of the Moonshot/mission-oriented approach to innovation which accelerated after the Soviet's Sputnik success. These include, as mentioned, the global positioning system (GPS), the Internet, lasers, Microsoft Windows, and even Google's search algorithm. However, as Caverley (2023) and Ridley (2020) explain,

---

[6] Baily (2003: 6) summarized and discussed the findings of an OECD research project into the sources of economic growth in the OECD, pointing out that "R&D activities by the business sector had high social returns, and hence contributed to growth, but there was no evidence in this analysis of positive effects from government R&D." Similarly, Sveikauskas (2007: 1) reported that "the overall rate of return to R&D is very large, perhaps 25 percent as a private return and a total of 65 percent for social returns. However, these returns apply only to privately financed R&D in industry. Returns to many forms of publicly financed R&D are near zero."

[7] There is a growing literature dealing with the question whether government R&D crowds in, or crowds-out, private R&D—see, for example, Becker (2015) and Görg and Strobl (2007). The literature is largely inconclusive, and neglects the question whether, even where crowding-in may occur, as in the defense industry, whether this crowding-in is distortive.

these examples are cherry-picked. They show that government-back innovation programs just as often, if not more often, funded failures or completely missed identifying opportunities for successful innovation. These include, as Caverley (2023) catalogues, the UK government refusing to support Charles Babbage's analytical engine, the precursor to the modern computer; the US government refusing to support the Wright brothers, rather investing in the failed motor-aircraft project of Samuel Langley; the Japanese government not wanting Honda to build cars, but only motorcycles. He also discusses the US$1.6 billion the Nixon administration invested in "cancer research with its National Cancer Act" but with no notable successes—on the contrary, as Hiatt and Beyeler (2020) warn, cancer is set to become the leading cause of death in most countries in the twenty-first century.

The Moonshot approach launched by President John F. Kennedy in 1961 was successful to achieve a landing on the moon, but not to sustain such a program. In December 1972, the last US lunar landing took place. It took 50 years before the US would land another craft on the moon, which was accomplished by the *Odysseus* lander on 23 February 2024 after four previous attempts failed. Concerned with this failure, Sample (2024) asked "Shouldn't landing on the lunar surface today be, if not quite trivial, then at least straightforward? Hasn't the rocket science of the mid-20th century become the basic knowledge of the 21st?" The answer seems to go right to the heart of innovation as a process that depends on learning from failures, for which, as discussed in the previous paragraphs, the state directed approaches as during the Soviet Union has showed. Hence, the Odysseus landing was not accomplished by the entrepreneurial state but was outsourced to the private sector—at a cost of US $ 188 million. Apparently, if NASA had to do it, it would have required up to a billion US$ (Cassidy, 2024).

Finally, it is not only that mission-directed, dirigiste innovation policies are ill-suited to the nature of the process of innovation, and hence not sustainable, but it is also ill-suited to a world facing a myriad of crises. The Moonshot approach worked when it had a single mission to land a person on the moon. This is not the type of challenge which the world is facing. An editorial in *Nature* Magazine in 2019 emphasized that the Moonshot/Mission oriented approach to the challenges faced by the world—the polycrisis in today's terms—is less than ideal for addressing complex problems. It used the example of climate change, pointing out that addressing it "will require not just money and expertise, but also reconciliation of competing political ideologies, especially in richer countries; satisfaction of demands for equity from poorer countries; and recognition of the citizen voice" (Editorial, 2019).

3.5 The Oligarchy and the Decline of Science

The consequences of the decline in innovation and science have contributed to the Great Stagnation and what has been termed the "Ossified Economy" (Naudé, 2022a, 2022b). The Great Stagnation is marked by a decline over time in GDP growth, productivity growth and in entrepreneurship.

As far as entrepreneurship is concerned, the US startup rate, defined as the share of new employers as a fraction of all employers, decreased by roughly 25% between 1979 and 2007, and has been referred to as the "startup deficit." It has been observed across various industries and geographic areas within the US, and predates the Global Financial Crisis, suggesting that it reflects a long-term structural shift in the US economy (Karahan et al., 2019).

Oligarchs, oil and guns explain much of the decline in innovation and science in the West—although, of course, not everything. Innovation and science are complex undertakings, that may benefit-mainly over the short-term—from oligarchic control and conflict. Moreover, the slowdown in population growth and population ageing in much of the West has robbed the West of a "demographic dividend" in that a growing and more youthful population tend to be associated with higher risk-taking, innovation, and economic growth.

The oligarchy, in particular the increasing dominance of large firms in the economy, tends eventually to stifle innovation. As a few powerful companies control larger market shares, they face fewer incentives to invest in risky research and development or to bring disruptive innovations to market. This dominance of established players can create barriers to entry for smaller, more innovative firms, potentially hindering the emergence of new technologies and ideas.

In the Soviet Union, science was often rejected on ideological grounds. As Chan (2015a, 2015b: 5) relates, some scientific theories were rejected as "bourgeois." For instance, "Einstein's theory of relativity was dismissed as bourgeois, reactionary, and incompatible with Marxism-Leninism, until—ironically—the imperative of building a nuclear bomb forced Soviet scientists to accept Einsteinian physics." Millions died of hunger under

Josef Stalin because the latter implemented pseudoscientific ideas, such as Lysenko's "vernalization" (Hotez, 2021).

Today in the West, there is a growing rejection of science as well as the capturing of science for special interest, often profit-driven. As a result, just as in the Soviet Union, despite large sums of money and people being invested in science, it is increasingly failing to reinvigorate society and innovative entrepreneurship. Even worse, "rejection of scientific information is costing lives" as Philipp-Muller et al. (2022: 1) argue, pointing to anti-vaccination campaigns and denial of climate change as but two instances where rejection of science is directly harming society.

Peter Hotez has chronicled and warned against the rise of antiscience activism in the West (Hotez, 2020, 2021). He defines antiscience as "the rejection of mainstream scientific views and methods or their replacement with unproven or deliberately misleading theories, often for nefarious and political gains. It targets prominent scientists and attempts to discredit them" (Hotez, 2021: 1).

Antiscience is fuelled by the spread of postmodernist notions of the subjectivity and equal relevance of all forms of knowledge acquisition as well as by profit and political motivations—which often misuses and thrives on pseudoscience and scientific illiteracy. For example, some student movements have even, under its influence, been insisting that science is only one way of knowing and that witchcraft is a legitimate alternative (Pluckrose, 2017). The epistemic relativism characterizing postmodernism "underlies the 'post-truth politics' that is endemic to contemporary populism," as Bonatti (2023: 21) points out.

Simultaneously, despite the antiscience rhetoric rising, "almost no US citizens can name a living scientist, and the few who did would name individuals such as Bill Nye and Neil deGrasse Tyson. The US public knows little about what scientists actually do" (Hotez, 2020: 1).

Postmodernism, referred to in popular memes as the "homeopathy of the social sciences" and stemming from the ideas of French scholars such as Jean-François Lyotard, Michel Foucault and Jacques Derrida is considered by many as trendy, politically correct, and "woke," and underpins much of the intersectional ideology that has affected science (Pluckrose, 2017). Sokal and Bricmont (1998) have called it "fashionable nonsense" and shown that postmodernists have "repeatedly abused scientific concepts and terminology: either using scientific ideas totally out of context, without giving the slightest justification [...] or throwing around scientific jargon in front of their non-scientist readers without any regard for its relevance or even its meaning" (Sokal and Bricmont, 1998: x).

The problematic hold of antiscience view has been illustrated by the EU's difficulties in allowing scientific research on New Genomic Techniques (NGTs). On 6 February 2024, more than 1000 scientists across 14 EU countries demonstrated[8] to press upon the European Parliament to vote in favour of changing its restrictive regulations on NGTs, which were holding back the application of gene-editing for supporting sustainable food production, using fewer fertilizers and pesticides in Europe. Preceding the demonstrations, 37 Nobel Laureates and over 1500 scientists wrote an open letter[9] to the European Parliament, calling for a vote "in favour of NGTs, thus aligning your decisions with the advancements in scientific understanding [...] We ask you to consider the unequivocal body of scientific evidence supporting NGTs, and make decisions that align with the European Union's and its citizens' best interests [...] and reject the darkness of anti-science fearmongering" (Lynas, 2024). In the end, on 7 February 2024, the call was heeded, but by a narrow margin of 307 to 263, with 41 abstentions—and mostly, it was the European Greens who opposed it (Stokstad, 2024).

As for the capture of science by business interests (destructive and unproductive forms of entrepreneurship), this has recently led Volker Türk, the UN High Commissioner for Human Rights to lament that "Too many governments, policymakers and big-industry leaders are willfully shutting their eyes to science," warning that "we still see heavy corporate influence on regulatory processes, direct attacks on scientific studies, smear campaigns against scientists, misleading literature and exploitation of scientific illiteracy" (Türk, 2023).

Examples of this include the tobacco and fossil fuel industry's manipulation of science. Supran and Oreskes (2021) outline how the fossil fuel industry, specifically ExxonMobil, has been undermining the science of climate change—anthropogenic global warming (AGW). As they put it, "One of the fossil fuel industry's primary AGW frames has been scientific

---

[8] See: https://allianceforscience.org/blog/2024/02/give-genes-a-chance-over-1000-scientists-in-14-countries-hold-historic-demonstrations-in-support-of-gene-editing/
[9] See: https://geneticliteracyproject.org/2024/01/22/viewpoint-nobel-laureates-and-1000-other-scientists-plead-with-european-parliamentarians-to-reject-the-darkness-of-anti-science-fearmongering-over-gene-editing/

uncertainty. Researchers have documented the industry's over-emphasis of uncertainty to deny climate science and delay action."

The rise of antiscience and the misused of science fuelled by postmodern ideologies and narrow business and political interests comes at a time when science in the west has been experiencing various headwinds, or pathologies in the way in which scientific research is organized. It is hitting western science at a time when its scientific edifice is showing cracks.

The evidence has been accumulating that the returns to science has been declining. Bloom et al. (2020: 1138) found that in the case of the US that it "must double the amount of research effort every 13 years to offset the increased difficulty of finding new ideas." Klüppel and Knott (2023) confirm that scientific productivity is declining and ascribed it to "contingent factors" or "pathologies in how R&D is organised," which results in "excess research" and "deterioration" of R&D practices on the firm level.

Archer (2020) suggests that the problem of declining scientific productivity may go deeper than only pathologies in how science is organized. It may also be due to an intellectual and moral decline in science. In this respect, he noted that the scientific establishment is increasingly incentivizing "shoddy research." For instance, as he puts it, "training in science is now tantamount to grant-writing and learning how to obtain funding. Organized skepticism, critical thinking, and methodological rigor, if present at all, are afterthoughts […] Retractions, misconduct, and harassment are only part of the decline. Incompetence is another" (Archer, 2020).

The following paragraphs will deal with the extent to which retractions, misconduct, harassment, and incompetence have come to obstruct science.

As far as the retraction rate of papers in scientific journals is concerned, this has more than trebled over the past decade (Van Noorden, 2023). A portion of the 10,000 or so papers retracted in 2022 are due to the rise in paper-mills, business-motivated initiatives that produce fraudulent scientific papers (McKie, 2024). They thrive on the fact that scientists' pay often depends on how much they publish. The extent to which scientific fraud undermines the credibility of science has now reached crisis proportions (McKie, 2024).

Misconduct and harassment have also become endemic to science. For instance, misconduct in terms of plagiarism is responsible for a large part of the growing number of papers that are retracted each year. Misconduct is not limited to plagiarism: falsification of results is also becoming problematic and is often linked to harassment. Lee (2021) relates the case of microbiologist Didier Raoult, who (now infamously) claimed that hydroxychloroquine is a cure for COVID-19. His results were scrutinized by Elisabeth Bik, a "science detective" who sounded alarm about the science. As a result, she suffered significant harassment. Similarly, Peter Hotez has reported being threatened and intimidated for his criticism of anti-vaxxers. These examples are few amongst many, which have led Türk (2023) to bemoan "direct attacks on scientific studies" and "smear campaigns against scientists."

Incompetence is another factor contributing to the intellectual and moral decline in science. One aspect, the misuse (hacking) of *p*-values, has motivated Ioannidis (2005: 1) to argue that this practice has led to the likelihood that "false findings may be the majority or even the vast majority of published research claims." Another aspect of incompetence is poor scientific and academic leadership, which has been driving what has been called "the great resignation" from academia. *Nature* magazine has reported a growing discontent amongst "early-career researchers, who must work longer and harder to successfully compete for a declining number of tenure-track or permanent posts at universities" (Gewin, 2023). It also interviewed "more than a dozen scientists leaving academia, who describe toxic work environments, bullying and a lack of regard for their safety and well-being as factors in their decisions." In addition, most universities do not welcome ambitious, cross-boundary scientists. They encourage hyper-specialization (Funk & Smith, 2022) and professorial appointments often reflect a hiring bias and not necessarily scientific merit (Nowogrodzki, 2022).

3.6 THE OLIGARCHY AND DECENTRALIZED, DEMOCRATIC DECISION-MAKING

A problem in the Soviet Union was, as Chan (2015a, 2015b: 8) explains, that

> the dominant vertical structures inherent within a statist environment, which came at the expense of horizontal linkages. Coupled with the tight control of information flow, this made for a toxic combination pernicious to innovation [...] the strict vertical separations imposed by this institutional logic meant that basic science, applied research, and industrial production took place within closed circuits, with little cross-pollination of ideas.

Compared to the Soviet Union, the West has a remarkably decentralized information gathering system—an "invisible hand." Harford (2006: 1–2) relates the example of "the Soviet official trying to comprehend the western system: 'Tell me … who is in charge of supply of bread to the population of London? The question is comical, but the answer—*nobody*—is dizzying."

The decentralized, horizontal flow of information in the West is facilitated by the activities of entrepreneurs who operate in a decentralized, democratic system. As knowledge filters, entrepreneurs spot profitable opportunities. Such an opportunity is "primarily a question of an entrepreneur recognizing the value of new information" (Mainela et al., 2018: 536). By acting on valuable new information, entrepreneurs have a demonstration effect—they illustrate (a cost-discovery function) what business activities can be feasible in a particular context, providing a positive informational externality (Hausmann & Rodrik, 2003).

In a manner different from the Soviet Union, but with possibly similar consequences for innovation and cross-pollination of ideas however, the flow of information in the West is increasingly being shackled, if not being subject to creeping attempts towards a "tight control" of information. It threatens the continued efficiency of the flow of information and the recognition of value in new information by entrepreneurs. It also threatens the flow of information necessary for open trade and for an open democratic political system to function. The pathologies in the flow of information in the West thus not only hinders productive and innovative entrepreneurship but also democratic decision-making.

With this finding suggesting that the flow of information (spillovers of knowledge) is facing obstacles, the question is, what is impeding the flow of information? In the Soviet Union, it was centralizing, dominating role of the state. In the West, it may be the increasing dominating and centralizing role of corporations, aided by information technology—the oligarchs or "techno-feudalists" as they have been referred to (Varoufakis, 2023).

Naudé (2022a, 2022b: 112–113) discusses growing concentration and corporate dominance, as well as the phenomenon of Zombie Firms[10] (pp. 113–114) which characterizes the "ossified" economy in which also the flow of information is getting ossified. Key studies that he refers to, where the evidence for growing concentration and Zombie firms are set

---

[10] Zombie firms are old firms with "persistent problems meeting their interest payments, on the edge of exiting but remaining in business" (McGowan et al., 2017: 3).

out, include Grullon et al. (2019), Covarrubias et al. (2019), Akcigit and Ates (2019b), Bessen et al. (2020), Crouzet and Eberly (2018), Andrews et al. (2016), and McGowan et al. (2017). Akcigit and Ates (2019a) discuss how "the use and abuse of patents" hinders the diffusion of new knowledge. As Naudé (2022a, 2022b: 113–114) adds to the use and abuse of patents, noting that the rise of digital platform capitalism and surveillance capitalism/surveillance states (Srnicek, 2016; Zuboff, 2015) has also created conditions wherein leading firms can act in ways to restrict the flow of information:

> Increasing evidence points to the impact of digital technologies, which relies on data-network effects that benefit firms with access to big data, often the firm who were the first movers [...] The upshot is that 'when knowledge diffusion slows down, market leaders are shielded from being copied, which helps establish stronger market power' (Akcigit & Ates, 2019b: 3). As a result, entrepreneurial entry declines, mark-ups rise, profits increase, and growth slows down. The slower knowledge diffusion is perhaps most apparent in the widening dispersion of productivity growth between leading and laggard firms referred to as 'best vs the rest' dynamics. (Andrews et al., 2016)

It is not only firms and new start-ups (often the sources of innovation in the past) that in particular suffer from the restricted flows of information by large incumbent and increasingly digital technology-based firms but also the democratic institutions of society, which are vital for ensuring the openness, good governance, and ultimately trust that are associated with productive entrepreneurship and efficient markets (Acemoglu & Robinson, 2011; Baumol & Strom, 2007).

Tirole (2021) has warned in this regard that the digital tools used by the rise of Surveillance Capitalism in the West can "rupture" the social fabric. These tools include surveillance and mis-and-disinformation. As far as surveillance is concerned, Tirole (2021) discusses the example of the secret police in the Soviet Union's East Germany during the Cold War, where spying on citizens reduced social trust. Surveillance destroys trust because people will avoid interacting with other people to avoid being possibly found "guilty by association." As Tirole (2021: 2010) warns,

> A government can use social graphs by allowing relationships with someone on a blacklist to taint the reputation of those who otherwise would not be on the blacklist. Such tainting can induce another social pressure (ostracism) on citizens to toe the line.

As far as mis- and-disinformation is concerned, Naudé (2023a) discusses how "the rise of the digital economy, and particularly of large digital platforms, have enabled the relativising of the truth—in the birth of what has been called the Post-Truth, alternative facts, and fake news society." Post-truth can be defined as "a deliberate strategy aimed at creating an environment where objective facts are less influential in shaping public opinion, where theoretical frameworks are undermined in order to make it impossible for someone to make sense of a certain event, phenomenon, or experience, and where scientific truth is delegitimized" (Bufacchi, 2021: 350). As Naudé (2022a) concludes,

> Post-truth strategies threaten political outcomes, undermine trust in government, induce and deepen polarization weaken collective decision-making and weaponise the Internet and its associated tools. It leaves social destruction in its wake, its only gains accruing to business or political entrepreneurs pursuing their own 'profits or prestige'. It is a prime example of destructive and unproductive entrepreneurship within the Baumol framework.

The oligarchy also threatens democracy, and through it the flow of decentralized information. How does the oligarchy undermine democracy?

According to Hartmann (2023) one way is by eroding trust in the government. It also fuels a sense of inequality and unfairness.

Fundamentally, though, oligarchs do not like democracy. There has, as Chomsky (2017) for instance explains, always been a tension between the oligarchs who want to control the levers of political power, and the ordinary citizen, who wishes to expand democracy. For the oligarchs, the aims of ordinary citizens to obtain better wages and working conditions, safeguard the environment and agitate for peace, is bad for business. The policies governments implement as a service to and under influence of the oligarchy, typically frustrates the desires of ordinary citizens. As their prospects worsen, as have been the case in the West over the past decades, they will increasingly protest. As Faber (2023: 1) discusses, the decline of the West has increasingly seen "a wide range of popular struggles, strikes, mass protests, riots, and political mobilizations aimed at challenging the neoliberal agenda and unjust capitalist development models." The response of the threatened oligarchs has been severe, and this is seen in the contemporary West in the oligarchy doubling down in its assault on democracy. According to Faber (2023), the West is, anno 2023, in the grip of a "reinvigoration of more authoritarian neoliberal regimes of capitalist development." This is what Monbiot and Hutchison (2024) refer to as the "Attack of the Killer Clowns," as was discussed in Chap. 2. As Faber (2023: 2) warns,

> One of the most alarming is seen in the resurgence of far-right reactionary or neo-fascist demagogic leaders. In recent years, Right-wing figures such as Vladimir Putin (Russia), Narendra Modi (India), Recep Tayip Erdogan (Turkey), Benjamin Netanyahu (Israel), Viktor Orban (Hungary), Giorgia Meloni (Italy), Rodrigo Roa Duterte (Philippines), and Jair Bolsonaro (Brazil) have become household names for the repressive tactics unleashed on sectors of their own and neighbouring populations (including immigrants). The list goes on and includes former U.S. President Donald Trump.

3.7 Concluding Remarks

This chapter critically examined the oligarchy as a significant and immediate threat to Western societies. This chapter was structured around several key themes: the definition and rise of the oligarchy, how the oligarchy exerts its influence, and its impact on innovation, science, and democratic decision-making.

In Section 3.2, the oligarchy was defined as a system where a small, wealthy elite wields significant economic and, consequently, political power. Oligarchs turn democracies into plutocracies. This section highlighted three dimensions characterizing the oligarchy: the concentration of wealth and power, the translation of wealth into political influence, and the erosion of democracy.

Section 3.3 examined the tactics used by oligarchs to maintain their grip on power. These include the weakening of regulatory bodies, the suppression of dissent, the undermining of public services to justify privatization, the control of the media, and the use of political donations. This section also raised tax avoidance by oligarchs and the use of stock buybacks to enrich wealthy shareholders and increase inequality.

Section 3.4 studied the detrimental impact of the oligarchy on innovation and entrepreneurship. Parallels were drawn between the West and the former Soviet Union. While both systems initially achieved technological successes through centralized, mission-oriented approaches (e.g. the Space Race), these approaches ultimately proved unsustainable.

Section 3.5 discussed the apparent stagnation of science in the West. It was argued that it is—among other factors—the consequence of the increased rejection of science and the capture of science for profit. This has similarities with the case of the former Soviet Union, where ideological rejection of specific scientific theories hampered scientific progress. Similarly, the rise of antiscience activism in the West, fuelled by postmodernism, has contributed to "post-truth" politics and the erosion of trust in scientists. At the same time, society has seen the corporate capture of science, exemplified by the fossil fuel industry's efforts to undermine climate change science and the pharmaceutical industry's influence on medical research.

Finally, in Section 3.6, it was argued that in addition to undermining innovation and science, the oligarchy threatens the decentralized information flow. The decentralized flow of information is essential for effective markets and democratic decision-making. The rise and influence of digital platform firms are allowing oligarchs to restrict information flow, stifle competition, and extract rents—threatening the very foundations of a free and open society and making the pursuit of the Permanent War Economy (see Chap. 5) more likely.

In conclusion, under the ideology of neoliberal capitalism, an oligarchy has increasingly taken control of Western society. Its stranglehold contributes to the West's economic decline by reducing innovativeness when needed most, undermining science and education, and exacerbating a loss of sensemaking and democratic decision-making. In short, the oligarchy leads to a less democratic, less equitable, and more divided West. It makes it more difficult for the West to deal with the problems of fossil fuel dependence (oil) and climate change, and to avoid destructive wars.

CHAPTER 4

Oil

4.1 Introduction

Oil merits particular attention. Oil is the largest proportion of total global primary energy needs [...] It is also expected to be the first global energy supply constraint. —Kerschner and Capellán-Pérez (2017: 425)

Even though energy may represent something like 10% of GDP, it's what makes the other 90% possible. It's not just another commodity like sneakers or widgets. —Murphy, (2011)

These quotes suggest that fossil fuels, especially oil, are exceptional. This is because of its energy density and ease of transport.

But using oil as an engine of economic growth releases carbon dioxide into the atmosphere, trapping heat, and causing global warming. The scientific literature—as reflected in successive reports of the Intergovernmental Panel on Climate Change (IPCC)[1] warns that global warming can cause a "ghastly future" characterized by mass extinction, societal collapse, and a planet increasingly hostile to human life (Bradshaw et al., 2021).

In addition to the threat of climate change, the world faces Peak Oil—the point at which oil production reaches its maximum rate (Layton,

---

[1] See: https://www.ipcc.ch

2008). The West is dependent on oil, exposing it to declines in the quality, quantity, and affordability of oil.

Over time, more and more energy is required to extract the same amount of oil, which means that less net energy is available for other sectors of the economy. This prolongs and deepens the Great Stagnation by slowing economic growth and raising the cost of living and doing business. The social and political tensions this will cause will be exacerbated by disruptions to the global supply chains on which the West depends and has been optimized for cheap energy.

These effects of more expensive oil have been percolating through the West since the 1970s to a more or lesser degree, and its manifestation in a Great Stagnation has been met in the West by attempts to try and maintain some economic growth through debt. However, the West's reliance on debt-fuelled growth is unsustainable in a future of declining energy availability. Debt represents a claim on future energy (Hagens, 2020), and as that energy becomes more scarce, servicing and repaying debts becomes increasingly challenging, potentially triggering financial crises.

Thus, the West faces a future of higher inflation, lower living standards, social and political strife, supply chain disruptions, and financial crises, on top of the growing costs of climate change, as a result of what can be called an Energy Trap into which it has fallen (Murphy, 2011b). As these pressures intensify in the West, geopolitical tensions will escalate, raising the spectre of further and more intense resource wars (Greenpeace International, 2024).

In light of the end of the era of affordable and abundant fossil fuels, this chapter discusses how they will contribute to the economic decline of the West. The rest of the chapter is structured as follows:

Section 4.2 explains the energy-economy nexus and analyses indications that the hydrocarbon age is declining.

Section 4.3 discusses the Energy-Environment Nexus, extending the discussion started in earlier chapters and describing the rise and impact of an oil oligarchy.

Section 4.4 discusses the Energy-Conflict Nexus. It outlines how oil generates conflicts and explains the links between the oligarchy and the military-industrial complex.

Section 4.5 concludes this chapter.

4.2 The Energy-Economy Nexus

This section shows that oil has been the lifeblood of the West and the Rest of the world. Fossil fuels provide for 80% of the world's energy consumption. However, with the era of fossil fuel abundance slowly coming to an end, so is the West's hegemony.

4.2.1 The Nature of Fossil Fuels

Fossil fuels have desirable and unique features as a source of energy. These help explain why fossil fuels are a double-edged sword and why moving away from fossil fuels will be an arduous and painful process for modern civilization (Gross, 2020).

The first characteristic of oil that makes it highly desirable as an energy source is its exceptional energy density coupled with ease of access and transport: Fossil fuels, particularly oil and gas, possess high energy density—the amount of energy stored per unit volume or mass. *"Gasoline is ten quadrillion times more energy-dense than solar radiation, one billion times more energy-dense than wind and water power, and ten million times more energy-dense than human power"* (Layton, 2008: 441).

The second desirable characteristic of oil is that it is extractable at human timescales: Unlike renewable energy flows (solar, wind), which are relatively diffuse and available at a fixed rate, fossil fuels exist as concentrated stocks that humans can extract and transport at a pace determined by demand. This means oil energy can be rapidly scaled up in response to demand (Gross, 2020). Thirdly, oil has, historically, been a cost-effective source of energy, enabling the Industrial Revolution (Gross, 2020; Smil, 2018).

These three characteristics make fossil fuels an ideal source of energy. There is, however, a downside. Using fossil fuels releases carbon dioxide, a greenhouse gas, into the atmosphere. These emissions have been unequivocally shown to lead to global warming and a cascade of dangerous climate impacts, including rising sea levels, more frequent and intense extreme weather events, disruptions to agriculture, and threats to human health and biodiversity (IPCC, 2021; Bradshaw et al., 2021). In short, fossil fuels have facilitated an ecological overshoot (Rees, 2021a, 2021b).

4.2.2 Energy Blindness and the Tooth Fairy Syndrome

Energy is the "Currency of Life" (Hagens, 2020). Economic growth is nothing but an energy conversion process, subject to the laws of thermodynamics. Students in economics get taught that since the beginning of the nineteenth century, global GDP—and the world's population—has grown exponentially—and that this is due to a combination of entrepreneurship and technological innovation enabled by appropriate "institutions" (such as property rights and rule of law—preferably those of the Global North according to Acemoglu & Robinson, 2011) that are supposedly good for business and investment (Acemoglu & Robinson, 2011; Mokyr, 2016).

They are rarely told that the commercial exploitation of energy—in the form of fossil fuels—kick-started the Industrial Revolution and made possible the subsequent unprecedented growth in world GDP (Hagens, 2020; Naudé, 2023a; Smil, 2018). The importance of fossil fuels—energy—to the modern economy has been described by Nate Hagens (2020), who pointed out that the "110 billion barrels of oil that were needed in 2018 to power the world economy is equivalent to more than 500 billion human workers toiling day and night."

Hagens (2020) refers to the neglect and underestimation of energy in modern mainstream economics—which translates into economic policies—as energy blindness. Energy blindness stems from a tendency in economics to focus on monetary flows and market dynamics while overlooking the biophysical foundations of all economic activities. Mainstream economics considers energy as just another input to production, similar to labour or capital, and do not recognize its uniqueness—essentially and ignoring the laws of thermodynamics in economic growth models. Arnoux (2022) described this ignorance as the "Tooth Fairy Syndrome," a metaphor for the widespread societal belief in economics as a perpetual motion machine, divorced from the laws of thermodynamics and the reality of resource constraints. He argues that much like a child who believes in the Tooth Fairy, modern society often clings to economic beliefs that defy the fundamental laws of physics and the finite nature of resources. This "magical thinking" leads to decisions based on financial abstractions, the promise of perpetual growth and techno-optimism, ignoring the tangible constraints of energy availability and the environmental consequences of resource extraction (Arnoux, 2022).

Another consequence of energy blindness is that, while mainstream economics recognizes the possibility of substitution between energy sources, it fails to account for the fact that this is not a simple one-to-one substitution—for reasons that will be set out below.

Another problem of energy blindness is that it helps sustain belief in absolute decoupling between economic growth and resource consumption (Haberl et al., 2020).

Finally, energy blindness leads to underestimating the decline in quality and quantity of oil and overestimating the monetary value of GDP growth. For example, while the expansion of shale oil production in the US raised GDP growth, this growth should be evaluated in light of the declining energy rates of return of shale oil and its associated environmental impacts (Hagens, 2020; Arnoux, 2022).

4.2.3 The Hydrocarbon Age and Its End

Figure 4.1 shows the close relationship between economic output and fossil fuel energy since the Industrial Revolution.

The West's first commercial oil wells were drilled in Ontario, Canada, in 1858 and 1859 in Titusville, Pennsylvania, USA (Habashi, 2000). The impact is evident in Fig. 4.1: Around the 1870s, there was a noticeable increase in GDP. Today, the average inhabitant of the Earth has "nearly 700 times more useful energy than their ancestors had at the beginning of the 19th century [...] it is as if 60 adults would be working non-stop, day and night, for each average person" (Smil, 2019: 19). In future, humans may describe the period 1820 to the 2020s not as the industrial age or the age of entrepreneurship, but as the fossil fuel age, or the hydrocarbon age (Murphy et al., 2021).

The hydrocarbon age was, however, a temporary "windfall" for the economy in terms of growth. As Hagens (2018) explains,

> the constant growth we've experienced was correlated with human inventions and economic theories, but the cause was finding a bolus of fossil sunlight. We behave like squirrels living in a forest where a truck full of hazelnuts crashed, living off the freight and thinking it will last forever.

The hydrocarbon age will not last forever. What will happen if the world runs out of fossil fuels, particularly oil? History—mainly since the 1970s—provides some preview of what could be expected to happen more

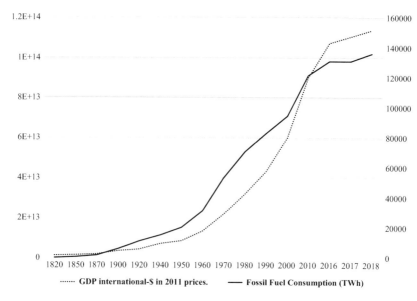

Fig. 4.1 World GDP and fossil fuel consumption, 1820–2018. (Source: Naudé, 2023a: 50)

frequently. Given that growing GDP requires growing fossil fuel consumption, if the latter is cut, GDP growth will inevitably decline—as the world dramatically experienced in the 1970s and more recently before the global financial crisis of 2008—see Fig. 4.2.

Figure 4.2 shows that the post-war period until 1973 was the golden age in terms of plenty of cheap fossil fuels. This was also the golden age of economic growth, at least in most advanced Western economies, which had access to this cheap oil (Cairncross, 2014).

However, since 1973, oil prices have been permanently on a higher level and have continued to rise—making a further structural increase to higher levels after 2003. These increases in oil prices are associated with a decline in overall world GDP growth (although some individual oil-producing countries benefited) and more substantial declines in growth in energy-dependent advanced economies because these economies are using more oil in total, even if they are using oil more efficiently. Bradford DeLong (2022: 431) explains the start of the Great Stagnation in the

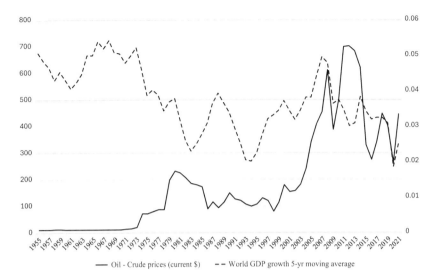

Fig. 4.2 Rising oil prices dampens economic growth: World GDP growth and oil prices, 1955–2021. (Source: Author's compilation based on data from the World Bank Development Indicators Online and Our World in Data)

1970s partly because "*energy diverted away from producing more and into producing cleaner would quickly show up in lower wage increases and profits.*"

For a while, the world and advanced economies enjoyed a temporary respite—from the early 1990s—by throwing money at the problem (debt-fuelled growth)—by liberalizing the financial sector and the US printing large quantities of money to ensure that the economic system was flush with credit to keep firms in business and interest rates and inflation low (Boccia & Lett, 2024; Lin & Tomaskovic-Devey, 2013).

So much credit has been pumped into the world economy since the 1970s that interest rates dropped in the past decade to levels not seen in 5000 years (Goldstein, 2021; Homer & Sylla, 2005). The average debt level of the industrial economies rose from 165% of GDP in 1980 to 320% by 2010 (Chan, 2011).

It planted the seeds for the Global Financial Crisis of 2007–2009 and remains a threat to global financial stability: during the COVID-19 pandemic, the US Federal Reserve printed an additional US$ 4 trillion (Boccia & Lett, 2024). The US, as the issuer of the world's reserve currency, indeed believes that it can print as many dollars as it wants and spend its way out of stagnation—a former chair of the US's House Budget Committee voiced this, saying[2] that

> We are a sovereign currency, we can print all the money we want to serve the people whom we serve [...] why do we borrow money anyway? We can print it and put it in the Treasury.

In addition, Western economies started in the 1970s and 1980s to massively offshore their manufacturing industries to developing countries where wages and costs were lower to reduce inflation and maintain competitiveness (Vietor et al., 2008). The emergence of the digital economy following the creation of the World Wide Web (WWW) in the early 1990s also gave a temporary respite to falling economic growth (and helped with offshoring) (Borenstein & Saloner, 2001). The digital platform firms that came to dominate (see Chap. 3) soon realized that the digital economy was one of the last extraction zones available—except perhaps for mining the sea floor or expanding into outer space (Gilbert, 2023; Weinzierl, 2023).

With fossil fuels a limited resource that will run out, the implications for the world economy of losing the equivalent of 500 billion workers will, of course, be catastrophic—unless, somehow, the world can find renewable, clean energy sources to replace the oil and gas that we will be running out of. This will inflict a heavy blow on the world's Petrostates, including the US. Carbon Tracker[3] estimates that the energy transition from fossil fuels would result in "*28 of the 40 petrostates losing more than half of expected revenue under a moderate-paced transition in line with governments' current climate pledges. $8 trillion worth of expected revenue would be wiped out between now and 2040, with different petrostates affected significantly differently.*"

Based on the Maximum Power Principle, one may assume that little of the fossil fuels that the Petrostates possess will be left in the ground and that despite the energy transition, most oil will be used. This raises two questions: how much oil is left? And how realistic is the possibility of finding adequate renewable and clean substitutes for fossil fuels in time through technological innovation?

Regarding the first question, the issue of how much fossil fuels are left has been analysed under "Peak Oil." Peak oil refers to the maximum oil

---

[2] Reported by Boccia and Lett (2024).
[3] See: https://carbontracker.org/reports/s-of-decline/

production rate, after which production would decline (Campbell & Laherrere, 1998; Layton, 2008). Hubbert (1956) predicted this for the US in the 1970s. His prediction, updated to the present, is shown in Fig. 4.3:

His prediction was pretty accurate until 2008, when technological innovations made the extraction of shale gas feasible and, thus, increased the available crude oil (Kapoor & Murmann, 2023). By 2015, the US lifted its prohibition on the export of oil that had been in place since 1973 because shale oil refineries had reached maximum capacity and became a Petrostate (Naím, 2016).

However, the shale gas revolution can only kick the can down the road, and there seem to be indications that this is also close to a peak. Naudé (2023b) refers to Fix (2020b), who argues that only a fraction of the roughly 1 trillion barrels of shale oil is possibly extractable and that it will only extend the timing of peak oil from the 1970s to the mid-2020s (Fix, 2020b). One commentator pointed out that *"more and more oil experts*

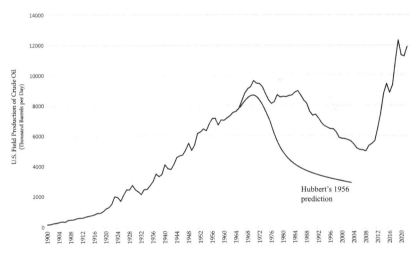

Fig. 4.3 Peak Oil: Hubbert's prediction for the US. (Source: Naudé, 2023a: 53, which is adapted from Fix [2020b, Fig. 2])

[…] warn that US shale production is set for a rapid decline. Five to six years is not very far out into the future. It is around 2028-29, two presidential election cycles from now" (The Honest Sorcerer, 2023).

Calculations by Murray and King (2012), Hall (2017), Hallock et al. (2014), and Mohr et al. (2015) point to total peak oil being reached around the 2050s at the latest. And recently, Goehring and Rozencwajg (G&R, 2023) reported that:

> The most crucial development in global oil markets is depletion in the Permian basin. We first warned about this in 2018, predicting the Permian would peak in 2025. In retrospect, our analysis was too conservative. We now believe the basin could peak within the next twelve months. The implications will be as profound as when United States oil production peaked in 1970, starting a chain of events ultimately sending prices up five-fold over ten years.

Regarding the second question, how likely is it that the world will provide the technologies to transition from fossil fuels to sufficiently reliable and appropriate renewable energy sources in time to avoid a massive economic collapse when fossil fuels run out?

It should be remembered that around 80% of world energy comes from fossil fuels. The challenge of replacing so much fossil fuel energy is daunting, and according to many, it is not clear at all at present whether this is possible (see also Gross, 2020). Indeed, the decline in science, research productivity, innovation, and entrepreneurship, as documented in Chap. 2, does not suggest that there is a cause for optimism. Naudé (2023b), referring to the work of Floyd et al. (2020) and Friedemann (2021), suggests that an "energy descent" is inevitable.

The end of the hydrocarbon age will spell the end of Western hegemony. Fix (2020b) argues that an empire's history is written in the language of energy. This is because "*a successful empire centralizes the flow of energy. This means that energy use (per person) in the empire's core will dwarf energy use in the periphery. The degree to which this is true marks the degree that the empire is successful.*" He justifies this notion of centralization of the flow of energy towards the empire by discussing the case of the British Empire, which

> plundered the resources of the world at the same time that it plundered the coal reserves under its belly. The results were spectacular. From an unre-

markable nation in 1600, Britain accumulated so much power that by the late 1800s, it was effectively the world's administrator. This rise is written in the language of energy. At the empire's peak, the typical Brit consumed about 7 times more energy than the world average.

If, following Fix (2020b), one plots energy use per capita in the West, the decline in the flow of energy towards the West, is notable in Fig. 4.4.

As Fig. 4.4 shows, over the post–World War II period, there has been a steady decline in the energy centralization to the US, with an acceleration from the end of the 1990s. From the end of the 1999s, as will be elaborated in more detail in Chap. 5, there was an acceleration in the number of US military interventions abroad. At the same time, there has been a steady increase in the ability of China to obtain and use energy, both fossil fuels and renewables (see also Chap. 5) to the extent that it is now about to exceed Europe. Fig. 4.4. is consistent with the narrative of the economic decline of the West.

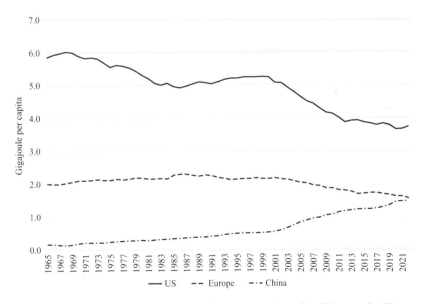

Fig. 4.4 Relative energy consumption per capita, the West and China, 1965–2022. (Source: Author's compilation based on data from BP's Energy Institute Statistical Review of World Energy)

4.3 The Energy-Environment Nexus

The previous section outlined how closely energy—in the form of oil—and economic production and growth are intertwined. In the face of declining fossil fuels, the possible hazards that this creates, especially for the West, in terms of collapsing growth and the implications thereof, have been described.

While fossil fuels were the driving force behind the unprecedented economic growth of the past two centuries and broadly supported the rise of the West and its "empire," it has also, as already alluded to, been responsible to a large extent for global climate change. Thus, while the decline in the use of fossil fuels is to be welcomed from the climate and ecological perspective, two problems remain. The first is that the process of climate change has already begun, so the decline and phase out of fossil fuels comes too little, too late. Second, although peak oil has been reached or will be soon, it will still be decades before fossil fuels will remain playing an essential role in meeting energy demand. Thus, the decline of fossil fuels is too late and will not be deep enough, in all likelihood, to halt or reverse global climate change. What about the hope of rapidly substituting oil for renewables? The rest of this section provides an answer.

4.3.1 The Driver of Climate Change[4]

Around 252 million years ago, the Siberian Traps, a volcanic complex, erupted, causing much carbon dioxide to be emitted. Nearly 90% of all species went extinct. This event, known as the Permian-Triassic extinction, illustrates the dangers of climate change (Sun et al., 2024).

The Industrial Revolution unleashed a force perhaps similar to the volcanoes that erupted in Siberia 252 million years ago: burning fossil fuels to enable perpetual economic growth.

Figure 4.5 shows the steady increase in CO_2 emissions since 1850, roughly when the modern industrial era started, and close to when the first commercial oil wells were drilled first in Enniskillen in Ontario, Canada, in 1858, and then in 1859 in Titusville, Pennsylvania, US—by the *Seneca Oil Company* (Habashi, 2000). It shows that by 2022, around 36.8 billion tons of CO_2 were emitted globally and that global average temperatures were around 0.8-degree Celsius (almost 1 °C) higher than

---

[4] This section is drawn from and extends Naudé (2023a).

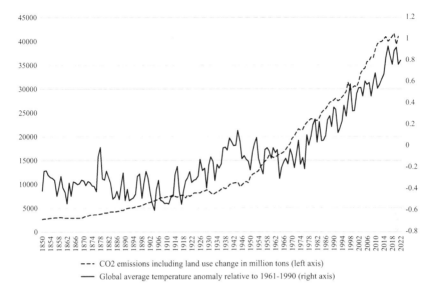

Fig. 4.5 Carbon emissions and global warming, 1850–2022. (Source: Author's compilation based on data from Our World in Data: https://github.com/owid/co2-data)

the 1961–1990 average—which was 1.15°C above the 1850–1900 (preindustrial) average (WMO, 2023).

The bulk of the emission increase depicted in Fig. 4.5 is due to human activity, hence the conclusion by the IPCC (2021) and the scientific consensus (see Oreskes, 2004) that there is certainty that global warming is due to humans—hence the term *anthropogenic warming*.

For thousands of years before the onset of the Industrial Revolution and the rise of the West, atmospheric CO_2 levels remained relatively stable, hovering around 280 parts per million (ppm). However, by October 2024, as this book was being finalized, there were 423.5 parts per million (ppm) of carbon in the atmosphere, as measured by the Mauna Loa Observatory in Hawaii. This was the highest level since the Observatory started measurements in 1958.[5] It is also the highest for millennia, as

---

[5] See https://www.climate.gov/news-features/understanding-climate/climate-change-atmospheric-carbon-dioxide

Osman et al. (2021) report that the "rate and magnitude of modern warming are unusual relative to the changes of the past 24 thousand years."

To prevent catastrophic climate change, it has been recommended that global warming stabilizes at not more than 1.7 degrees warming before pre-industrial times, which in turn implies limiting carbon in the atmosphere to not more than 350 ppm—based on assumptions about *climate sensitivity*,[6] which is the extent to which increased carbon leads to higher global mean surface temperatures (GMST) (Hansen et al., 2008). In the Paris Agreement of 2015, the EU and 194 countries of the United Nations committed themselves to limit global warming to preferably 1.5 °C above pre-industrial levels (and not more than 2 °C) and that doing so would require reducing carbon emissions by around 50% by 2030. Suppose the world succeeds in reducing carbon in the atmosphere to 450 ppm. In that case, the Intergovernmental Panel on Climate Change (IPCC) only gives the Earth a 66% chance of keeping global temperature increases below 2 °C (Bradshaw et al., 2021).

The IPCC has produced scenarios indicating that given past trends, there would be between 2 °C and 3 °C of global warming above pre-industrial levels by 2100 (the median is 2.2 °C), which means that the world is off-target from its Paris commitments (Pielke et al., 2022). The World Meteorological Organization (WMO), using a climate model,[7] has indicated a 66% probability that Global Mean Surface Temperature (GMST) would exceed 1.5 °C above pre-industrial levels for at least one year between 2023 and 2027 (WMO, 2023). By the time of writing, the average global temperature was already 1.35 °C above pre-industrial levels.[8]

According to Griffen (2017), if trends in fossil fuel use, the major contributor to GHG emissions, continue as in the recent past, GMST would

---

[6] Equilibrium Climate Sensitivity (ECS) is the eventual long-run outcome of temperatures of high CO_2 ppm in the atmosphere. According to estimates, there is a 90% probability that ECS is between 2.3 and 4.7 °C (Hausfather et al., 2022).

[7] Many climate models, also known as Integrated Assessment Models (IAMs), are used to forecast GMST changes. Most prominently, the Intergovernmental Panel on Climate Change (IPCC) refer to IAMs for various climate change scenarios (Beek et al., 2020). According to Hausfather et al. (2020), "climate models published over the past five decades were skilful in predicting subsequent GMST changes, with most models examined showing warming consistent with observations." But IAMs are also subject to severe criticism and shortcomings—for example, Pielke and Ritchie et al. (2021) and Hausfather et al., 2022).

[8] See: https://gml.noaa.gov/ccgg/trends/gl_trend.html

increase to as much as 4 °C above pre-industrial levels by 2100. Lenton et al. (2023) conclude that based on current climate mitigation policies in terms of the Paris Agreement, GMST would still be at least 2.6–3.1 °C above pre-industrial levels by 2100.

4.3.2 A Ghastly Future

> The danger of the climate crisis and the possibility of a planetary collapse can no longer be confined to a purely financial issue (solvable by a hypothetical allocation of 3% of world GDP) or a strictly technical-engineering challenge (solvable by the advancement of a successful energy transition —Fuentes (2023)

Civilization evolved within a relatively stable climate during the Holocene epoch, starting around 11,000 years ago. However, climate change may result in climate instability that may overwhelm the ability of societies and ecosystems to adapt.

Bradshaw et al. (2021) describe the future under unchecked climate change as "ghastly." They inventoried the current evidence of climate change impacts, noting high species extinction rates, accelerated ice sheet melting, and significant ecosystem degradation. For instance, species extinction rates are currently 100 to 1000 times higher than background rates; the Greenland Ice Sheet is losing mass at a rate that could contribute up to 7 meters of sea-level rise; and critical ecosystems such as kelp forests have declined by approximately 40%, and the biomass of large predatory fish has been reduced to less than 33% of its level a century ago. Furthermore, ocean warming and acidification, driven by climate change, may lead to a loss of 99% of tropical corals if the global average temperature rises by 2 °C (Lenton et al., 2019).

Bradshaw et al. (2021) further argue that the full scope of climate change is underestimated due to the time lag between environmental damage and its socioeconomic consequences, which creates a false sense of security, an "optimism bias" in human thinking that can lead to downplaying the severity of crises; and the consistent failure to implement practical solutions on a global scale.

This underestimation and complacency is made more dangerous by the likely existence of so-called climate tipping points, which are nonlinear in occurrence and impact and challenging to foresee or predict. A tipping point is "a critical threshold at which a tiny perturbation can qualitatively alter the state or development of a system" (Lenton et al., 2008: 1). Less formally, a tipping point is marked by sudden changes once it is crossed: *"Everything's fine until it's not [...] And then everything goes to hell,"* as Douglas Erwin from the Smithsonian National Museum of Natural History is quoted to have said (Truscello, 2018: 262).

Earth systems where tipping points could occur to trigger abrupt climate change include the Arctic Sea Ice, the Greenland Ice Sheet (GIS), the West Antarctic Ice Sheet (WAIS), the Atlantic Thermohaline Circulation (THC), the El Ninō-Southern Oscillation (ENSO), the Indian Summer Monsoon (ISM), the Sahara/Sahel and West African Monsoon (WAM), the Amazon Rainforest, and the Boreal Forest (Lenton et al., 2008; Lenton et al., 2019).

Crossing tipping points in the Earth System may threaten societal collapse,[9] and even pose an existential risk (Richards et al., 2021; Willcock et al., 2023). It may even happen sooner rather than later, given the multiple stresses on the environment (Dearing et al., 2023). "The prospect of civilization collapse has now entered the mainstream of scientific and popular discourse" (Gowdy, 2020: 2).

Collapse is possible for several reasons (Kemp et al., 2022). One is that global warming directly threatens agriculture and food supply. According to Gowdy (2020: 2), some *"Climate models indicate that the Earth could warm by 3°C-4 °C by the year 2100 and eventually by as much as 8 °C or more. This would return the planet to the unstable climate conditions of the Pleistocene when agriculture was impossible."* He refers here to the fact that climates have been comparatively stable over the past 12,000 years (the Holocene), which allowed human societies to switch from hunting and gathering to large-scale farming. The West is so dependent on agro-food supply on complex and vulnerable global supply chains—dominated by a few oligarchic firms (see Chap. 3) that the collapse of food production due to climate change would be catastrophic.

---

[9] There are many estimates of the economic costs of climate change, which are estimated using so-called climate damage functions (see, e.g. Auffhammer, 2018). These, like the IPCC's scenarios, all assume continuing economic growth until 2100 and thus ignore the potential growth collapse from ecological overshoot (including fossil fuel depletion). They thus allow commentators such as Bjorn Lomborg to proclaim that despite climate change, the world will be better off economically in 2100 than at present (Lomborg, 2020). The potential economic cost of ecological overshoot is unknown in terms of GDP.

A second reason the crossing of tipping points would hasten the economic decline of the West—and the collapse of global civilization is because environmental change is implicated in all past mass extinction events (Kemp et al., 2022). Song et al. (2021: 1) point out that mass species extinctions[10] in the past have been associated with tipping points in climate change of >5.2 °C magnitudes. Bradshaw et al. (2021) and Dirzo et al. (2022) consider the current biodiversity loss rate so significant that it signifies that humans have triggered the planet's sixth mass extinction. A growing number of authors and scientists indeed warn that a sixth mass extinction may be beginning or imminent—for example, Barnosky et al. (2011), Cowie et al. (2022), Kaiho (2022), Kolbert (2014), and McCallum (2015).

Other reasons that have been cited for the breaching of climate tipping points as terminal threats to the West is that environmental collapse, say due to climate change, water scarcity, or biodiversity loss, could cause global conflict, could increase vulnerability to other shocks, cause systemic crises, and reduce humanity's ability to recover from other catastrophes (Kemp et al., 2022). Climate change can trigger failures across interconnected systems.

For example, climate change-induced crop failures could trigger food shortages, inflation, and economic instability, potentially fuelling social unrest, conflict, and mass migration. It would leave society with a diminished capacity to recover from future catastrophes like nuclear war or pandemics (Kemp et al., 2022).

Despite these risks to the economies of the West and even the existential dangers posed to all people on the planet, "existential risk is not a narrative or term that has been widely adopted or further developed by the climate change research community. Neither the concept of existential risks nor the term 'existential' was used in the IPCC 5th Assessment Report (AR5), nor the IPCC Special Reports of the 6th Assessment Cycle" (Huggel et al., 2022: 4). And climate catastrophe remains "relatively under-studied and poorly understood" (Kemp et al., 2022: 1).

---

[10] A mass extinction occurs when "the Earth loses more than three-quarters of its species in a geologically short interval" (Barnosky et al., 2011: 51). There have been five mass extinctions—444, 372, 252, 201, and 66 million years ago (Cowie et al., 2022; Kaiho, 2022).

4.3.3 Energy Cannibalism and the Complexities of the Energy Transition

Given the dangers of ecological overshoot caused by fossil fuels, the need to transition towards renewable energy sources (e.g. solar, wind, hydro, and geothermal power) is clear. There are, however, hugely significant challenges facing a successful energy transition. These challenges include (current) technological limitations, economic realities, political inertia, and the ingrained societal dependence on fossil fuels—the world is just profoundly dependent on fossil fuels. The failure of the energy transition will result in the significant shrinking and possible collapse of economies deeply dependent on oil, including those of the West and the major oil-producing and consuming countries in the Global South. The rest of this section discusses why the energy transition may fail.

The first challenge is "energy cannibalism." Energy cannibalism can occur when the energy required for the energy transition, for example, mining green minerals or constructing solar panels or wind farms, demands existing fossil fuels. It may offset some of the intended emissions reductions (Heinberg, 2024a).

A second challenge related to energy cannibalism is that energy cannibalism makes the energy investment costs required to build new renewable energy infrastructure particularly burdensome, especially during energy decline. This could cause a further energy deficit (Murphy, 2011b).

A third challenge is the sheer scale and speed of the transition required. The current world energy system has been built for over a century at an enormous cost. It represents a massive sunk investment with significant vested interests. To replace this in the time frame required to stave off catastrophic climate change may be impossible.

Fourth, and related to the scale and speed required, is the political and economic power of the fossil fuel industry—of Big Oil (see Chap. 3). The industry undertakes immense lobbying efforts and has substantial financial influence over the government and the mainstream media.

Fifth, intermittency and storage challenges continue to characterize wind and solar energy (Heinberg, 2024a). The battery technology needed to overcome this is still limited, characterized by high costs and limited storage capability, which results in devastating environmental impacts as a result of the mining of the critical metals required for their production (such as nickel, lithium, and copper). Integrating renewable energy sources into existing electricity grids is still costly and time-consuming. Moreover, the investments and extensions to facilitate this integration often face public opposition, particularly regarding the placement of new transmission lines (Heinberg, 2024a; Michaux, 2021; B, 2024a, 2024b, 2024c, 2024d).

Sixth, as mentioned at the outset of this chapter, renewables have a much lower energy density than fossil fuels (Heinberg, 2024a; Layton, 2008).

Finally, mainstream energy and climate crisis solutions rely on technological fixes. This has been criticized, for instance, by Heinberg (2024b) and others who make the vital point that more than just technologies (or finance) will be needed but also a fundamental shift in societal values and consumption patterns. The critical insight is that infinite economic growth is incompatible with ecological limits, even if renewable energies drive such growth—there is no such thing as genuinely green growth (Murphy, 2011a, 2011b).

As described in Chap. 3, the current global economic system is addicted to continuous growth, which, as this chapter has shown, demands ever-increasing energy. This Growth Spiral in which firms and countries are caught in the system of global capitalism makes it politically and socially challenging to implement policies that prioritize energy conservation or a shift towards a steady-state economy. This challenge is accentuated by adherence to the Maximum Power Principle (MPP) (Tverberg, 2024a, 2024b). The MPP implies that human societies always strive to maximize energy consumption (B, 2024a, 2024b, 2024c, 2024d). Thus, adding renewable energy will unlikely reduce fossil fuel use.

4.3.4 The Fossil Fuel Oligarchy

A particular feature of the fossil fuel industry is that it is a powerful, concentrated industry. The dominance of "big oil" in the US spans more than a century. The US Library of Congress documents[11] that "In 1909, antitrust laws forced Standard Oil into 34 different companies, but by the 1940s, three of them, along with four other international companies, grew to dominate the market and were nicknamed the "Seven Sisters" " (Sampson, 1991). The *Seven Sisters* comprised Standard Oil of New Jersey, New York, and California, Royal Dutch Shell, Texaco, Gulf Oil, and British Petroleum. These companies were all founded between 1870 and

---

[11] See: https://guides.loc.gov/oil-and-gas-industry/history#note7

1909. By the time of the oil crisis of the 1970s, the Seven Sisters reportedly controlled around 85% of world petroleum reserves.[12]

Since the oil crisis, the rise of OPEC, the consolidation of the Seven Sisters, and the rise of state-owned oil companies in the 1990s and 2000s, the world's Big Oil companies today consist of six large private companies and the "new" Seven Sisters. The six largest private companies are ExxonMobil, Chevron, Shell, BP, Eni, and TotalEnergies. The New Seven Sisters are Saudi Aramco, Gazprom (Russia), CNPC (China), NIOC (Iran), PDVSA (Venezuela), Petrobras (Brazil), and Petronas (Malaysia) (Hoyos, 2007).

At the time of writing, around 100 fossil-fuel companies are responsible for 71% of "global industrial GHG emissions" (Griffen, 2017: 8). The top 21 of these fossil-fuel companies, who generate close to 36% of global industrial GHG emissions (Grasso & Heede, 2023: 461), are listed in Table 4.1.

In the US, the fossil fuel industry's spending on lobbying has been around U$1.25 billion over the past decade. In addition to direct lobbying, the industry also poured over $650 million into political campaigns in the US over the same period (Lakhani, 2024). Such is the influence of the fossil fuel industry that despite the knowledge that oil drives climate change and despite the Paris Agreements, these fossil fuel companies continue to receive substantial government subsidies and licences to continue expanding the extraction of even more fossil fuels. For instance, wealthy Western countries, including the US, UK, Canada, Norway, and Australia, have been responsible for two-thirds of all new oil and gas licenses since 2020. This trend contradicts their pledges under the Paris Agreement to limit global warming to 1.5 °C above pre-industrial levels.

The US, in particular, has historically stood out for its hypocritical stance on oil and climate change. Despite the Biden administration's pledges to address the threat of climate change, the US has become the world's pre-eminent oil and gas producer—the world's leading petro-state—surpassing traditional petro-states like Saudi Arabia. This resulted from the shale gas (fracking) revolution and the 2015 lifting of the crude oil export ban. Under President Joseph Biden, the US has issued a record number of new oil and gas licenses, exceeding even those approved during the first Trump era. As described by Milman et al. (2024)

---

[12] Source: Wikipedia at: https://en.wikipedia.org/wiki/Big_Oil#cite_note-34

Table 4.1 Top 21 fossil-fuel companies in the world

Company	Country	Percentage of global GHG emissions
Saudi Aramco	Saudi Arabia	4.78%
ExxonMobil	USA	2.06%
Shell	UK	1.82%
BP	UK	1.65%
Chevron	USA	1.43%
Abu Dhabi	UAE	1.37%
Peabody Energy	USA	1,23%
TotalEnergies	France	1.05%
Kuwait Petroleum Corp	Kuwait	1.04%
ConocoPhillips	USA	0.90%
BHP	Australia	0.85%
Gazprom	Russian Federation	4.49%
Pemex	Mexico	1.65%
PetroChina	China	1.62%
Rosneft	Russian Federation	1.00%
Iraq National Oil Co	Iraq	0.94%
Petrobras	Brazil	0.87%
National Iranian Oil Co	Iran	2.60%
Coal India	India	2.33%
Petroleos De Venezuela	Venezuela	1.15%
Sonatrach	Algeria	1.07%
TOTAL		35.9%

(Source: Naudé, 2023a: 51 and based on Table 1 from Grasso & Heede, 2023: 461)

Under the Biden administration, the US has handed out 1,453 new oil and gas licences, accounting for half of the global total and 83% of all licences by wealthy nations. This is 20% more than during the term of Donald Trump, who has promised to "drill, baby, drill" should he return to the White House.

Not surprisingly, then, As BailoutWatch and Friends of the Earth (2022) document, the 18 most prominent Oil CEOs in the US have increased their collective wealth by over $8 billion since President Biden's inauguration in 2021. With Trump assuming the Presidency for a second term in January 2025 all pretences to address climate change was swept away by a full fontal assault on climate science and efforts to combat climate change. At least, there is no hypocrisy anymore, which has been replaced by a clear determination to bulldozer any resistance against the full exploitation of fossil fuels.

It is not only the US that has acted hypocritically. The UK, despite its 2024 newly elected Labour government's promises, was on track to issue a record number of oil and gas licenses in 2024: "The UK is forecast to hand out 72 oil and gas licences this year, which would result in an estimated 101 m tonnes of planet-warming pollution, a 50-year high" (Milman et al., 2024).

And in Australia, the world's third-largest exporter of fossil fuels, after Russia and the US, and the world's second-largest exporter of CO_2 emissions, Hare (2024) laments that *"between 2023 and 2035, Australia's fossil fuel exports alone would consume around 7.5% of the world's estimated remaining global carbon budget of about 200 billion tonnes of CO_2. This is the amount of CO_2 that could still be emitted from 2024 onwards if we are to limit peak warming to 1.5°C with 50% probability."*

Fossil fuel companies and their CEOs often gain from conflict (see section 4.4 for a discussion on the energy-conflict nexus). In the US, for example, top oil executives sold significant portions of their company shares following the start of the war in Ukraine, when oil prices increased, increasing their fortunes during a period of global instability and rising fuel costs (BailoutWatch and Friends of the Earth, 2022).

The message of this section is thus that economic growth, which requires energy as input and results in goods and services that stimulate further energy demand, is very closely associated with the rise of industrial superpowers—and a highly oligarchic and robust fossil-fuel industry. The very structure and nature of global capitalism are predicated on plenty and cheap fossil fuels to allow more and more extraction—with the consequence, as this chapter has shown, greenhouse gas emissions that are now threatening the habitability of the planet.

In this light, the question has arisen: Should Big Oil pay reparations for the damages that oil emissions have caused? According to Grasso and Heede (2023), Big Oil has significantly contributed to climate change despite knowing they are doing so. Moreover, they argue that Big Oil has trivialized and suppressed climate science, which puts them under further moral obligation to pay reparations (Grasso & Heede, 2023).

The question is, how much in reparations should the fossil fuel industry pay? Grasso and Heede (2023) calculate potential reparations based on Big Oil's historical emissions from 1988, when scientific consensus on human-caused climate change solidified, and assign a larger share of reparations to Big Oil in more wealthy countries. According to Grasso and Heede (2023), the top Big Oil companies (listed in Table 4.1) should pay a cumulative total of $5.4 trillion in reparations between 2025 and 2050. For the top 99 "Carbon Major" companies responsible for 54.3% of global emissions from 1988 to 2022, they estimate reparations of $12.6 trillion are due.

4.4 The Energy-Conflict Nexus

Fossil fuels frequently breed oligarchy and empower dictators who incite aggressive conflicts. —Razom We Stand (2023)

It is not only the decline of oil and the ecological damages caused by greenhouse gas emissions from oil production and consumption that are economically undermining the West; it is also the geopolitical conflicts and tensions caused by the importance of energy for driving the relentless expansion of global capitalism's extraction that are diminishing the West's stature and influence globally.

This section discusses energy's role in global conflicts.

4.4.1 The Future Tinderbox

Jones (2012: 208) describes how US President Franklin D. Roosevelt hosted Abd al-Aziz Ibn Saud, Saudi Arabia's founding monarch, aboard the USS *Quincy* on Egypt's Great Bitter Lake in 1945, in a meeting that

> Permanently linked Middle Eastern oil with American national security. It also helped forge one of the twentieth century's most important strategic relationships, in which the Saudis would supply cheap oil to global markets in exchange for American protection. A bargain was made. And so too was a future tinderbox.

The next chapter, Chap. 5, will explore how this future tinderbox has exploded and contributes to the West's economic decline.

Oil can be a tinderbox that causes war, which has generated an extensive literature. Colgan (2013), for instance, pointed out that "between one-quarter and one-half of interstate wars since 1973 have been connected to one or more oil-related causal mechanisms. No other commodity has had such an impact on international security."

Kaldor et al. (2007) discuss the cases of conflicts in Iraq, Nigeria, Angola, Chechnya, Nagorno-Karabakh, Indonesia, and Colombia as instances of oil wars. Hurst (2022: 20) studies the US-Iraq wars, showing how "American policy towards Iraq since 1979 has been driven, ultimately, by the need to maintain a dominant position in the international oil system." Jones (2012: 210) has made a case that

American oil wars have not been about establishing direct control over oil fields nor about liberation or freedom, at least not political freedom for the peoples of the region. Instead, they have primarily been about protecting friendly oil producers. The objective has not necessarily been to guarantee that Middle Eastern oil made its way to the United States, although meeting basic domestic energy needs remained a vital part of the broader calculation. Keeping prices stable (not low) and keeping pro-American regimes in power were central to U.S. strategic policy.

Oil can play a role in both inter-country and intra-country conflicts. Ross (2012), for instance, concludes that oil-rich countries are 50% more likely to be ruled by autocrats and twice as likely to descend into civil war than countries without oil.

4.4.2 How Oil Fuels War

Colgan (2013) discusses eight distinct mechanisms through which oil influences international conflict. The first is "simple" resource wars, where states engage in conflict explicitly to capture oil reserves. Colgan (2013) argues that while such wars occur, they are less common than other oil-related conflict mechanisms.

The second is what is called Petro-Aggression. This occurs when oil wealth can embolden aggressive leaders by providing them with the financial resources to suppress domestic opposition and project power abroad. Chapter 5 discusses the high and rising oil and gas revenues facilitating and emboldening Russia's invasion of Ukraine in 2022 as an example of such Petro-Aggression.

The third entails the externalization of civil wars. Conflicts within oil-producing states can draw in external actors seeking to protect their oil interests or influence the outcome. This can escalate internal conflicts into regional or even global crises. Smith (2015) describes how oil significantly motivates countries to intervene in other nations' civil wars. He examined 69 civil conflicts between 1945 and 1999. He found that countries with substantial oil reserves were more likely to experience interventions from external forces. In contrast, countries heavily reliant on oil imports were more inclined to intervene in oil-producing nations facing civil unrest.

A fourth is that oil money can finance insurgencies and terrorist groups. Lee (2018) outlines how oil is linked to terrorism and that "oil-producing countries have a higher tendency to sponsor terrorism" (Lee, 2018: 903). Colgan (2013) mentions the funding from Iran to Hezbollah in Lebanon (see also Chap. 5).

Fifth, pursuing control over the global oil market, rather than just physical possession of oil fields, can trigger conflicts. The 1991 Gulf War, where the US intervened to prevent Iraq from controlling a significant portion of global oil supplies, is, according to Colgan (2013), an example. Smith (2015) discusses Western (US) involvement in Angola's civil war (1975–2002) from 1975 to the end of the Cold War, highlighting the role of oil as a motivating factor for intervention. Smith (2015) noted that the US frequently aligns with "conservative autocratic states in oil-rich regions," of which their involvement in Angola was a typical strategy to secure access to oil resources. In the case of Angola, the country became embroiled in the Cold War rivalry between the US and the Soviet Union, its civil war becoming a proxy war between the US and the Soviet Union.

Six, war can arise over control of strategically vital oil transportation shipping lanes and pipelines. In Chap. 5, the Suez Canal Crises of 1956 and 2023–2024 are discussed as examples.

Seven, oil-related grievances can stoke conflict. The presence of foreign oil workers in oil-producing states, particularly if accompanied by environmental damage and socioeconomic disparities, can fuel local resentment—and create a breeding ground for extremist recruitment (Lee, 2018; Colgan, 2013; Basedau & Richter, 2014).

Eight, a country's dependence on oil-producing states can stand in the way of international cooperation on security issues. An example of this is the US becoming a petrostate and oil exporter in 2015 and increasingly becoming important to Europe for energy following the Russian invasion of Ukraine. This will likely make Europe more dependent on the US and hence more pliable to follow the US agenda on global affairs, even if this may lead to conflict with China (see Chap. 5).

Colgan (2013) focused on conflicts driven by fossil fuels, including "Green Imperialism," "Green Colonialism," and "new" resource wars (Almeida et al., 2023; Radley, 2023; Lang et al., 2024).

Renewable energy technologies will require a massive increase in the extraction of critical minerals, such as lithium, cobalt, and rare earth elements. These are essential ingredients for solar panels, wind turbines, and batteries. This demand for critical minerals could lead to new resource conflicts, particularly as these minerals are often concentrated in specific geographic regions. The Democratic Republic of Congo (DRC) is an example. Historically, this country has been the victim of the global scramble for natural resources. Radley (2023: 322) discusses the case of the DRC, pointing out that

> Hegemonic powers are seeking to position the Congolese economy as an exporter of low-cost, low-carbon metals and an open market for the entry of renewable energy finance and technologies. To date, the political response to green imperialism in the DRC has reproduced a model of mining-led national development that historically has delivered little by way of material improvements for most of the population, thus undermining the prospects of prosperity in the country.

Another critical analysis of green imperialism is Almeida et al. (2023), who critically discuss the European Green Deal (EGD), whose "pro-growth orientation of the EGD reproduces a *colonial and capitalist ecology* by deepening the hegemony of resource imperialism and in greening a historically Euro-centered empire."

Furthermore, as fossil fuel use declines, countries reliant on oil and gas exports may experience economic and political instability, potentially leading to conflicts as they adapt to a changing energy landscape (Vakulchuk et al., 2020; IRENA, 2024). As has been already pointed out, but worth repeating, Carbon Tracker[13] estimates that the energy transition out of fossil fuels would result in "*28 of the 40 petrostates would lose more than half of expected revenue under a moderate-paced transition in line with governments' current climate pledges. $8 trillion worth of expected revenue would be wiped out between now and 2040, with different petrostates affected in significantly different ways.*" This impact could also result in resource nationalism, with countries restricting access to fuel and critical minerals, (Dou et al., 2023).

Finally, energy security in a world dependent on renewables will require new approaches to protect energy infrastructure. Renewable energy's intermittency and reliance on transmission networks to distribute energy, could create new points of vulnerability that could be targeted in conflicts, or exploited for political gain (Vakulchuk et al., 2020).

---

[13] See: https://carbontracker.org/reports/s-of-decline/

4.5 Concluding Remarks

This chapter dealt with fossil fuels as part of the Guns-Oil-Oligarchy nexus.

Section 4.2 discussed the energy-economy nexus. It emphasized Western nations' dependence on fossil fuels. The relationship between energy and the economy was explained with reference to the nature of fossil fuels, energy blindness, and the Tooth Fairy Syndrome. This section explained why the end of the Hydrocarbon Age—the age of plenty and cheap oil—also spells the end of the West's hegemony.

Section 4.3 discussed the energy-environmental nexus. The section started by drawing parallels between the current era and the Permian-Triassic extinction, a period of massive volcanic eruptions—emitting many millions of tons of greenhouse gases—that ultimately led to a climate catastrophe. Section 4.3 stressed the need to transition to renewable energy sources and explained that this is a tall order. Challenges include the sheer scale of the existing energy system, the political and economic power of the fossil fuel industry, the intermittency of renewable sources, the lower energy density of renewables, and the limitations of relying only on technological solutions. The implication is that the dominant paradigm of endless economic growth, described in Chap. 3, is incompatible with ecological limits, even if renewable energy can fully substitute for fossil fuels. Section 4.3 also dealt with the role of the concentrated fossil fuel industry in perpetuating the energy-climate crisis.

In Section 4.4, eight mechanisms by which oil influences conflict were outlined, including petro-aggression, civil wars, and control over oil transportation routes.

In conclusion, the world is on the precipice of an energy transition that will have dire consequences for Western nations accustomed to abundant and cheap energy. The Guns-Oil-Oligarchy nexus exacerbates these to the extent that the energy transition, whether undertaken voluntary or involuntary, will fatally undermine the economic prosperity and dominance of the West.

CHAPTER 5

Guns

5.1 Introduction: The Road to Barbarism

The Permanent War Economy, in brief, offers no hope of solving humanity's basic problems. It represents a further stage on the road to barbarism—Vance (1951:44)

One country among the world's more than 190 nations, is responsible for over 70% of global military spending annually, maintains 902 military bases around the Globe (Global South Insights, 2024) and has around 100 tactical nuclear weapons[1] deployed in its vassal, Europe—in Belgium, Germany, Italy, and the Netherlands (Masters & Merrow, 2023). This country is the United States (US), home to the world's most effective oligarchy and also the world's newest Petrostate.[2] Together with its

---

[1] The US thermonuclear arsenal in Europe consists entirely of B61 gravity bombs. These bombs are designed to be dropped from allied bombers or fighter aircraft (Masters & Merrow, 2023). The explosive power of a B61 bomb can be up to 320 kilotons, which is around 20 times more than that of the atomic bomb dropped on Hiroshima by the US in 1945.

[2] In November 2015, the US lifted the prohibition it had had since 1973 on oil export. This is a result of the development of hydro fracking which resulted in a shale oil boom (Naím, 2016). Carbon Tracker analyses 40 Petrostates globally; see: https://carbontracker.org/reports/petrostates-of-decline/

© The Author(s), under exclusive license to Springer Nature Switzerland AG 2025
W. Naudé, *The Economic Decline of the West*,
https://doi.org/10.1007/978-3-031-82299-5_5

European partners, it is the world's epicentre of weapon production and exports, responsible for 72% of global sales of weapons between 2019 and 2023 (Wezeman et al., 2024).

This chapter presents why the high level of militarization in the West—primarily in the US and its European partners—undermines its prosperity and contributes to its decline. This is consistent with the arguments of historians who have pointed out that increased militarization often precedes the collapse of an empire, as it did in the Soviet Union (Chan, 2015a, 2015b; Eckhardt, 1990). Militarization precedes collapse, as it contributes in various ways, explored in this chapter, to economic decline over the long term. It is also a symptom of collapse or economic decline—a declining "empire" is more prone to resort to militarization. In this respect, Foster and McChesney (2014:30) are correct in concluding that "*Its very economic exploitation of the world population, as well as its own, has left the U.S. imperial system open to attack, producing ever greater attempts at control. These are signs of a dying empire.*"

The term War Economy was defined in Chap. 1. In Sect. 5.2 of this chapter, the notion of the Permanent War Economy as an outflow of the war economy is described as the growing basis of economic growth in the West, an economic engine of growth which began to emerge in the US at the beginning of the twentieth century, and which rose to ever greater importance after World War II, and paradoxically (because a peace dividend was expected) after the Cold War. Today, the Permanent War Economy is more prominent in the West than ever. In describing the Permanent war Economy, Sect. 5.1 highlights the US's massive military spending, global military presence, and dominance in weapons production and exports. It shows that the US and its European partners are the epicentre of weapon production and exports, responsible for 72% of global arms sales between 2019 and 2023.

The military-industrial complex (MIC) was defined in Chap. 1. With this definition in mind, Sect. 5.3 discusses the rise of the MIC as an oligarchy that benefits from its monopolization of the arms industry and political influence. The MIC has a deep vested interest in the militarization of the West and has become deeply entrenched in the US government and society. Section 5.4 examines how the Silicon Valley oligarchs (which were described in more detail in Chap. 3) are increasingly pivoting to the MIC, with tech giants like Palantir, Amazon, Microsoft, Google, and Starlink increasingly being reported to profit from war.

Section 5.5 considers that the US oligarchy not only benefits from hot conflicts but has increasingly entered into economic wars—in fact, by 2024, the US was waging an economic war against a third of all countries in the world. The dominance of the US dollar in global finance allows the US Treasury to control access to the global financial system, enabling it to target entities worldwide. As in the case of arms production and sales, the waging of economic war has created a rentier class in the US, which benefits from sanctions—a lucrative sanctions industry has arisen in the US. Section 5.5 also explains why economic sanctions rarely achieve their intended effects and often lead to unintended negative consequences.

Section 5.6 outlines eight key harms caused by increased militarization to the economies of the West. These are the misallocation of resources and opportunity costs, the illusion of job creation, the distortion of market forces and entrenching of oligarchy, the perpetuation of a cycle of militarization and conflict, the undermining of Western standing, the unsustainability of military-based economic growth, the Thucydides Trap, and military overextension.

Section 5.7 concludes that the Permanent War Economy, while enriching a select few, is detrimental to the West's long-term security and economic well-being. The US's maintenance of global hegemony through militarism and economic warfare is both delusional and dangerous. The spectre of nuclear war has never been as acute: as Morris (in Wiblin & Harris, 2023) has warned, the

> Number one threat to humanity—even more severe than climate change or anything else you might want to talk about—is nuclear war [...]. So, I think abrupt, sudden, violent extinction is a genuine possibility.

5.2 From the Business Plot to Bombenomics

This section traces the historical evolution of the US military-industrial complex (MIC). It describes how the MIC has effectively shaped US foreign policy.

5.2.1 Gangsters of Capitalism

Jonathan M. Katz's 2022 book *Gangsters of Capitalism* relates the experience of Major General Smedley Butler during the early twentieth century, which saw the US embroiled in several conflicts such as the

Spanish-American War, the Philippine-American War, the Boxer Rebellion, and the Banana Wars. As described by Katz (2022), during this period the Marine Corps was transformed from a naval force into a leading instrument of US interventionism.

With reference to the Philippine-American war during this period, Farnia (2022) discusses how US President Theodore Roosevelt justified US imperialism in the Philippines by forwarding the paternalistic view that the country was not yet ready for self-government.

It was during this period that Major General Smedley Butler emerged as a critic of American imperialism and war profiteering—after having supported the US occupation of Haiti in 1915. As South (2022a, 2022b) relates in his book review and interview with author Jonathan M. Katz, Butler's initial belief in the righteousness of American expansionism waned as he witnessed firsthand the realities of US interventions in Latin America and the Philippines. In particular, "*Nicaragua was an extremely aggressive, extremely overt war of colonialization and annexation. It was pretty dark, with rhetoric about 'benevolent assimilation' from President William McKinley at the end of the Spanish-American War in 1898*," according to Katz (as related in South, 2022a, 2022b).

5.2.2 War Is a Racket

This disillusionment culminated in Butler's 1935 book, *War Is a Racket*, which exposed the military-industrial complex (MIC) and its corrosive effects on American democracy. He argued that corporations, driven by profit, were all too willing to use the military to advance their economic agendas, often at the expense of human life and global stability (Katz, 2022). Butler (1935) was also critical of his own earlier embrace of the MIC, writing that[3]

> I helped make Mexico, especially Tampico, safe for American oil interests in 1914. I helped make Haiti and Cuba a decent place for the National City Bank boys to collect revenues. I helped in the raping of half a dozen Central American republics for the benefit of Wall Street. The record of racketeering is long. I helped purify Nicaragua for the international banking house of Brown Brothers in 1909–1912. I brought light to the Dominican Republic for American sugar interests in 1916. In China I helped see that Standard Oil went its way unmolested.

---

[3] Sourced from Wikipedia at: https://en.wikipedia.org/wiki/War_Is_a_Racket

In 1934 Major General Smedley Butler testified under oath before the MacCormack-Dickstein Committee that in 1933 he was approached by wealthy Wall Street financiers to lead a military veterans' association to overthrow President Franklin D. Roosevelt and install a fascist government in the US (Denton, 2022). This conspiracy is now known as the "Business Plot," or Wall Street Putsch.[4] It never went through.

The Spanish-American War, the Philippine-American War, the Boxer Rebellion, the Banana Wars—and the foiled Wall Street Putsch with which the oligarchs got away (see Denton, 2022)—laid the basis for the MIC and what would soon become the Permanent War Economy. The Permanent War Economy emerged directly from the US's experience in World War II (WWII). The US economy massively benefited from the consumption and investment boom of taking part in WWII—the production of military goods raised the US's GDP between 1940 and 1945 by 72% (Fishback, 2020a, 2020b). At the end of the war, it established what has become known as the Permanent War Economy, with the military-industrial complex (MIC) being the primary beneficiary in terms of government contracts to produce military supplies and tech (Duncan & Coyne, 2013a, 2013b).

Writing in 1944, Walter Oaks described how the US's industrial and political elite realized that a Permanent War Economy would be a valuable permanent source of economic growth. He defined a war economy as "*whenever the government's expenditures for war (or 'national defence') become a legitimate and significant end-purpose of economic activity*" (Oakes, 1944). This is evident that between 1940 and 1996, the US spent $16.23 trillion on the military compared to only $1.70 trillion on healthcare (Hedges, 2003).

From 1945 to 1990, much of this trillions of US dollar spending on the military was justified in the context of the Cold War. The immediate aftermath of World War II saw the subordination of Europe through the Marshall Plan and the establishment of 171 military bases in Germany, essentially permanently occupying Europe.

Following the end of the Cold War, in roughly 1989–1990, the broad expectation in the West was of a "peace dividend" from the fact that the end of the Cold War meant that defence spending could be scaled down. Initially, this happened; however, without the war stimulus, the US economy fell into an economic slump. To revitalize it, defence spending had to

---

[4] See: https://en.wikipedia.org/wiki/Business_Plot

find new justifications. In due course, plenty of excuses were found to ratchet up US military spending and even accelerate it. Hence, as Tuft University's Military Intervention Project (MIP), which tracks US military interventions over time, shows,[5] over 100 military interventions, a quarter of all US military interventions ever, took place after 1999—in other words, *after* the end of the Cold War. Most of these military interventions, at least the significant interventions, ended poorly for the US, suggesting perhaps that the point is not for the US to win wars but to wage wars as a justification for diverting resources to the MIC.

The following subsections of this chapter will recount these "War-as-a-Racket "projects of the MIC in furtherance of the Permanent War Economy. In particular, the focus will be on four big war-as-rackets post–Cold War projects of the US that entrenched the Permanent War Economy: the War on Terror, the militarization of Africa, the expansion of NATO, the so-called reshaping of the Middle East, and the containment of China.

5.2.3 The War on Terror

One of the first post–Cold War hot wars or MIC "projects" was the wars in Afghanistan and Iraq. These followed as the US's response to the 9/11 attacks in 2001, which the Bush administration saw as a chance to reshape the Middle East according to US interests under the banner of the "War on Terror." The Iraq War, in particular, has become much discussed as an example of a conflict that the West was so eager to have that it did all it could to manufacture consent. Moeini (2022) refers to the Bush administration's claims about Iraq's weapons of mass destruction (WMDs) as a clear example of how a "noble lie" was used to justify a war that served the interests of the military-industrial complex and the pursuit of US hegemony.

The subsequent wars in Afghanistan and Iraq provided a huge monetary boost to the MIC. The 20-year US war in Afghanistan cost the US between US $825 billion and US $2.3 trillion (Cercone, 2023).

Even after these wars, Afghanistan and Iraq have remained client states of the MIC—the US's arms sales to Afghanistan and Iraq between 2009 and 2021 amounted to almost US$12 billion.[6]

---

[5] See: https://sites.tufts.edu/css/mip-research/
[6] According to the Cato Institute, see: https://www.cato.org/policy-analysis/2022-arms-sales-risk-index

The War on Terror is, moreover, far from over. Brown University's Cost of War project notes[7] how

> From 2018 to 2020, the United States government undertook what it labelled "counterterrorism" activities in 85 countries. [...] in an outgrowth of President George W. Bush's "Global War on Terror." These operations include air and drone strikes, on-the-ground combat, so-called "Section 127e" programs in which U.S. special operations forces plan and control partner force missions, military exercises in preparation for or as part of counterterrorism missions, and operations to train and assist foreign forces [...] Despite the Pentagon's assertion that the U.S. is shifting its strategic emphasis away from counterterrorism [...] If anything, counterterrorism operations have become more widespread in recent years.

The total costs of the War on Terror between 2001 and 2022 have been estimated to be around US$8 trillion.[8]

5.2.4 The Militarization of Africa

A second post–Cold War military project supporting the MIC was the US's military interventions in Africa. US military involvement in Africa goes back to before the end of the Cold War and included US support for the apartheid regime in South Africa until the 1980s (Thomson, 2008); involvement in the Angolan Civil War in the 1970s, supporting the UNITA anti-government rebels and waging a proxy war through South African forces (Minter, 1991); supporting the Ethiopian government against the Eritrean separatist movement in the 1970s, and shifting this support to the rebels in the 1980s (Baissa, 1989; Schmidt, 2023); keeping the Mobutu Sese Seko regime in power in Zaire (now the Democratic Republic of Congo) (Afoaku, 1997; Plunk, 1986). This is not an exhaustive list.

Since the end of the Cold War, military intervention in Africa rapidly accelerated and became comprehensive through establishing the US-AFRICOM command in 2007–2008. Notably, US-AFRICOM has its headquarters not in Africa but in Stuttgart, Germany, due to strong opposition from South Africa and other African nations channelled through the

---
[7] See https://watson.brown.edu/costsofwar/papers/2021/USCounterterrorism Operations
[8] See: https://watson.brown.edu/costsofwar/figures/2021/BudgetaryCosts

Table 5.1 US Arms Sales to African Countries, 2009–2021, US$ millions

Country	Arms sales in millions of US dollars
Egypt	8.517
Morocco	1.978
Tunisia	381
Algeria	359
South Africa	163
Kenya	150
Nigeria	137
Mauritius	88
Mauritania	27
Niger	27

Source: Author's compilation based on data from the Cato Institute's 2022 Arms Sales Risk Index, available at: https://www.cato.org/policy-analysis/2022-arms-sales-risk-index

African Union (AU) (Tricontinental, 2023). Unfortunately, the opposition of the African Union could not prevent more, and since then, there has been a surge in US military presence across Africa: it has 29 known military facilities across 15 African countries (Tricontinental, 2023). According to Tricontinental (2023) US-AFRICOM has two primary objectives: to safeguard Western corporate interests and to counter China's growing influence. The "safeguarding" of Western corporate interests continues a historical pattern when Western powers used military force during the colonial period to ensure access to African resources and markets. Africa's economic development is of little concern to US-AFRICOM—in 2023, a total of US$36 billion in official development assistance (ODA) was allocated to the entire continent of Africa, around only one-third of the aid the US has provided to one country—Ukraine—since 2022.

The MIC not only sells arms to the US Military for its growing operations in Africa, it also sells these countries arms directly. Between 2009 and 2021, the US has sold weapons to the value of US$12 billion to 46 African countries, according to the Cato Institute.[9] Table 5.1 lists the top 10 destinations of US arms sales to African countries over this period.

It shows that Egypt receives by far the most military support. The relationship with Egypt, as a US ally in the Middle East, is a historic one to be

[9] See: https://www.cato.org/policy-analysis/2022-arms-sales-risk-index

seen in the context of the US's strategic interest in Middle Eastern Oil (see the discussion on this in Chap. 4) and the Suez Canal trade route. The relationship with the other African states is more recent and, concerningly, will no doubt be considered a new zone of extraction that will grow in value over time—just as in other zones of US military involvement, states become customers of the MIC—see, for example, the cases of Afghanistan and Iraq already mentioned.

For instance, to get an idea of the acceleration in US arms sales to Africa, Hartung and Moix (2000) report that during the Cold War, the US's total arms sales to Africa amounted to an estimated US $1.5 billion. Thus, in a mere twelve years after establishing US-AFRICOM, the US has sold *ten times* as much weaponry to African countries as during the entire forty-plus years of the Cold War.

With reference to the neocolonial ambitions of US-AFRICOM, Tricontinental (2023) have pointed out that the presence of US military bases often exacerbates existing conflicts, particularly in regions abundant in resources. Tricontinental (2023) discusses the case of the discovery of significant oil reserves near the Congo-Uganda border in 2007, following which the US provided training to the Congolese army and designated local armed groups as terrorist organizations, often based on questionable evidence.

Tricontinental (2023) also points to the dubious role of the US military in helping to externalize Europe's border control efforts into the Sahara Desert by referring to the US drone base in Agadez, Niger, which is used to surveil and limit migration. Olumba (2024) discusses the proliferation of Western drone bases in Africa such as these, describing these as "aerial technologies of domination" which ensure " subjugation under aerial colonialism" (Olumba, 2024:1).

That the US and other Western military operations in Africa would be seen as a perpetuation of colonialism is understandable, especially in light of the limited public scrutiny, hence a lack of transparency and accountability surrounding US military operations in Africa. In countries where US-AFRICOM operates, its troops have legal immunity from local prosecution—effectively, African countries have surrendered their sovereignty to the US Military (Moorsom & Raber, 2024).

Furthermore, the expansion of the US military presence through Africa has inevitably drawn in other foreign powers, which has fuelled the rise of Private Military Companies (PMCs) in Africa, often with the backing of Russia (Moorsom & Raber, 2024). An example is Sudan and the role of

Russia's Wagner Group, which is reportedly supporting the RSF led by Mohamed Hamdan Dagalo (Howell et al., 2023; Žižek, 2024a).

Finally, although the discussion in the previous paragraphs has focused on US-AFRICOM, many other Western countries are involved or have been involved in military conquest and control in Africa and have also been working closely in recent years with US-AFRICOM. A notorious example of continued colonial imperialism and control that has been reported in Africa is by France (one of the largest arms manufacturers and exporters in Europe) and its oligarchy. As Valdespino (2023) relates

> Many French citizens unknowingly rely on the rapacious neocolonial industries. Nigerien uranium mines have long fueled France's massive nuclear power plants. Meanwhile, mineworkers and local communities live with the deadly consequences. Gas stations across France pump Gabonese oil into their cars, sending riches to French executives and, until a recent coup, the coffers of the country's long-ruling Bongo family. Similar dynamics play out across France's former colonies. Extractive industries destroy landscapes and livelihoods, pushing millions to find new ways to sustain themselves and their communities.

In October 2023, the French military was expelled from Niger, a country that is the world's seventh largest producer of uranium and which supplies around 25% of the European Union's uranium used to generate electricity to millions of Europeans. The people of Niger have seen little benefit from these resources,[10] which had to be sold to France at below-market prices, with the country having to use the French-imposed CFA Franc—called by Pigeaud and Sylla (2021) "Africa's Last Colonial Currency." It was imposed after the independence of former French Colonies, robbing these countries of monetary independence and cost competitiveness, and creating dependence on French imports. And around 90% of people in Niger have no access to electricity.[11] Following the French military expulsion from Niger, Burke (2023) commented in *The Guardian* that

> Across Africa, France is now reaping the consequences of decades of self-interested interference and commercial greed in their former colonies at a moment of widespread and vocal resentment of the western nations that exploited the continent for so long.

---

[10] See: https://reliefweb.int/report/niger/niger-uranium-blessing-or-curse
[11] See: https://www.opensocietyfoundations.org/voices/who-benefits-niger-s-uranium

5.2.5 The Expansion of NATO and the War in Ukraine

A third big post–Cold War "project" from which the MIC benefitted was the expansion of US-led NATO. Rather than morph NATO, founded in 1949, into a political organization at the end of the Cold War, such as the Conference on Security and Cooperation in Europe (CSCE), the US "looked to expand NATO even as the dust settled from the Cold War" (Goldgeier & Shifrinson, 2023:5). Between 1999 and 2020, 14 countries from Central and Eastern Europe joined the alliance, and in 2023 and 2024 respectively Finland and Sweden joined.

Goldgeier and Shifrinson (2023) critically discuss NATO's expansion policies within a shifting geopolitical context of the times, noting that East-West relations increasingly deteriorated after the Cold War and that mutual suspicion between the US and Russia grew worse over time. They recognize that

> Although one might have expected these developments to call for a reassessment of the principles undergirding NATO expansion, the main consequence has instead been to reinforce the logic of NATO enlargement. Since the mid-2000s, Russian officials from President Vladimir Putin down have highlighted NATO enlargement as a particular problem for East-West relations, just as reciprocal fears of Russian behaviour have driven many NATO members (particularly in Eastern Europe) to focus on using the alliance to confront and deter Moscow […] In effect, this process has redivided Europe as post-Cold War Russian leaders (and many Western officials and analysts) once feared. (Goldgeier & Shifrinson, 2023: 10)

While Goldgeier and Shifrinson (2023) note that the motivations for the expansion of NATO related to the US's desire to reinforce and grow Western influence, and to dominate Europe by limiting "Western European states' ability to pursue a separate security policy" (p. 7), it has been argued elsewhere that there was also an essential economic motivation driving the US to continue the expansion of NATO, even in the face of Russian opposition, which had been clear and unambiguous since 1991 (Menon & Ruger, 2023). According to Serge (2024), *"The prospect of long-term arms sales was part of the attraction in expanding NATO. All of the new members are required to replace their Eastern Block weaponry with nice new Western stuff. That is a lot of guaranteed money over several decades, with most of it going to the USA."*

On 24 February 2022, Russia invaded Ukraine, starting a War of Aggression that continues at the time of the writing of this book. One of the heated controversies surrounding the illegal Russian invasion of Ukraine is about its ultimate causes. As Zubok (2023:145) noted, "in the chorus of indignation and condemnation of the Russian invasion, it became near-impossible to speak and write about the causes and consequences of the NATO expansion in a balanced, dispassionate way." This also marks the portrayal of the invasion in the Western mainstream media, which has, as Zollmann (2024: 373) had shown, de-emphasized the role of NATO's expansion as the cause of the war and marginalized "non-military solutions to solve the conflict."

On the one side of this chorus of indignation and condemnation, many have blamed Vladimir Putin's aggression and ambitions for a greater Russia as the sole and ultimate reason for the invasion. Zubok (2023:146) points out, "*For the Western elites, the cause of the war lies in the authoritarian and aggressive nature of the Russian regime, not its geopolitical grievances.*" Brunk and Hakimi (2022:688) point as an example of the authoritarian and aggressive nature of Russia to Vladimir Putin's 2021 essay, which was "full of conspiracy theories and lies, but the message was clear: 'true sovereignty of Ukraine is possible only in partnership with Russia.' Russia would no longer tolerate a truly independent Ukraine, free to distance itself from Russia and align more closely with the West."

An important dimension that has facilitated Vladimir Putin's Russia's aggression is oil. Russia is one of the world's major producers and exporters of oil and gas. In 2022 and 2023, it exported 12,3% and 11,3% of the world's crude oil daily—around 5000 barrels. As a result of its oil exports, it has always managed to run a trade surplus, as Fig. 5.1 shows.

Figure 5.1 shows the extent of Russia's trade surpluses since the turn of the century. In 2023, it managed to earn a US$30 billion trade surplus per quarter (Vakulenko, 2024). As a result of this, the country has built up significant gold and foreign exchange reserves, worth more than US$ 580 billion by the end of 2023.[12] Russia's government budget deficit is estimated to be around US$580 billion in 2024. It also has a National Wealth Fund (NWF) worth US$130 billion and little foreign debt. Despite steep increases in military expenditures, its government budget deficit is estimated to be around a manageable 5% of GDP in 2024 (Vakulenko, 2024).

---

[12] Around half of this was frozen as part of comprehensive economic sanctions by the West following the Russian invasion of Ukraine in 2022 (McCauley et al., 2024).

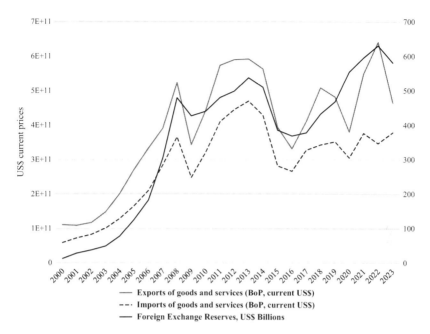

Fig. 5.1 Oil Revenue and a War Chest: Russia's Imports, Exports, and Foreign Exchange Reserves, 2000–2023 (Source: Author's compilation based on data from the World Bank Development Indicators Online and Yermakov, 2024, p. 3)

Thus, as a result of the significant oil revenue, Russia has been able to literally build up a "war chest," which facilitated—or emboldened—its decision to invade Ukraine in 2022. Moreover, it no doubt expected that higher oil prices as a result of the conflict would swell its coffers and that the price of evading sanctions would be worth paying. As Vakulenko (2024) concludes, "Russia has the resources for a long war in Ukraine."

With the Russian economy having access to significant gold and foreign reserves due to oil, and in light of the West's lack of signalled—or interpreted—commitment to support Ukraine, Russia may have calculated that it is in its best interest to invade Ukraine sooner rather than later. According to Zubok (2023:155–156),

> Bolstered by oil profits after 2000, he and his corrupt entourage, as well as the hierarchy of the Orthodox Church, wanted to play the role of a regional

hegemony in Ukraine, in both financial and cultural spheres. The Western alliance's lack of clear strategy regarding Ukraine abetted his ambitions. Western politicians and NGOs, especially in North America and the UK, stopped short of a clear pro-active policy of integrating Ukraine into NATO and the EU. Ukraine for them was too large, too poor, and too corrupt, and Putin was given enough leeway to act with impunity.

Zubok (2023) here refers to the West's decision based on resistance from especially France and Germany, after the Bucharest Summit 2008, to not formally accept Ukraine as a NATO member but to promise such membership[13] at some "future date." In this analysis, the West signalled to Putin that NATO would not be willing to come to the defence of Ukraine, and that if it was ever in future to give Ukraine such membership, it would be in Russia's interest to strike early to depreciate whatever threat a future Ukraine could pose. As such, it was NATO hesitancy in 2008, as well as the soft response to Russia's annexation of Crimea in 2014 by US President Barack Obama, that emboldened an aggressive Russia to invade Ukraine in 2022: "Ukraine was left exposed to Putin's fury" (Zubok, 2023: 158; see also Anghel & Stolle, 2022).

Others have argued that, although the invasion is indeed illegal and has rightly been condemned by the UN,[14] and that the International Criminal Court (ICC) has appropriately issued an arrest warrant[15] for Vladimir Putin, Russia has ultimately been provoked to start a war that could have

---

[13] NATO's promise to allow Ukraine as a member at some future date was reiterated by its new Secretary General, Mark Rutte, in October 2024, although, as always, no specific date is committed to it (Skujins, 2024). This begs the question, if NATO is not willing to accept and defend Ukraine in 2024, why would it do so at a future date? According to Mearsheimer (2014:12), the answer is no because "the United States and its European allies do not consider Ukraine to be a core strategic interest […] It would, therefore, be the height of folly to create a new NATO member that the other members have no intention of defending."

[14] The UN's General Assembly adopted its Resolution ES 11/4 on 12 October 2022 in which it demanded that Russia "immediately, completely and unconditionally withdraw" from Ukraine and reverse course on its "attempted illegal annexation." See: https://news.un.org/en/story/2022/10/1129492

[15] On 17 March 2023, the ICC issued a warrant of arrest for Vladimir Putin stating that he is "allegedly responsible for the war crime of unlawful deportation of population (children) and that of unlawful transfer of population (children) from occupied areas of Ukraine to the Russian Federation (under articles 8(2)(a)(vii) and 8(2)(b)(viii) of the Rome Statute). The crimes were allegedly committed in Ukrainian occupied territory at least from 24 February 2022"—see: https://tinyurl.com/3mturx72

been avoided through diplomacy. Major proponents of this view are John J. Mearsheimer, Jeffrey D. Sachs, and Yanis Varoufakis.

Mearsheimer (2014) claimed, almost a decade before the invasion of Ukraine, that "the Ukraine Crisis Is the West's Fault" when he argued that

> The taproot of the trouble is NATO enlargement, the central element of a larger strategy to move Ukraine out of Russia's orbit and integrate it into the West […] For Putin, the illegal overthrow of Ukraine's democratically elected and pro-Russian president—which he rightly labelled a "coup"— was the final straw. He responded by taking Crimea, a peninsula he feared would host a NATO naval base, and working to destabilize Ukraine until it abandoned its efforts to join the West. (Mearsheimer, 2014:1)

Mearsheimer's (2014) argument is based on the view of the School of Offensive Realism in International Relations, which emphasizes the importance of power and competition in international relations. It argues that states are driven by a desire for power maximization and security and that this leads to a perpetual state of competition and conflict. Hence, according to economic historian Adam Tooze, allowing Ukraine to join NATO, from Moscow's perspective, would represent an intolerable security risk, effectively moving a hostile military alliance directly to Russia's borders. This fear of encirclement and vulnerability shapes Russia's determination to prevent Ukraine from aligning itself with the West militarily (Tooze, 2022a, 2022b).

Anghel and Stolle (2022) provide a criticism of Mearsheimer's Offensive Realism in the context of the Ukraine war, arguing that Mearsheimer ignores Putin's imperialistic ambitions as well as Ukrainian agency; as they put it, "the Ukrainian people expressed their desire for a democratic, European future, divorced from their authoritarian past […] As the war of 2022 continues, we are all witnesses to the same struggles for freedom and dignity."

Sachs (2023) criticizes Western leaders and the media's description of the Russian invasion of Ukraine as "unprovoked," stating that there

> were in fact two main U.S. provocations. The first was the U.S. intention to expand NATO to Ukraine and Georgia to surround Russia in the Black Sea region by NATO countries (Ukraine, Romania, Bulgaria, Turkey, and Georgia, in counterclockwise order). The second was the U.S. role in installing a Russophobic regime in Ukraine by the violent overthrow of Ukraine's pro-Russian President, Viktor Yanukovych, in February 2014. The shooting

war in Ukraine began with Yanukovych's overthrow nine years ago, not in February 2022 as the U.S. government, NATO, and the G7 leaders would have us believe.

For Sachs (2022), these provocations should be seen in the light of the fact that as NATO expanded eastwards, it ceased to become a mere defensive alliance and became an aggressor. He cites in this regard NATO's bombing of Serbia in 1999, the NATO intervention in Libya in 2011, and the NATO occupation of Afghanistan (2001–2021). The latter suggests NATO's willingness to engage in protracted military interventions beyond its own borders.

For further reading about NATO's bombing of Serbia, which has been argued to be illegal because it bypassed the UN Security Council in violation of Article 53 of the UN Charter, see Mirković (2001), Mandel (2001), Davies (2020), and Amnesty International (2000). Terry (2015) and Ulfstein and Christiansen (2013) review the NATO intervention in Libya, which has been argued to have overstepped the Security Council's mandate and hence to have been illegal; and Williams (2024) discusses NATO's (failed) intervention in Afghanistan between 2001 and 2020 and draws lessons for the conflict in Ukraine, arguing that "with Ukraine, NATO leaders are committing many of the same mistakes" they made in Afghanistan, leading to an endemic war, the result of which he believes is that "Ukrainian victory today are hardly credible […] NATO has sown the seeds of failure in Ukraine, and in the coming months the continent will reap this deadly bounty."

Varoufakis (2024a, 2024b) asks, given the complexities of the Russian-Ukrainian war, wherein NATO stands central (whether by commission or omission), it is still fit for purpose, and suggests in Europe, a more fundamental reconsideration of NATO has become necessary in light of the war. He argues that

> Ever since Putin's regime invaded Ukraine, we have lost our capacity, as Europeans, to have a rational and historically-grounded debate about whether NATO membership is detrimental to, or essential for, European liberal democracies. Of course, some would argue that NATO membership is about defending a country from external threats, rather than guaranteeing democracy. But, arguably, NATO membership is neither necessary nor sufficient for a country's defence. […] So, what is the point of NATO? A decade or so ago, I enjoyed an informal conversation with a former Chief of Staff of NATO's forces in Europe. The American, a staunch Republican, was candid when I asked him whether NATO remained fit for purpose. "It

depends on how you define its purpose," he replied with a smile. I asked how he defined it. "It's three-fold," he said. "First, to keep us in Europe. Second to keep the Russians out. Third, to keep Germany down." No analysis of NATO's role in Europe that I have encountered since has been more accurate or prescient.

Those subscribing to the arguments of John Mearsheimer, Jeffrey Sachs, and Yanis Varoufakis suggest that—if negotiations had been made a priority from the start instead of only conflict—millions of Ukrainian and Russian lives could have been spared. It is argued that Ukraine will not be able to militarily defeat Russia and hence eventually will have to negotiate a peaceful resolution—but then in a weakened position having suffered the loss of millions of lives, a demographic collapse, and billions of US dollars in a destroyed economy (Benjamin & Davies, 2024a, 2024b; Williams, 2024).

If a negotiated settlement is unavoidable, Sachs (2024) asked why the US keeps avoiding a peaceful settlement and prolonging the war? He discussed various attempts or suggestions by Russia in the past to push for a negotiated settlement, each of which was, in his analysis, torpedoed by the US and its allies. Sinclair (2022) reports on accusations that in March 2022, soon after the start of the war, that an outline peace agreement was reached between Ukraine and Russia but that the West allegedly torpedoed this,[16] in particularly through UK's then Prime Minister Boris Johnson, who, according to Sinclair (2022), "appeared in the capital [Kyiv] almost without warning" on 9 April, bringing *"two simple messages. The first is that [Putin] is a war criminal, he should be pressured, not negotiated with. And the second is that even if Ukraine is ready to sign some agreements on guarantees with Putin, they [The West] are not."*

Perhaps one answer is that the Russian invasion of Ukraine in 2022 has, according to some analysts, provided the EU and the UK with a smokescreen to throw further largesse at the MIC (Akkerman et al., 2022a). For example, Freynman (2024) reported that "Of the $61 billion earmarked for Ukraine, 64% would flow back to US defense contractors that make the weapons […] since Russia invaded Ukraine nearly two years ago, industrial production in the US defense and space sector has surged 17.5%." Since February 2022 the US has approved more than US$111

---

[16] In a March 2023 Open Letter to Jeffrey Sachs a "group of economists" are highly critical of this allegation, claiming that "Peace negotiations in early 2022 broke down not because of nonexistent US intervention but because Russia demanded unconditional capitulation of Ukraine" (see https://voxukraine.org/en/open-letter-to-jeffrey-sachs)

billion in aid to Ukraine. And former NATO Secretary General Jens Stoltenberg has indicated that NATO should commit itself to providing US $43 billion worth of arms and military equipment to Ukraine each year for an unlimited time (Benjamin & Davies, 2024a).

In conclusion, whether Russia was provoked, or the war the outcome of an aggressor who stepped into a gap left open by the West's (and NATO's) strategical blundering, the West's handling of the war in Ukraine—and its possible loss of the war—reveals strategic blunders and policy failures and ends up enriching the MIC and perpetuating the Permanent War Economy. Thus further erodes its leadership position, making it appear incompetent and out of touch with global realities. This is accelerating the decline of Western influence and contributing to the emergence of alternative global orders that challenge Western dominance. The West's actions in Ukraine have alienated many countries in the Global South, who see the conflict as a regional European issue fuelled by NATO expansion (or bungling) and Western interventionism—rightly or not. This alienation is driving a shift away from Western-led institutions and towards alternative alliances and leadership models, such as the BRICS+ nations, which may seem to offer a more multipolar and less Western-centric vision of global governance. Ultimately, if Mearsheimer, Sachs, Varoufakis and others who have argued that the Ukrainian war is not in the West's self-interest, and moreover cannot end in a military victory of Ukraine, then it will indeed perhaps be the case, as Emmanuel Todd has argued, that the task of Donald Trump's second Presidency which started in 2025, would be to manage the defeat of the West.

5.2.6 *Reshaping the Middle East*

In sub-sections 5.2.3–5.2.5 several "War-as-a-Racket "projects" of the MIC were discussed, namely the War on Terror, the militarization of Africa, and the expansion of NATO and how it relates to the war in Ukraine. This sub-section will deal with a fourth such a project, the attempted reshaping of the Middle East. It should be read in conjunction with sub-section 5.2.3 on the War on Terror.

The Middle East's role in the global production and supply of oil has meant that it is of strategic interest to the West (Prifti, 2017). Seen through this filter, the West has not been adverse in the past to attempt to "reshape" the Middle East, even through military intervention, in the service of its geopolitical interests. For a historical overview, see Yergin (1990). *Guns,*

Oil and Oligarchs have been extremely intertwined in the West's longstanding troubled relations with the Middle East.

Take the Suez Canal as an example. The Suez Canal, built between 1859 and 1869, is a crucial link in the global trade and military networks of Western powers, providing a vital trade artery for the West, transporting more than 60% of Europe's oil (Prifti, 2017), as well as a providing conduit for quicker deployment of naval forces in the Middle East. In July 1956 Egyptian President Gamal Abdel Nasser nationalized the Suez Canal, which led the European powers of Britain and France to secretly collude with Israel to launch a joint military attack on Egypt—to seize control of the canal, ensure control over supplies of Middle Eastern oil, and topple Nasser's government (Office of the Historian, n.d.). However, US President Dwight Eisenhower refused to support this action and pressurized Britain and France to stop their aggression.

As a result, "aghast that their supposed NATO ally could betray them, several European countries began their turn towards what was then Soviet, and is now Russian, oil. In the 1970s, this Soviet European energy relationship was extended to gas" (Thompson, 2022b: 364). In this respect, the Russian invasion of Ukraine in February 2022 gave windfall gain to the US's Big Oil by severing the buying of Russian oil by Western European countries (the EU imposed a ban on Russian crude[17] on 5 December 2022) in addition to sending oil and gas price skyrocketing. Global Witness (2024) documents that since the Russian invasion of Ukraine, Big Oil (e.g. Shell, BP, Chevron, ExxonMobil, and TotalEnergies) have made profits of more than $281 billion. Nerlinger and Utz (2022) noted that following the invasion, the stock prices of 1630 energy firms outperformed the stock market, and those in the US performed the best. The EU reduced its imports of Russian fossil fuels "from a high of $16 billion per month in early 2022 to around $1 billion per month by the end of 2023" (McWilliams et al., 2024). It is still, however, dependent on imports for 62% of its energy needs,[18] of which an increasing share is coming from the US. For example, by October 2023, the EU was importing 226 million

---

[17] Despite EU sanctions against Russia, the EU will remain the single largest importer of Russian LNG and pipeline gas by 2024 (see: https://energyandcleanair.org/january-2024-monthly-analysis-of-russian-fossil-fuel-exports-and-sanctions/)

[18] See: https://www.cleanenergywire.org/factsheets/germanys-dependence-imported-fossil-fuels

cubic feet of LNG per month from the US, up from 157 million cubic feet per month—an increase of 44% in a little over a year.[19]

Back in the 1950s, following the Suez Canal crisis which pivoted European countries to greater oil and gas imports from Russia and other central Asian countries, and with European control over the Middle East declining and shifting to the US, the latter formulated the policy approach that is known as the Eisenhower Doctrine (Office of the Historian, n.d.). The Eisenhower Doctrine "aimed at preventing the expansion of Soviet influence in the region and the emergence of a regional aggressor state" (Prifti, 2017:71). It authorized the use of the US Military and provision of military assistance to countries in the region in pursuit of this objective, even to the extent to authorize the US to "to employ, for economic and defensive military purposes, sums available under the Mutual Security Act of 1954, as amended, without regard to existing limitations" (Prifti, 2017:71). The rest is, as they say, history (see also sub-section 5.2.3). Since the Suez Crisis, as Brzezinski (2003:11) points out, "the area from the Suez to the Persian Gulf has effectively been an American protectorate. Gradually, the protector shifted from a pro-Arab to a pro-Israeli preference while successfully eliminating any significant European and, later, Soviet political influence from the region."

Fast-forward to December 2023, major shipping lines, including MSC, Maersk, NYK Line, and Hapag-Lloyd, stopped using the Suez Canal for sea-borne transportation, and started re-routing their ships around South Africa's Cape of Good Hope. The reason was that Yemen's Houthi Rebels have been attacking ships passing through the Bab al-Mandeb Strait which connects the Red Sea to the Gulf of Aden and the Arabian Sea. Around 10% of global seaborne oil flows through this narrow strait (Gnana et al., 2023). Denamiel et al. (2024) describe the global economic impact of the Houthi attacks on shipping through the Suez Canal, noting that in addition to the disruption of global supply chains around the Cape, which is a 40% longer distance for most EU bound traffic, it has also caused an increase in freight insurance, up from around 0.6% of the value of a ships freight to 2%. They also mention that the average price of transporting a 40-foot (ft) container on a cargo ship increased "from $1,521/40 ft on December 14, 2023, to $3,777/40 ft as of January 18, 2024."

The reason for the Houthi Rebels' attacks on seaborne trade through the Suez Canal was in support of the Palestinians in the War in Gaza,

---

[19] See: https://www.politico.eu/article/europes-risky-new-energy-reliance/

which erupted following unprecedentedly vicious attacks[20] by Hamas on Israel on 7 October 2023. Israel reacted by invading Gaza in a manner that has drawn wide international condemnation for going far beyond its right to self-defence, including a warning that it is plausibly committing genocide by the International Court of Justice (ICJ). In 2024 Israel extended its invasion of Gaza to Lebanon targeting Hezbollah, and carried out various attacks on targets in Iran. Increasingly, commentators have been arguing that Israel's disproportionate response to the October 7 Hamas attacks is not so much an attempt to limit further attacks or bring the perpetrators to justice, but to reshape the entire Middle East—a project for which it has the US support (Barthe & Rémy, 2024; Kelly, 2024; Wood, 2024). As Barthe and Rémy (2024), however, point out, every US and Israel attempt to "reshape" the Middle East since the 1980s has "had the opposite effect to that which had been expected."

Indeed, according to Joschka Fischer, German foreign minister and vice chancellor between 1998 and 2005, instead of reshaping the Middle East according to some Western ideals, the wars in Gaza and Lebanon has the potential to trigger a global economic crisis:

> In a dramatically changing, increasingly unstable world, the century-old Middle East conflict has become something new. All the great powers are already involved—since Iran is a close partner to Russia and China—and the region's status as a major energy exporter means that any further escalation will bring severe global economic disruptions. As in the 1970s, the Middle East has the potential to trigger a global economic crisis. This time, however, no viable solutions are in sight. (Fischer, 2024)

The War in Gaza is, moreover, undermining the moral status and integrity of the West. The West's staunch support for Israel, despite the immense suffering inflicted upon Palestinians in Gaza, is perceived as a blatant display of hypocrisy, particularly in light of the West's vocal condemnation of Russia's actions in Ukraine. The US readily provides military aid and intelligence sharing to Ukraine, actively supporting its fight against Russia while simultaneously acting as an accomplice to Israel's aggression and

---

[20] The immediate motivation for the 7 October 2023 attacks by Hamas is, as explained by Gelvin (2024), due to the "Abraham Accords" which refers to the normalization of relations with Israel since 2020 by Middle Eastern and Arab countries such as the UAE, Bahrain, Sudan, and Morocco in exchange for significant US financial and military support. By 2023 it seemed that Saudi Arabia was to join suit, and moreover that the long-standing Israeli-Palestine crisis was being put on the "back burner."

plausible genocide in Gaza by supplying weapons, shielding it from international pressure through UN Security Council vetoes, and obstructing aid efforts.

In sum, the 70-year-plus conflict in Palestine, which deeply intensified after October 2023 with Hamas's attacks on Israel and the latter's response of invasion and occupation of Gaza, and further invasion of Lebanon in October 2024, coupled with attacks on Syria and Iran and Yemen, together with the West's support, represents a significant turning point in global perceptions of Western leadership. The erosion of moral authority, the loss of trust, and the empowerment of alternative narratives have undermined the West's ability to act as a moral leader and champion of human rights on the world stage. The jettisoning of diplomacy in both Ukraine and Gaza, however, and the loss of economic, political, and moral power by a declining West raise a terrible spectre. Oberg (2023) sees this spectre as the only eventual outcome to which a permanent war economy, with no diplomatic solutions in sight, can lead to: mass killing. As he puts it, *"Since the decision-makers in Western capitals have lost on both economic, political, cultural, diplomatic and moral power dimensions, there is only one left—as in all falling empires in history: Militarism. Mass killing. Ethnic cleansing. Kill the people instead of the problem that stands unsolved between the parties and causes the violence in the first place."*

5.2.7 The Grand Chess Board: Containing China

> It is imperative that no Eurasian challenger emerges, capable of dominating Eurasia and thus of also challenging America—Brzezinski (1997: xiv).

A fourth big post–Cold War military "project" of the US is its (relatively) apparent obsession to contain China. The motivation for the West to want to contain China, and the basis of this motivation in the *Guns-Oil-Oligarchy* nexus, is explained in this sub-section.

One motivation is provided by the Heartland Theory proposed by Halford Mackinder. Mackinder (1943) argued that the "heartland" of Eurasia is the key to world domination. Zbigniew Brzezinski, a National Security Advisor to President Jimmy Carter, took this idea up and combined Europe and Asia into the concept of *Euroasia* and argued in his book *The Grand Chessboard. American Primacy and Its Geostrategic Imperatives* that "a power that dominates Eurasia would control two of the world's three most advanced and economically productive regions. A mere glance at the map also suggests that control over Eurasia would almost automatically entail Africa's subordination" (Brzezinski, 1997: 31).

The US—and its oligarchs—already has control over Europe, not only through NATO, as was noted, but also in terms of being an increasingly important supplier of Europe's oil, following the war in Ukraine, through which Europe's link to Russian oil and gas has effectively been severed. The Soviet Union had collapsed and fragmented, leaving Russia much weakened, facing NATO on its western flank and being further exhausted in economic and military terms by an endemic war in Ukraine coupled with unprecedented economic sanctions. In the Middle East, the central strategic block of Europe, the US's efforts at reshaping the region have been noted in the previous sections, and to an extent, the apparent unlimited support that the US is providing to Israel may reflect a belief that the region has become a US protectorate (Brzezinski, 2003; Rubin, 1990). This essentially leaves China to be controlled to ensure continued US world domination—according to the Heartland Theory.

In the past, the US/West has to a great extent contained China, hence the apparent confidence, or hubris, that it can continue to do so. This historical containment has been referred to as China's "Century of National Humiliation" which is a period in Chinese history from around 1839 until 1949, marked by a series of military defeats, territorial losses, and economic exploitation by Western powers and Japan (Lac, 2024). One of the territorial losses that China has not so far recovered is that of Taiwan. According to Lac (2024), the recovery of Taiwan remains an essential objective of the modern Chinese state.

It is not only that Taiwan was a part of China before the Century of National Humiliation and hence needs to be returned, but it is also the case that China perceives the West as wanting to continue its containment (and humiliation) by encircling it. As Radtke (2007:392) points out, Taiwan occupies a strategically vital position on China's flank. Similarly, on its other flanks, Iran and North Korea occupy strategical positions. According to Radtke (2007: 389), "*US failure to bring about a regime change [in Iran and North Korea] also amounts to a victory of sorts for China, since it will make it so much more difficult for the US to increase its strategy of encirclement, for which basic changes in Iran and North Korea are essential.*"

Thus, it is perhaps no surprise that following the West's wars against Russia in Ukraine and the escalating war in Gaza, with the latter also extending to attacks on Iran and on Iran's proxies in Lebanon, China has been moving strategically closer to Iran, Russia, and North Korea (Chivvis & Keating, 2024). China is fighting its encirclement.

The US motivation to contain (encircle) China and hence to maintain control over Euroasia is made more acute by China's economic rise, accompanied by progress in the fields of science, ICT, and renewable energies. These erode not only the military lead of the US and the profits its Silicon Valley oligarchs can extract from the digital economy but also its direct access to and affordability of oil. As Noam Chomsky describes it in Polychroniou (2023), "since the discovery of oil in Saudi Arabia in 1938, and the recognition soon of its extraordinary scale, controlling Saudi Arabia has been a high priority for the U.S. Its drift towards independence—and even worse, towards the expanding China-based economic sphere—must be eliciting deep concern in policy-making circles. It's another long step towards a multipolar order that that is anathema to the US." In other words, it is not only China's economic, military, and scientific prowess that is a threat to the US domination of Euroasia, but its steps to establish a multipolar world order in which it plays a growing role in the Middle East—the US's "protectorate." Ehteshami and Horesh (2020) discuss the growing role of China in the Middle East, noting in particular the country's dependence on oil from Iran.

And it is not only fossil fuel access and affordability that may be threatened by China's Middle East approach, as discussed by Thompson (2022b: 364) "There is a discernible fear in Washington DC that an age of green energy will be the age of China. Renewables infrastructure depends heavily on rare-earth minerals, whose production China almost entirely dominates."

The US, grappling with relative economic decline, has already resorted to aggressive measures, including sanctions and protectionist policies (a trade war), and attempts to counter China's Belt and Road Initiative (for instance, by promoting its own infrastructure projects through initiatives like the G7's Partnership for Global Infrastructure Investment (PGI). The US MIC is of course, also profiteering from the new "red" (communist) threat, In 2022, *The New York Times* unveiled how the US plans to create a "giant weapons depot" in Taiwan, making the island a "porcupine" with enough firepower to defend itself against a potential Chinese invasion (Wong & Ismay, 2022).

5.2.8 *Bombenomics*

By 2024 the Permanent War Economy is deeply entrenched and becoming even more essential given that other sources of economic growth and extraction are drying up, as was discussed in Chap. 2. Evidence for this is, amongst others, contained in the Biden administration's 2023 National Defense Industrial Strategy[6] and in what has been termed "Bombenomics" (Gould, 2023). The National Defense Industrial Strategy focuses on rapidly expanding the US's military-industrial capacity, prioritizing rapid production when facing "crisis period acquisition." This has been interpreted as preparing for a state of perpetual readiness for conflict, a "permanent war footing," designed to accelerate weapons production and procurement and bypassing customary oversight mechanisms (Gledhill, 2024).

The term *Bombenomics* refers to the economic benefits derived from war and military spending, particularly in the context of the Biden administration's efforts to garner support for continued funding of the war in Ukraine. Thus, to counter resistance to further Ukraine aid, particularly among sceptical Republicans in Congress, the Biden administration has emphasized the economic benefits of this aid for US states. Gould (2023) relates how the Biden administration has presented lawmakers with a map illustrating the distribution of billions of dollars in defence contracts across various states, emphasizing the economic gains associated with the production of munitions and military equipment intended for Ukraine (Gould, 2023). For example, the state of Pennsylvania is reported by Gould (2023) to have received US$2.4 billion in defence from the war in Ukraine, and the state of Arizona US$2.3 billion. The Biden administration's argument centres on the idea that supporting Ukraine has revitalized the US defence industrial base, translating into job creation and economic growth in numerous states, essentially emphasizing the dependence of the US economy on war.

Commenting on this use of defence contracts for votes, Ottenberg (2024) exclaimed in horror that

> What a profitably blood-soaked investment our Ukraine proxy war is! Hundreds of thousands of Ukrainian men get to die fighting for the U.S., which doesn't have to risk any soldiers, while back home armaments makers fatten on the carnage, and the politicians promoting this gory fiasco have the nerve to try to get re-elected! For the U.S., the Ukraine War has truly been a win/win business enterprise.

The US's experience from the Business Plot to Bombenomics is one of the MIC becoming "more powerful than ever" (Hartung & Freeman, 2023a, 2023b). This is despite President Dwight Eisenhower's prescient 1961 warning[7] that we *"must guard against the acquisition of unwarranted influence, whether sought or unsought, by the military-industrial complex. The potential for the disastrous rise of misplaced power exists and will persist."*

The misplaced power that Eisenhower warned against has built an US economy, and under the US-led NATO a Western economy, where making war has become a major business incentive. It has become a Military Trap, a dimension of the Growth Trap, in the sense that without war and its military expenditure providing a demand injection into stagnating Western economies, these economies will decline fast; however with ever more military expenditure and wars to justify it, the West is undermining its own global standing, moral integrity, and ultimately its long-term security and survival.

How the Permanent War Economy, whose projects were discussed in this section, facilitated the rise—and rise—of the military-industrial complex (MIC), and the outlines and mechanisms of the MIC is discussed in the next section.

5.3 The Rise and Rise of the Military-Industrial Complex

This section examines the global reach and influence of the military-industrial complex (MIC), also further considering its impact on Europe. It explores how the MIC has become deeply entrenched in Western economies, driving militarization and shaping government policies to prioritize military spending, often at the expense of social well-being and economic stability. The section examines the MIC's structure and mechanisms for maintaining its power, and describes how as an oligarchy, composed of a few dominant corporations, it exerts considerable influence over US government policy and public perception.

5.3.1 *Diplomacy by Armed Force Alone*

Section 5.2.1 described the origins of the MIC within the overall notion of the War Economy, when it related how during the early twentieth century the US was embroiled in several conflicts such as the Spanish-American War, the Philippine-American War, the Boxer Rebellion in China, and the Banana Wars, which transformed the US Navy from a naval force into a leading instrument of US interventionism.

Dunne and Sköns (2009) describe the rise of the MIC during World War II and afterwards, during the Cold War. They summarize this rise as follows:

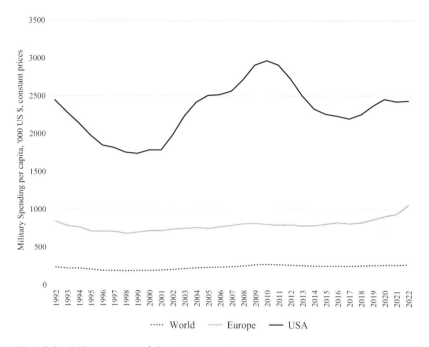

Fig. 5.2 Militarization of the USA and Europe, Relative to the World (Source: Author's calculations based on SIPRI Military Expenditure Database)

The Second World War spurred unprecedented technological innovations and created huge demand for industry. Industry, universities and the military were linked and huge government funded R&D efforts led to patents that were given to companies, with aircraft and electronics production given special status. This represented a fundamental change in attitudes and at the end of the war procurement cuts led to this new defence industry lobbying for arms procurement to maintain its size. The fall of the 'iron curtain' answered their calls, with the Soviet Union threat requiring the maintenance of a permanent army and a permanent defence industry to protect US interests. The Soviet nuclear explosion of 1949, the Communist take-over in China in the same year, and the Korean War (1951-1953) contributed to halting the downward trend of US military spending and set the scene for the development of a mature MIC. (Dunne and Sköns (2009:5)

Thus, the MIC matured during the Cold War. During the Cold War, but moreover even more so after the Cold War, the rise of the military-industrial complex has driven the militarization, not just of the US, which spends more on its military than the rest of the world put together, but of the entire West (Williamson, 2007a, 2007b). As the Stockholm International Peace Research Institute (SIPRI) documents,[21] in 2022, total world military spending exceeded US$2.2 trillion. By far the most militarized regions are the US and Europe, as Fig. 5.2 shows, plotting military spending per capita (in real terms).

Three things stand out from this chart: one is the steep rise in militarization in the US after 2000, following the end of the Cold War (it was interrupted by the global financial crisis in 2009 and the Covid-19 pandemic in 2020); the second is the upswing in militarization in Europe, which started around 2016; and the third is the fact that military spending per capita in Europe and the US is a factor of five to ten times the world average. It is thus indeed not far-fetched to label the West a *Warfare Economy* (Foster & McChesney, 2014). See also Turse (2008).

The MIC has fuelled and profited from the almost relentless expansion of the US's military interventions in the rest of the world, as was described in the previous sections of this chapter.

As the MIP points out, *"with the end of the Cold War era, we would expect the US to decrease its military interventions abroad, assuming lower threats and interests at stake. But these patterns reveal the opposite—the US has increased its military involvements abroad."*

Increasingly, the US is jettisoning traditional diplomacy for what has been labelled kinetic diplomacy: "diplomacy by armed force alone" (Toft, 2018a, 2018b). It includes not only the scuttling of diplomatic solutions and ceasefires in the case of hot conflicts such as in Ukraine in 2022 and Lebanon in 2024, but also the increased use of covert interventions, including the use of special operations forces and drones, and is accompanied by domestic surveillance, oppression and misinformation[22] (Foster & McChesney, 2014; Toft, 2018a, 2018b). It is therefore no surprise then, as Duncan (2022a:5) notes, that by 2021, US military spending reached $768 billion, which was 10% higher than the $698 billion in spending in 1986 "at the height of the Cold War."

As noted by Peltier (2023), almost half of the US federal government's discretionary budget is allocated to the Department of Defense (DoD)—an amount of US$849 billion (out of $1.82 trillion) in the 2023 fiscal

---

[21] See: https://www.sipri.org/media/press-release/2023/world-military-expenditure-reaches-new-record-high-european-spending-surges

[22] Foster and McChesney (2014:23) describe the rise of military interventions abroad and deep domestic surveillance in the US as a military-digital complex, defined by "a tight interweaving of the military with giant computer-Internet corporations."

year. When funding for the Department of Homeland Security (DHS) and Veterans Affairs is included, the total allocation from the discretionary budget rises to approximately 55%.

Peltier (2023) shows how this prioritization of military spending has come at the expense of other essential areas of government investment, such as healthcare, education, and infrastructure which receives considerably less funding than the military. Moreover, Peltier (2023) finds that healthcare creates almost twice as many jobs, while education supports nearly three times as many jobs per million dollars spent compared to the military. The implication is that the rise and power of the MIC has created a budgetary imbalance in the US government that obstructs investments in crucial sectors, ultimately hindering the country's long-term economic prosperity and societal well-being.

5.3.2 The Military-Industrial Complex as an Oligarchy

Hartung and Freeman (2023a, 2023b) details why the military-industrial complex, more than 80 years after WWII, is more powerful than ever—as the substantial taxpayers' money it receives, implies. The power and influence of the MIC is maintained and extended by a fourfold approach, essentially all mechanisms oligarchs everywhere use to extend and entrench power.

First, the MIC has consolidated into several dominant corporations, which is essential for the establishment of an oligarchy. This military oligarchy dictates prices, leading to inflated costs for weapons systems and reduced accountability for performance. The top defence companies/contractors[23] in the West (US and Europe) in 2023 were Lockheed Martin, RTX Corp, Northrop Grumman, Boeing, General Dynamics, BAE Systems, L3Harris Technologies, Leonardo, Airbus, HII, Thales, Leidos, Amentum, Booz Allen Hamilton, Rheinmetall AG, Dassault Aviation, Elbit Systems, Rolls-Royce, Honeywell, Naval Group, and General Electric (Lu, 2023).

Second, the MIC invests heavily in lobbying efforts and campaign contributions to influence politicians, including maintaining a "revolving door" between the defence industry and government.

---

[23] For a list of corporations who received US government contracts between 2006 and 2026, see: https://www.militaryindustrialcomplex.com/companies.php

Third, it exerts considerable influence over public perception of national security through strategic funding of think tanks, influencing media coverage, and collaborating with Hollywood to produce pro-military entertainment. For example, "*more than 75% of the top foreign-policy think tanks in the United States are at least partially funded by defence contractors. Some, like the Center for a New American Security and the Center for Strategic and International Studies, receive millions of dollars yearly from such contractors and then publish articles and reports largely supportive of defense-industry funding*" (Hartung & Freeman, 2023a, 2023b).

Hartung and Freeman (2023a, 2023b) further note how experts from think tanks receiving MIC funding were cited far more frequently in major newspapers' coverage of the Ukraine War than those without such ties, and relates how the Pentagon collaborates with Hollywood, providing resources, expertise, and even script revisions for movies so as to embed pro-military narratives into popular culture. This normalization of militarism within government and society contributes to the perception that military solutions are the primary means of addressing global challenges, perpetuating the MIC's power.

Fourth, the MIC maintains and extends its power through increased partnership with Silicon Valley, as will be discussed below in more detail (Hartung & Freeman, 2023a, 2023b).

Finally, as is necessary for oligarchs under global capitalism, the grow-or-die rule necessitates continued expansion, and this has entailed that the MIC in the US also extends its reach abroad, not only in the form of conflicts, but also driving other countries and regions to become buyers of US weapons. In Sect. 5.2.4 the case of the militarization of Africa has been discussed as one example of this. The expansion of NATO has been another—discussed in Sect. 5.2.5. Of course, with the expansion of NATO, the MIC has been extending itself into Europe—and it goes beyond this. The next subsection details how Europe is becoming a cash cow for the MIC.

5.3.3 *Europe as Cash-Cow for the Military-Industrial Complex*

"Europe is a garden [...] The rest of the world is not exactly a garden. Most of the rest of the world is a jungle, and the jungle could invade the garden."— Josep Borrell, the European Union's foreign policy chief, October 2022, as reported in Liboreiro *(2022)*.

Although Josep Borrell did apologize for these remarks, it perhaps betrays the deep-seated view amongst European elites and provides a justification—or excuse—to agitate for the further militarization of Europe, and the strengthening and expansion of NATO, claiming the rest of the world is a "jungle" ready at any moment to invade the European "garden."

Such views, coupled with pressure from the US, are making the European, the military-industrial complex becoming more and more powerful. It has become "a cash cow for the military industry, without proper parliamentary control and with the collusion of decision-makers" (Ruiz et al., 2021a, 2021b:28). The European arms lobby has even proposed[24] to get privileged access to finance as a sector that is safe for sustainable finance, which means that European "arms companies should be exempted from any form of assessment of the risks of corruption or bribery, or of possible negative impacts on the environment, climate or human rights" (Sédou, 2023a, 2023b).

Since 2016 the EU has taken several strategic initiatives to further militarize and strengthen the military-industrial complex, including adopting a *Global Strategy* (2016), an *EU Security Union Strategy* (2020), an *EU Roadmap on Climate and Defence* (2020), and an *EU Strategic Compass* (2022)—for a discussion see Ruiz et al. (2021a, 2021b). These have already resulted in significant increases in European countries' military expenditure, such as the €100 billion spending announced by Germany in 2023, and the intention of the Netherlands to double military spending by 2025 (Akkerman et al., 2022a, b).

The EU itself plans to raise military spending from €0,5 billion in 2017–2020 to at least €10 billion in 2021–2027.[25] And as Bonaiuti et al. (2023b: 3) documents:

> In the last ten years, military expenditures of NATO EU countries (according to NATO definitions and data) have increased by almost 50%, from €145 billion in 2014 to a budget forecast of €215 billion in 2023 (measured in constant 2015 prices) [...] Such a rise in military expenditure and arms procurement contrasts starkly with the stagnation of EU economies. In the aggregate of NATO EU countries, between 2013 and 2023, real GDP has increased by 12% (just over 1% per year on average), total employment by

---

[24] See: https://enaat.org/wp-content/uploads/2023/02/2022_ASDnote_financbanquesindusdefense-noteasd221011enw.pdf

[25] See: https://commission.europa.eu/system/files/2020-11/mff_factsheet_agreement_en_web_20.11.pdf

9%, and military expenditures by 46%, four times faster than national income. The picture in the area of new investment is even more dramatic: while capital formation has risen by 21%, arms acquisitions have increased by 168%.

In the EU, it is the French arms industry that is turning out to be one of the biggest profiteers of the increased arms production enthusiasm—between 2014 and 2018 France's arms exports increased a whopping 47% (Wezeman et al., 2024). It is now, after the US, the world's second largest seller of weaponry.

In the UK, which boasts the second largest military network globally after the US with 145 military bases in 42 countries, the Johnson government in 2020 announced an additional £16.5 billion for the military (a 10% increase), with then Prime Minister Boris Johnson reportedly declaring that "*I have decided that the era of cutting our defence budget must end and ends now [...] Our plans will safeguard hundreds of thousands of jobs in the defence industry*" (Kampmark, 2020).

Varoufakis (2024a, 2024b) has lamented, consistent with the trends mentioned in the previous paragraphs, that the EU is becoming increasingly militaristic and nationalistic rather than the peaceful, unified entity it was once envisioned to be. He warns that the EU is moving towards a more authoritarian and militarized future, characterized by nationalism and isolationism, reliant on "expensive missile launchers and tall electrified fences" rather than diplomacy and cooperation (Varoufakis, 2024a, 2024b).

5.4 Silicon Valley's Pivot to the Military-Industrial Complex

If war is not impossible, every advance in scientific technique means an advance in mass murder—Bertrand Russell, 1952. (quoted in Wheeler, 1952a)

5.4.1 Silicon Valley Hawks

In Sect. 5.3.2 it was mentioned that one of the ways how the oligarchs of the MIC extend and entrench their influence and power is through a deepening partnership with the oligarchs in Silicon Valley—the digital "Tech Bros." The nature and modus operandi of the Silicon Valley oligarchs was discussed in Chap. 3, where it was described how a few large—"superstar"—firms have succeeded in capturing the digital economy through large dominant—digital platform firms, concentrating industries and wealth to an unprecedented degree (see, e.g. Autor et al. (2017a, 2017b), Bajgar et al. (2023a, 2023b), Qureshi (2023a, 2023b), Sadowski (2020a, 2020b), UNCTAD (2021))—and maintaining monopolistic domination through building of "moats" around the digital economy.

The billionaires who head these digital platforms are amongst the wealthiest humans who have ever lived, constituting a global elite that has been described by Goodman (2022) as *Davos Man*, "*who wield unsurpassed influence over the political realm while promoting the notion that [...] when the rules are organized around the greater prosperity for those who already enjoy most of it, everyone's the winner.*" This is pretty much the strategy that the MIC has adopted as well, increasingly trying to manufacture consent for the necessity of raising military expenditure in the West.

Author Robert Wright has devoted part of his weekly newsletter to highlighting the role and views of Palantir CEO Alex Karp, who is characterized as a "Silicon Valley hawk" for his militaristic and pro-Western ideology. Wright (2024) argues that Karp embodies a growing trend of tech-driven militarization, with venture capitalists pouring significant funding into military tech startups. Wright (2024) further notes that Karp believes the West is locked in an existential struggle with authoritarian powers like China, Russia, and Iran, and that AI-enhanced weaponry is essential for the West to achieve security and prevail in this contest. This worldview increasingly aligns with the views of many influential figures in Silicon Valley and Washington.

5.4.2 A Seat at the Table of the Permanent War Economy

But the deepening partnership between the MIC oligarchy and the Silicon Valley oligarchy is about more than just manufacturing consent. The MIC wants to weaponize Silicon Valley's (digital) technology, and Silicon Valley wants to profit from a new and growing extraction zone that the zones of conflict in a Permanent War Economy offer.

In fact, Silicon Valley may need the MIC more than the MIC need Silicon Valley. To see this, keep in mind the analyses in Chap. 2, which described the grow-or-die rule, and which outlined how new extraction zones are being exhausted and over-exploited by capitalism's relentless growth imperative. Keep in mind also the analysis in Chap. 3, where it was described how, after 2009, the digital platform oligarchy had, in essence, eaten the digital economy's low-hanging fruits—and that the digital economy itself had even come to be seen as a potential cause of further economic stagnation.

In this context, the emergence of AI—an outcome of the digital platforms' harvesting of "big data" from their online platforms—was promoted as a hoped-for saviour technology—to allow the big tech firms another instrument with which to extend their extraction of profits from the digital economy. After 15 years, however, it seems that the profit potential of AI has been largely extracted. The Great Stagnation is coming, also for the digital economy and AI.

With neither consumers nor businesses generating sufficient demand, AI companies are not doing well. For example, although OpenAI rakes in around $2 billion from ChatGPT and about $1 billion from access fees from the current consumer demand for its products, these do not seem to be sufficient—it is reported to be suffering losses to the extent that it is estimated to require at least US$5 billion per year in new investments to cover these losses (Barrabi, 2024; Shields, 2024). According to one reckoning, companies would have to earn US $600 billion per year to justify their current level of investment in AI: this is about six times the revenue projected for the AI industry in the best-case scenario (Shilov, 2024). At the same time, stricter regulations and a consumer backlash threaten the industry, making it even more costly to profitably sell AI products (Candelon et al., 2021a, 2021b; Longpre et al., 2024a, 2024b; Di Placido, 2024a, 2024b).

Whereas AI's extraction potential from traditional markets such as consumers and firms is diminishing, there is one area left where it may still be wildly profitable: war and conflict. Silicon Valley's Tech Bros are thus embracing the MIC to get a seat at the table that offers the fares of the Permanent War Economy (González, 2024).

5.4.3   Counting the Spoils of War

The potential for profits from war, conflict, and surveillance is enormous. As was mentioned, total world military spending exceeded US$2,2 trillion in 2022 and is rising. In 2021, US military spending was $768 billion, around 10% higher in real terms than the spending in 1986 "at the height of the Cold War" (Duncan, 2022a, 2022b). Between 2009 and 2021, the US is estimated to have sold more than US$444 billion in arms to foreign countries.[26]

---

[26] As reported by the Cato Institute at: https://www.cato.org/policy-analysis/2022-arms-sales-risk-index

González (2024) relates how

> Years of AI hype generated by tech leaders, venture capitalists, and business reporters, among others, has played a crucial role in sparking the interest of military leaders who have come to view Silicon Valley's newest innovations as indispensable warfighting tools [...] As Defense Department officials have sought to adopt AI-enabled systems and secure cloud computing services, they have awarded large multi-billion dollar contracts to Microsoft, Amazon, Google, and Oracle.

He further reports that between 2019 and 2022, the top five defence department contracts to Silicon Valley tech firms were worth at least $53 billion in total and that between 2021 and 2023, venture capital firms invested more than US$100 billion in defence industry tech start-ups in the USA. Against this, the US$2 billion that OpenAI earns from ChatGPT pales into insignificance.

Specifically, incorporating AI into the MIC is the latest deepening of a relationship between Silicon Valley and the US's security state, which has been ongoing. As Foster and McChesney (2014, p.23) point out, "*Edward Snowden's revelations of the NSA's Prism program, together with other leaks, have shown a pattern of a tight interweaving of the military with giant computer—Internet corporations, creating what has been called a -military-digital complex.*"

One of the ways in which the MIC and Silicon Valley are integrating their interests is through the leveraging of increased amounts of Venture Capital (VC) for investment in military technologies and equipment. The US government utilizes venture capital to drive military technological development primarily through two main avenues: direct investment through dedicated entities and indirect influence by shaping the investment landscape.

Direct VC investment into the MIC is channelled by the Department of Defense (DoD) and the CIA, who have established their venture capital arms to invest actively in startups developing technologies with military applications. These include the Defense Innovation Unit (DIU), founded in 2015 and focusing on technologies like AI, robotics, data analytics, cybersecurity, and biotechnology. By September 2022, the DIU had awarded $1.2 billion in contracts to over 320 companies. Direct VC initiatives also include In-Q-Tel, which provides VC to startups working on technologies related to surveillance, intelligence gathering, data analysis, and cyberwarfare (González, 2024).

Indirect VC investment is done via US government influence, providing a "Halo Effect" to steer private investment towards defence technology. Here, DIU and In-Q-Tel will provide funding with the aim of sending out a signal to private venture capital firms, hence amplifying the impact of government funding by attracting considerably larger sums from private investors seeking potentially lucrative returns from future government contracts. In-Q-Tel claims that, on average, for every dollar it invests, it leverages $28 in private VC funding (González, 2024).

5.4.4 Murder on an Industrial Scale

While the AI tech giants regularly pontificate about their commitment to ethical AI and human-centred AI, they seem to have no qualms about their products being profitably provided to the MIC and being actively used in war, even when civilians are slaughtered and used to plausibly commit genocide. For example, on 26 January 2024 the International Court of Justice (ICJ) found[12] that Israel has plausibly violated the Genocide Convention in its war in Gaza, where at the time of writing[13] an estimated 41,118 people, including nearly 16,500 children, had been killed by the Israeli military. And, on 20 May 2024, the Prosecutor of the International Criminal Court (ICC), indicated that it was seeking arrest warrants for Israeli Prime Minister Benjamin Netanyahu and Defense Minister Yoav Gallant for war crimes.

Despite these concerns of genocide, ethnic cleansing, and war crimes, the US and its MIC have been providing Israel with unprecedented amounts of weaponry, providing another bonanza for the Permanent War Economy. Between 1951 and 2022, the value of the US military and related aid to Israel is estimated to top *US $317 billion* (Bilmes et al., 2024). Brown University's Cost of War Project[27] documents that

> U.S. spending on Israel's military operations and related U.S operations in the region total at least $22.76 billion and counting. This estimate is conservative; while it includes approved security assistance funding since October 7, 2023, supplemental funding for regional operations, and an esti-

---

[27] See: https://watson.brown.edu/costsofwar/papers/2024/USspendingIsrael. See also Bilmes et al. (2024).

mated additional cost of operations, it does not include any other economic costs.

To put this amount of military assistance in context, recall from the preceding section on the militarization of Africa that the entire continent of Africa, with a population around 1.2 billion, received a grand total of about US$36 billion in ODA in 2023. Thus, one small country receives in one year, in the form of weapons, 60% of all the aid from the West that goes to Africa.

Furthermore, the Israeli war machine has been reported to be allegedly receiving significant support from big tech companies, including Amazon's Cloud servers, on which the military stores "intelligence on almost everyone" in Gaza, which is used "to confirm aerial assassination strikes in Gaza—strikes that would have also killed and harmed Palestinian civilians." AI, in particular, is being weaponized (Abraham, 2024b). The Israeli military's AI systems are reported to be known as "The Gospel" and "Lavender" and respectively target infrastructure and people to be bombed—and are allowed to "kill up to 15 or 20 civilians" in each attack as collateral damage (Abraham, 2024a).

Similarly, as noted, the expansion of NATO and the proxy war between the US and Russia in Ukraine have created a further bonanza for the MIC and the Silicon Valley Hawks. Since the Russian invasion of Ukraine in 2022, the US has provided around US$111 billion in aid to Ukraine (Cercone, 2023). This is, again, using the benchmark of total ODA to the entire African continent, three times as much as aid as Africa receives annually.

The Silicon Valley Hawks have not been left out of this war economy "feast"; indeed, the tech giants have "turned Ukraine into an AI War Lab" (Bergengruen, 2024). The firm of Palantir has been described as "the AI arms dealer of the 21st century" (Bergengruen, 2024). It provides AI to analyse satellite imagery, open-source data, drone footage, and reports from the ground to steer the Ukrainian army's targeting of enemy troops. Other involved tech companies have been reported to include Microsoft, Amazon, Google, and Starlink (Bergengruen, 2024).

In September 2024, the second Responsible AI in the Military Domain (REAIM) summit was held, during which around 60 countries endorsed a non-binding "blueprint for action" (Lee, 2024a, 2024b). The problem with REAIM is not only that its recommendations are non-binding—and even if it were binding on the few countries who endorsed it, a powerful military would simply ignore it—there is no agreement on what "responsible" AI even means (Assaad et al., 2024a, 2024b).

The oligarchs—or Broligarchs—that run Silicon Valley have, like oligarchs everywhere, a problem with democracy—democracy is bad for profits as people tend to vote for peace, a clean environment, and better wages and working conditions (Harrington, 2024; Lingelbach & Guerra, 2023; Monbiot & Hutchison, 2024; Pillay, 2024). In the US, billionaires frequently aim to turn their money into political power to prevent the population from meeting their demands for peace and better environmental and working conditions. Hartmann (2023) notes that the US's billionaires are spending more and more influencing elections: in 2010 they spent US$31 million on elections campaign funding; by 2020 it had risen to $2,3 billion. Many US oligarchs have in 2024 indicated their support for Donald Trump as president in the 2024 US elections, expecting that Trump will be soft on regulating AI, reduce taxes, and continue the economic and kinetic warfare that helps the oligarchs to have continued access to an extraction zone. The Campaign on Digital Ethics has warned that

> the unchecked influence of tech billionaires in politics threatens to undermine the principles of accountability, transparency, and fairness in technology governance. If the rules are written by those who prioritize profit and power over public good, the digital rights of individuals and communities will be at serious risk. (Pillay, 2024)

When considering the dystopia that is the integration of Silicon Valley into the MIC and the US's Permanent War Economy, one should take very serious Bertrand Russell's warning (Wheeler, 1952a, 1952b) that "If war is not impossible, every advance in scientific technique means an advance in mass murder." Mass murder may, terrifyingly, characterize the last days of a terminally sick West.

5.5 Economic Warfare with a Third of the World

It is not only hot, but kinetic wars are also profitable to the MIC and the Silicon Valley Tech Bros' AI. Possible competitors from outside the US are increasingly being dealt with through economic warfare, which helps maintain the moats around their business. Such economic warfare consists of sanctions and prohibitions against countries that present a threat to US business interests. This is part of the modus operandi of the Permanent

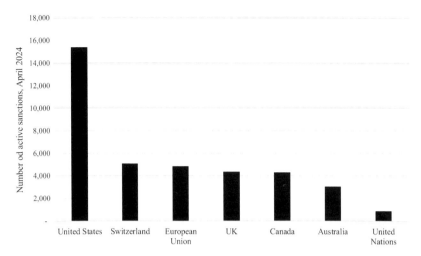

Fig. 5.3 Economic Warfare by the West, Active US Sanctions, April 2024 (Source: Author's compilation based on data from Stein & Cocco, 2024a, 2024b)

Warfare Economy. It has led the US to engage in economic warfare with a third of the world.

A 2024 *Washington Post* investigative report details how "*The United States imposes three times as many sanctions as any other country or international body, targeting a third of all nations with some kind of financial penalty on people, properties or organizations. They have become an almost reflexive weapon in perpetual economic warfare*" (Stein & Cocco, 2024a, 2024b).

Figure 5.3 shows the number of active economic sanctions that has been imposed by the US and other Western countries in comparison to that of the UN.

In this perpetual economic warfare, China, in particular, as the country with the second largest global AI industry and the only viable global competitor to the US tech giants, has become the prime target of technology sanctions (Bradford, 2023a, 2023b) to secure Silicon Valley's global dominance (Mirrlees, 2021a, 2021b) and contain China (see also subsection 5.2.7).

With the rise of the MIC there occurred a dramatic shift in the US's approach to sanctions, evolving from a rarely used tool to a central instrument of foreign policy, aimed to support the US's oligarchy and Permanent War Economy. Essentially, the US has transitioned from employing sanctions sparingly to a state where they have become an almost reflexive response in foreign policy (Stein & Cocco, 2024a, 2024b).

The extent of US sanctions, as noted, impacts a significant portion of the globe targeting roughly one-third of all nations, with some form of financial penalty imposed. The impact is particularly acute for less developed nations, as over 60% of low-income countries are subject to some type of US financial penalty. This expansive reach stems from the US dollar's dominance in global finance, allowing the US Treasury to exert significant control over access to the global financial system and target entities worldwide, even those without direct ties to the US (Stein & Cocco, 2024a, 2024b). Farnia (2024) stresses that US sanctions disproportionately affect nations in the Global South, particularly in Africa, Asia, and Latin America—regions with a history of colonialism. She argues that the underlying logic and implementation of these sanctions reflect white supremacy (Farnia, 2024).

Several factors have contributed to the proliferation of US sanctions, all related to the rise of the MIC and the US oligarchy. Hence, sustained pressure for economic sanctions has been forthcoming from the US Congress, motivated by a desire to protect US industries from foreign competition. This has been coupled with the weaponization of the dollar, which, due to the US dollar's global dominance as reserve currency, allows the US Treasury to exert control over the global financial system. Indeed, the US has crafted a system where in particular the economies of many formerly colonized nations are dependent on the US dollar, and wherein these countries are de facto forced to hold US dollar reserves—which effectively finances the US deficit and domestic investment. This dependence and financial flows from the Global South to the wealthy West, which stems from the Bretton Woods agreement after World War II, reinforces a global hierarchy that continues to disadvantage these countries (Global South Insights, 2024).

Economic sanctions have also turned out in the case of the US to have gained an in-built and perhaps unstoppable moment. This is because sanctions have created a lucrative industry in Washington, D.C., attracting investments from foreign governments, multinational corporations, law firms, and lobbying groups seeking to extract gains (Stein & Cocco, 2024a, 2024b).

Rarely do economic sanctions have the desired effects, and most often result in unintended and negative consequences, which diminish and isolate the West. Stein and Cocco (2024a, 2024b) refer to the example of Venezuela, where US sanctions aimed at ousting President Nicolás Maduro have triggered Venezuela's economic collapse, leading to widespread shortages of food and medicine, primarily harming. They also refer to how sanctions often lead to the emergence of black markets and illicit trade networks—an example is how sanctions on Russia's energy exports have led to a "dark fleet" of ships operating outside international regulations to transport oil. And, increasingly, the one-third of the world against whom the US wages economic war are collaborating to circumvent sanctions, develop alternative financial systems and reduce their reliance on the US dollar. Stein and Cocco (2024a, 2024b) argue that the US's economic warfare against the rest of the world has reached a point where their efficacy is debatable, and their continued use may be counterproductive to achieving long-term peace and stability.

5.6 How the War Economy Contributes to the Decline of the West

Drawing on the discussion in the previous sections of this chapter, this section can now attempt to connect all the strands and provide a concluding discussion of how the Permanent War Economy and its MIC contribute to the economic decline of the West.

The first harm that increased militarization does is that it leads to misallocated resources and opportunity costs. The immense concentration of resources in the defence sector starves other critical areas of much-needed funding, creating a significant opportunity cost for the nation. The $886 billion budget proposed (2023) for the Pentagon and nuclear weapons programs in a single year dwarfs the budgets of essential government agencies and programs, demonstrating the prioritization of military spending over investments in public health, education, environmental protection, and job training. This imbalance leads to underinvestment in sectors crucial for long-term economic growth and societal well-being. Shifting resources from defence to areas like education, green energy, healthcare, and infrastructure would not only create significantly more jobs but also address pressing societal needs.

The second harm that is done is that an illusion of job creation is created. While the defence industry often justifies its massive spending by highlighting job creation, this challenge can be challenging. Despite receiving record levels of government funding, the defence sector has experienced job losses due to factors like automation, outsourcing, and a shift towards highly specialized engineering roles. Thus, the concentration of expertise in a single industry creates a "brain drain," depriving other sectors of skilled workers and potentially hindering innovation in fields crucial for addressing challenges like climate change and public health.

Thirdly, militarization undermines the economies of the West by distorting market forces and facilitating the emergence and strength of the oligarchy—see also Chap. 3. The consolidation of the MIC into a handful of powerful corporations has significantly reduced competition, creating a system where a few companies hold disproportionate leverage over the government. This allows the MIC to dictate prices, often resulting in taxpayers funding overpriced weapons systems that fail to deliver on their promises.

Fourthly, the rise and rise of the MIC is perpetuating a cycle of militarization. The MIC, with its vested interest in maintaining high levels of military spending, actively shapes public discourse and influences government policy to perpetuate a war economy" mentality. This influence, channelled through lobbying, campaign contributions, and the manipulation of public narratives through media and entertainment, creates a self-perpetuating cycle of military buildup and interventionism. This prioritizes military solutions over diplomatic efforts and diverts resources from addressing the root causes of global instability and insecurity, further hindering long-term economic prosperity and global well-being.

Fifth, as Brenner (2024) has suggested, the attachment of the US to its MIC and Permanent War Economy, and the falling under its sway by many other leaders in the West, seriously undermines the standing and respect of the West in the rest of the world. He points to what is being perceived as an absence of guilt and shame in Western leaders for the increasingly shameful and shocking violence that the West is inflicting. According to Brenner (2024), this lack of guilt or shame in Western leaders is due to a pervasive influence of nihilism in contemporary Western societies, undermining their sense of moral responsibility and accountability.

As an example, Brenner (2024) refers to the US airdropping a small amount of humanitarian aid into the sea off Gaza following the Israeli 2023 invasion as "grotesque" in light of the US role in enabling the Israeli offensive through the provision of weapons and diplomatic cover, and the US's actively hampering of aid efforts by withholding funding from the UN agency responsible for Palestinian refugees (UNWRO) and blocking attempts at a ceasefire through its UN Security Council veto power. This grotesque action creates, however, little guilt due to the decline of moral constraints and communal accountability in the West (Brenner, 2024). How this lack of shame and guilt leads the "Rest to reject the West" is explained by Gerges (2024), who states that the US's unwavering support for Israel's military campaign in Gaza has significantly harmed its relationship with the Global South, particularly in the Middle East, by solidifying the perception that the West disregards Arab lives.

McKern (2024) adds to this, explaining that the uneven portrayal of civilian suffering by Western leaders and media of the conflicts where they are involved adds to the increasing condemnation of the West. He refers to this portrayal, where Palestinian casualties are minimized or rationalized while Ukrainian suffering is emphasized, and argues that it erodes trust in the West's commitment to human rights. This disparity is compounded by the West's inconsistent responses to similar events, such as condemning alleged war crimes in Ukraine while remaining silent on comparable situations in Gaza. This perceived hypocrisy fuels scepticism towards Western moral authority in the Global South.

Sixth, in in spite of its "permanence," the Permanent War Economy cannot deliver permanent economic growth—which remains unattainable, as Chap. 2 explained. It provides, however, that the lure of short-term economic growth, together with debt-fuelled growth, has managed to keep economic growth rates higher in the West than it would have been. However, neither war nor debt-fuelled growth can be sustained. Over the longer term, Western economies will pay a steep economic price for their addiction to short-term militaristic growth strategies. In this regard, an Institute for Economics and Peace (IEP) study that examines the macroeconomic consequences of war spending on the US economy since World War II is insightful (Institute for Economics and Peace, 2012).

The IEP study explored the relationship between government spending on war and the military and its impact on GDP growth, public debt, taxation, consumption, investment, inflation, and stock market valuations. It does so over five distinct periods of conflict: World War II, the Korean War, the Vietnam War, the Cold War, and the Iraq/Afghanistan Wars. The study finds that, while war spending does generate short-term economic benefits, such as increased economic growth and employment, it ultimately leads to longer-term negative consequences, including higher inflation, budget deficits, and reduced consumption and investment. In this, the study is consistent with earlier studies, such as that of Rasler and Thompson (1985), who studied wars from the 1700s, finding that the economic growth impacts of wars are only positive over the short-term and come at a longer-term cost.

Seventh, a hegemon based on a Permanent War Economy may fall into what has been called the *Thucydides Trap*. Thucydides (ca 460–400 BC), an Athenian general and one of the world's first historians, described[28] in the *History of the Peloponnesian War* that, the rise to power of Athens was seen by Sparta as such a threat, that war became inevitable. This observation has lent the general's name to the notion of the Thucydides Trap (Allison, 2017). It is a historical pattern[29] that "when a rising power threatens to displace a ruling one, the most likely outcome is war." Allison (2017) has argued that the US is facing the Thucydides Trap, which has been sprung by the rise of China, which it considers its main geopolitical rival—and hence a country to be contained. In was already pointed out that indeed a major post–Cold War project of the US's MIC is to contain China, both through projecting US military power to the region, for instance in creating a "porcupine" Taiwan, and, as discussed in Sect. 5.2.7, to wage economic war against China. The moral of the *Thucydides Trap* story, and why it is a trap, is that it does not end well for the incumbent hegemon. In the case of Thucydides, his side lost: Sparta ultimately won the Peloponnesian War. Athens, once a powerful maritime empire, was defeated and forced to surrender.

Eighth, a Permanent War Economy inevitably overextends itself, like the Roman Empire or the Soviet Union. Rich (2024) cites as evidence of the US's overextended military reach, with its 902 foreign military bases and involvement in numerous conflicts over the past decade, the fact that the US has experienced several military defeats and that with NATO it is staring at defeat in Ukraine.

Thus, despite its heavy militarization, the US is less and less able to achieve its objectives in various regions of the world. As historian Jeff Rich describes it,

> In the last three years, the US has experienced effective defeats in Kabul, Ukraine, Africa, and West Asia. But it remains in denial. Its ranting supremacists want to forestall defeat in Taiwan, and ignore how the BRICS+ economies are larger than the G7. The US grows more isolated diplomatically, while the Global Majority asserts its voice. The US's humanitarian interventionism has been defeated by US disgraces from Serbia to Gaza. The greatest-ever army was undone by its own vanity. The empire of democracy was defeated by inventing too many of its own realities. Even its grand alliance, NATO, is tasting defeat in Ukraine. (Rich, 2024)

---

[28] See: https://en.wikipedia.org/wiki/History_of_the_Peloponnesian_War
[29] See: https://www.belfercenter.org/programs/thucydidess-trap

The increasing failure of the US and its European vassals to achieve its geopolitical objectives through military means is also stressed by Watkins (2024), from whom it is worth quoting, as he describes the US's failure in Syria and Ukraine:

> The limits of empire were spelled out in 2011, when the—then—loose association of China, Iran, and Russia stepped in to prevent the US neocons from conducting regime change in Syria ... a defiance which has undoubtedly fuelled neocon determination to conduct regime change in all three countries, beginning with Russia. But that, too, has failed. All of those hi-tech weapons that the Western arms manufacturers claimed would be war-winners have proved to be next to useless in a real war against a country with the resources to fight back. Moreover, the attempt at economic warfare against a country with most of what remains of the world's energy and mineral resources has proved disastrous for Western economies, whose main product is fiat currency and accounting services. Indeed—although you wouldn't know it from western establishment media coverage—the main consequence of the western attempt at regime change in Russia has been the development of a BRICS economic bloc containing more than 75 percent of the world's countries and more than 80 percent of the world's remaining resources.

At the same time the economic costs of keeping this ineffective military super-apparatus going and appeasing the MIC are also causing the US to be less and less effective in domestic economic issues, with a deterioration in living standard the consequence. Bello (2024) posits that military overextension has fuelled political turmoil in the US. He argues that this turmoil has led to the rise of far-right politics within the Republican Party, characterized by racism, anti-immigrant sentiment, and anxieties stemming from declining economic status among white Americans. For Bello (2024) the severe polarization of US politics suggests that the country is nearing a state of civil war.

The growing militarization of the West, as discussed in this chapter, paradoxically does little to promote the long-term security and economic development of the West. It entrenches the short-termism that characterizes the Growth Trap of global capitalism while enriching a select few. Moreover, in doing so it also hinders job growth in crucial sectors, distorts market forces, and traps the West in a cycle of militarization that prioritizes short-term security interests over long-term societal well-being.

5.7 Concluding Remarks: A Dangerous and Delusional Hegemon?

This chapter argued that the continued militarization of the West undermines its prosperity and contributes to its decline.

Section 5.2 traced the historical development of the military-industrial complex (MIC) and its role in establishing and entrenching the Permanent War Economy. It concluded that spending on the military and defence industry—the Guns Oligarchy—has become essential to economic growth in the West. The origins of the Permanent War Economy with its MIC oligarchy is traced back to the beginning of the twentieth century—and early warning was sounded in Smedley Butler's book *War Is a Racket* (1935), wherein he exposed the MIC's manipulation of US national interests to benefit corporations, laying bare the profit-driven motives behind US military actions. The massive economic boost that the US economy was provided laid the groundwork. The Cold War further solidified this system, providing justification for high military budgets and a global military presence.

After the Cold War, however, with the Great Stagnation setting in in the West (see Chap. 2), the militarization of the West paradoxically accelerated. Various post–Cold War "projects" were discussed in this chapter to illustrate this acceleration in militarization. These include the War on Terror following the 9/11 attacks which led to profitable wars in Afghanistan and Iraq for the MIC; the establishment of US-AFRICOM in 2007–2008 which significantly expanded US military presence in Africa, resulting in increased arms sales and interventions on the continent; NATO's expansion eastwards, despite Russia's security concerns, which fuelled tensions and created new markets for US weapons (including for testing Silicon Valley's Artificial Intelligence products), culminating in the conflict in Ukraine; the US (and Israel's) attempts to reshape the Middle East, and the US's focus on containing China's rise which has led to increased military spending and use of economic sanctions, aiming to curb China's global influence and encircle the country.

Section 5.3 critically examined the MIC extension into Europe. It was argued that Europe has become a new cash cow for the Guns Oligarchy, a continent that is economically stagnating to an even worse degree than the US.

Section 5.4 explored the burgeoning relationship between Silicon Valley and the MIC. It highlighted why and how tech companies want to and are profiting from the Permanent War Economy. It was pointed out that a generation of "Silicon Valley Hawks" considers tech-driven militarization essential for Western security. They see the Permanent War Economy as a lucrative new market for their technologies, particularly as profits from traditional markets diminish.

Section 5.5 dealt economic sanctions as an "economic warfare" tool against countries perceived as threats to Western interests, highlighting how this practice supports the US oligarchy and the Permanent War Economy. It was shown that the US imposes significantly more sanctions than any other country, targeting roughly one-third of all nations with financial penalties, particularly those in the Global South. The "weaponization of the dollar" has created a system where many countries, mainly former colonies, depend on the US dollar, effectively financing the US deficit and domestic investment. Sanctions have, however, mostly failed to achieve their intended goals and have led to unintended negative consequences, including economic hardship for targeted populations and the emergence of black markets.

Section 5.6 drew together the various implications from Sects. 5.2–5.5 for the economic decline of the West, stressing the myriad of ways in which militarization does harm and ultimately undermines the West.

In conclusion, the evidence and arguments presented in this chapter support conclusions elsewhere of the detrimental course that Western economies have embarked on in a desperate bid to continue economic growth. It is consistent with Sachs's (2022) conclusion that the US's pursuit of global hegemony is *delusional* because it is based on a misreading of the current geopolitical reality and the nature of economic growth, and is *dangerous* because it increases the risk of major further conflicts, including nuclear war.

In this respect, historian Ian Morris (in Wiblin & Harris, 2023) has importantly pointed out that

> When you look back over the long run of history, one of the things you repeatedly see is every time there has been a major transformation, a major shift in the balance of wealth and power in the world, it's always been accompanied by massive amounts of violence. And living in a world that has nuclear weapons, I would say the number one threat to humanity—even more serious than climate change or anything else you might want to talk about—is nuclear war. […] So, I think abrupt, sudden, violent extinction is a perfectly real possibility.

CHAPTER 6

The End

6.1 Introduction

> Since 1945 the world has been the best it has ever been. The best it will ever be. Which is a poetic way of saying this era, this world - our world - is doomed. (Zeihan, 2022:3–4)

In Chaps. 3–5 of this book, the simple thesis was advanced that Western economies, led by the US as the modern hegemon or "Empire," are in absolute and relative decline as a result of the simple economics of three interrelated aspects: the decline in cheap and easy oil, the rise of an oligarchy, and the growing militarization in the rise of the Military Industrial Complex (MIC) which has put the economies of the West on a Permanent War Economy footing. It is worth emphasizing that these factors are interrelated and do not only one-directionally drive the economic decline of the West, but as the West stagnates, the decline in energy, conflicts, and monopolization of the economic space will become more acute.

This thesis is not a thesis of collapse. This book, as was explained in Chap. 1, does not predict or expect the imminent collapse of the West, or the "end of the US Empire." It explains how, with the backdrop of the Great Stagnation, climate change, and the decline in affordable and easily accessible energy—and hence Peak Oil—the West is inflicting on itself further and avoidable damage through the perpetuation of oligarchies and war. Although it is unlikely that the West will reverse its relative decline as an economic power and reverse the Great Stagnation (that started in the 1970s), much damage, death, and destruction can be avoided if the West can jettison the Oligarchy and the Permanent War Economy.

What thus needs to collapse is not the West or its constituent countries but the system of neoliberal capitalism—explained in Chap. 2. Mitigating further climate change, adapting to a world that wreaks less havoc on Earth Systems, phasing out the use of GHG-emitting fossil fuels, and pulling the World back from the brink of a nuclear war necessitate an end to the system of neoliberalism capitalism whose slash and burn doctrine is not only hastening the economic decline of the West but moreover ultimately does threaten the prospects of the Earth as habitable planet.

Thus, in a sense, this book *is* about the collapse, not only of the West but of civilization, as the unchecked and out-of-control system of neoliberal capitalism is turning the world into a slaughterhouse. Chapter 4 outlined how global climate change may threaten civilization collapse, and Chap. 5 cautioned that the Permanent War Economy may result in a thermo-nuclear conflagration. Chapter 3 pointed out that many in the oligarchy expect (and perhaps hope for) such a civilizational collapse to be unavoidable, and they are building underground shelters and planning to leave the planet altogether.

In this light, this chapter explores how the economic decline of the West in the Great Stagnation and its acceleration as a result of Guns, Oil, and Oligarchs (the central thesis of this book) have been reflected in contemporary debates on the collapse of the West and the possible eventual collapse of human civilization.

Section 6.2 discusses the current broad narratives of collapse, starting by defining what is meant by collapse and referring to the main contributions to the idea that the West is collapsing. Section 6.3 outlines and explores four dimensions of the West's collapse, marked in the literature: economic, environmental, political, and population collapses. Section 6.4 points out that several authors also consider but reject the thesis that the West is facing collapse. This section explores some of the views of optimists as a counter to the declinist views that dominate this book. Section 6.5 concludes, asking whether an Ars Moriendi is possible for the West.

6.2 Broad Narratives of Collapse[1]

6.2.1 *Defining Collapse*

Civilizational or societal collapse is generally understood as a significant decline in a society's complexity and ability to function. This often manifests as a breakdown in social order, economic productivity, political institutions, and technological advancements.

Tainter (1988: 4) defined societal collapse as when a society "displays a rapid, significant loss of an established level of sociopolitical complexity." He describes the immediate aftermath of collapse as follows (Tainter, 1988: 20):

> The overarching structure that provides support services to the population loses capability or disappears entirely. No longer can the populace rely upon external defence and internal order, maintenance of public works, or delivery of food and material goods. Organization reduces to the lowest level that is economically sustainable so that a variety of contending polities exist where there has been peace and unity. Remaining populations must become locally self-sufficient to a degree not seen for several generations. Groups formerly economic and political partners now become strangers, even threatening competitors.

McAnany and Yoffee (2010) questioned the notion of "collapse," arguing that most previous societies described as having collapsed may rather have transformed and evolved indicating enduring resilience of human societies. For Ehrenreich (2020), like McAnany and Yoffee (2010), the notion of "collapse" underplays the nature of change, resilience, and adaptability of humans. He writes that

> If you close your eyes and open them again, the periodic disintegrations that punctuate our history — all those crumbling ruins — begin to fade, and something else comes into focus: wiliness, stubbornness and, perhaps the strongest and most essential human trait, adaptability [...]. Perhaps it is what we do best. When one way doesn't work, we try another. When one system fails, we build another. We struggle to do things differently, and we push on. As always, we have no other choice.

---

[1] This section draws on and extends the discussion in Naudé (2023a).

Greer (2005:11–12) prefers the term "succession" to collapse, arguing that the term collapse is associated only with negative connotations, while it may also entail opportunity for societal renewal and diversification, pointing out that the "Roman collapse enabled other societies to emerge from Rome's shadow, and launched major cultural initiatives such as vernacular literatures in the ancestors of today's Celtic, Germanic, and Romance languages." One could argue that modern Western Civilization and its Western Offshoots are the eventual succession to the Roman Empire.

6.2.2 From Spengler to the Eventual Todd

There is a substantial "Collapse of the West/US" industry. One of the earliest authors on the topic was Oswald Spengler, a German historian and philosopher who argued in his 1918 book, *The Decline of the West*, that Western culture, having passed through its periods of growth and maturity, was now in an irreversible state of decline (Spengler, 1918). He saw evidence of this decline in various aspects of Western society, including the dehumanizing impact of technology, the obsession with material wealth and consumption, wars and the rise of totalitarian regimes, and the growth of large, impersonal cities as a sign of cultural decline (Frye, 1974). Spengler's was, however, neither a scientific nor a serious historical account, and explained decline not very specifically, but rather broadly as some natural phenomenon of growth, stagnation, and decline.

Since the onset of the Great Stagnation since the 1970s (coinciding with the oil crisis—see Chap. 2), there have been several studies on the potential collapse of the West that have focused on more specific mechanisms of decline and collapse.

In the last years of the Cold War, Paul Kennedy's 1987 book, *The Rise and Fall of Great Powers*. Kennedy (1987) argued that "imperial overstretch" has been a recurring factor in the decline of great powers throughout history and that the US was at risk of overextending itself. In an evaluation of Kennedy's thesis, Porter (2015) concludes that while the US is unlikely to experience a sudden collapse, a gradual erosion of its relative power, as Kennedy (1987) warned, is a real possibility.

At roughly the same juncture in time, Joseph Tainter (1988) in his book *The Collapse of Complex Societies*, explained the collapse of the West with reference to the complexity of civilization. He argued that civilizations face various never-ending series of problems, which rising complexity is an approach to solve. However, at some stage, rising complexity as problem-solving mechanism becomes subject to diminishing returns (Tainter, 1988).

Turchin and Gavrilets (2009), very similarly, argued that as states attempt to control larger and larger populations, they construct larger and more complex hierarchies (bureaucracies) which at first have a politically and socially integrative result as it overcomes the collective action problem. However, at some stage, due to various reasons, amongst them the inter-elite conflict (see below), these hierarchies start to unravel, and the collective action problem and its correlates reassert themselves. They consider the EU already as past this point, which is leading to a "reversal of the dynamic of integration" in the EU (Turchin & Gavrilets, 2009:187).

Burja (2020) argues that societal collapse is the eventual outcome of a succession problem, namely how to ensure that the knowledge, expertise, and values required to manage a complex civilization get adequately transferred to new generations. When societies fail in doing so, the slow erosion of knowledge—rot—leads to an intellectual Dark Age which precedes an actual collapse. The succession problem is strongly related to the decline[2] in population growth experienced in the West, where generally fertility rates dropped below replacement rates in the 1970s.

One proponent of the notion that population growth (the succession problem) will lead to Western decline is Robin Hanson, who laments that Westerners just do not breed enough anymore—a result of what he labels "cultural drift." Hanson (2024b) links population and innovation a central plank of endogenous growth theory. One way to see this is to consider that a complex civilization needs constant innovation to tackle both the problems it was set up to tackle in the first place, as well as deal with the weight of its complexity and that a declining population creates success and innovation shortages that obstruct this. According to Hanson (2024b), the dystopia and collapse will happen as follows:

> World population will start to fall in a few decades [...] Falling population should then cause a more than proportionate fall in innovation rates [...] after innovation rates greatly fall due to population fall, innovation will seem a less important social phenomenon, making less of a difference to who wins

---

[2] Typically, and in contrast to Thomas Malthus (1798), there has been fear that too large a population would lead to a collapse. Kohr (1957) argued that larger populations, often concentrated in megacities, contribute to creating unwieldy and ultimately unsustainable political structures.

or loses. And then societies will prioritize it less, sacrifice other opportunities for it, and do less work to regain it when it randomly decays. Plausibly leading to widespread decline of cultural support for innovation. And also for liberality. [...] Having lost the taste and habit of innovation, the world might take a long time to revive it again, just as it took a long time for the ancient world to stumble into a way to create our current innovation levels. That is, while the coming post-population-peak economy might retain many industrial techs, such as cars and electricity, it might lose the capacity to innovate such techs, and not rediscover that for many centuries, or maybe even longer. And a world with a rising population and constant tech is much more likely to be a world of falling median income. So we may return to a world of poverty and low liberality, plausibly also with more war. A non-modern world, but with cars and electricity.

For Turchin (2023), it is not the level or growth of population that matters as much as the composition and nature of the population, particularly the number and power of elites—or Oligarchs. Turchin (2023) considers societal collapse to be the outcome of an Elite Overproduction and immiseration of non-elites, which leads to a counter-elite revolt, which results in rising inequality, growing distrust, and a breakdown of social resilience. The outcome is the eventual political disintegration of society. Using cliodynamics, Turchin (2023) finds that nations rise and fall through cycles of integration and disintegration, each lasting around ~100 years on average.

Kotkin (2020) warns that the oligarchy-dominated West is more and more resembling a Middle Ages-like Feudal order. He argues that, like in the Middle Ages, a rigid class structure is solidifying in the US. He identifies four distinct classes—the oligarchs, the clerisy, the yeomanry, and the new serfs—mirroring the hierarchy of medieval society—and which increasingly reduces social mobility in the US.

French historian and anthropologist Emmanuel Todd argued in his book *La Défaite de l'Occident* (*The Defeat of the West*) that Western societies, particularly the US, are in decline because of the decline of religious belief in the West. As a result, Todd (2024) laments that the West has entered an era of nihilism characterized by an emphasis on individual pursuits and material gain at the expense of collective well-being. He explains how against this post-Christian nihilism the pursuit of a global hegemony has stretched the resources of the West (the Paul Kennedy argument) and led to a series of foreign policy blunders, such as the conflict in Ukraine (Polonsky, 2024). For Todd, the main task for Donald Trump in his second term as President of the USA is to manage the consequences of what he describes as the USA's defeat in its proxy war in Ukraine.

6.2.3 Through the Kübler-Ross Grief Cycle

Roberts (2024) has used the *Kübler-Ross Grief Cycle*, a model for processing grief, to analyse how the US, or West more generally, might react to its declining global power and possible collapse due to the reasons explored in Sect. 6.2.2. This framework suggests that the West could experience stages of *denial, anger, bargaining, depression*, and ultimately, *acceptance* as it grapples with its diminishing influence.

Roberts (2024) uses the example of the US military withdrawal from Afghanistan to show how the Biden administration exhibited signs of denial in their attempts to downplay the severity of the defeat and portray the chaotic evacuation as a success. Thus, instead of acknowledging the implications of the Taliban's victory, President Joseph Biden focused on the scale of the airlift evacuation, trying to deflect attention from the US's defeat at the hands of the Taliban. It is clear, from the discussion in Chap. 5, that the US is likely in the stages of anger, bargaining, and depression but that it has not yet accepted its diminishing influence.

6.2.4 Over the Seneca Cliff

The contributions surveyed in Sect. 6.2.2 deal with the reasons offered since the start of the Great Stagnation for the decline—and likely collapse—of the West. The question of what the collapse, when it eventually takes place, will look like is answered by Ugo Bardi (2020). Bardi (2020) has proposed the *Seneca Effect or Seneca Cliff*, which depicts civilizations as collapsing much faster than they rise. The Roman Empire, for instance, experienced a gradual decline over several centuries but ultimately collapsed relatively rapidly.

Following Bardi's argument, the current "Western Empire" may similarly be on a slow, gradual economic decline which may rapidly collapse sometime in the future. It is described as a Seneca Cliff or Seneca Effect after the Stoic philosopher Lucius Seneca who emphasized that "increases are of sluggish growth, but the way to ruin is rapid" (Bardi, 2020, p. 68). This may explain why populations in such societies tend to be complacent, mostly not realizing that the end is near until collapse suddenly occurs. The Seneca Cliff is depicted in Fig. 6.1.

The Seneca Cliff may be associated with one of the very first theses of Western Collapse, and also more generally civilizational collapse, namely the Club of Rome's 1973 LtG study—at the outset of the Great

Fig. 6.1 The Seneca Cliff (Source: Naudé, 2023a:131, based on Bardi, 2020)

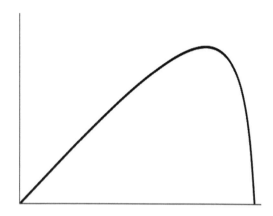

Stagnation—which predicted that by the 2020s/2030 the global economy would peak and then follow a decline due to the environmental limits to growth. The shape of the graphs that the LtG study prepared resembles the Seneca Cliff. Turner (2014), in an update and review of the LtG study, concludes that *"it would appear that the global economy and population is on the cusp of collapse."*

Once a society drops over the Seneca Cliff, the crisis may deepen following a *four-wave sequence*: environmental, economic, political, and population collapse. These waves are interconnected and influence each other, with environmental collapse potentially triggering economic collapse, which further leads to political and, eventually, population collapse (Genco, 2024).

These four factors, or waves, are four areas of concern in the current debate on the future of the West. In the next section, the views of commentators, scholars, and policymakers on these causes and manifestations of decline that trigger collapse will be explored in more detail.

6.3 War and Global Warming for the Rest of Us

> American politics has become a game of, by, and for corporate interests, with tax cuts for the rich, deregulation for polluters, and war and global warming for the rest of us—Sachs (2018).

This section outlines the main contemporary narratives of decline and collapse in the West.

6.3.1 Environmental Collapse

There is a notable concern in contemporary debates and scholarship that the West is spearheading an environmental collapse—although it is far from the only responsible party. There are two related perspectives on this. The one, which may also argue plays a role in most collapses of Empires, is resource depletion and energy constraints: Bardi (2024) for instance highlights the role of resources in the rise and fall of empires, citing the depletion of Roman gold mines and the Western reliance on fossil fuels as crucial factors. Additionally, the emergence of new trade routes, like the *Belt and Road Initiative*, can reshape global trade patterns and challenge the West's economic hegemony (Bardi, 2024). In Chap. 4 of this book, the case was made that the West faces increasing resource limitations, especially the decline in affordability and availability of oil.

A second, and closely related perspective due to the role of energy, is climate change. Engelhardt (2023) argues that the US's decline is unique because it coincides with climate change—which was not relevant in the case of previous empires (Engelhardt, 2023).

The rest of this subsection will discuss these two environmental dimensions of collapse, which are deeply intertwined with the model of neoliberal capital that the West championed but that is now threatening its economic foundations.

Chapter 2 emphasized the critical role of energy, particularly fossil fuels, in powering economic growth. Recent commentators, such as The Honest Sorcerer ("B") (2024b), argue that diesel and fuel oil consumption is the most significant metric for economic activity, as these fuels are essential for heavy industries, including mining and transportation. The plateauing of global diesel and fuel oil consumption, despite a growing global population and demand for goods, signals a potential decline in economic output. This decline is linked to the concept of "Energy Cannibalism" that was discussed in Chap. 4, where an increasing amount of energy is required to extract the remaining, less accessible fossil fuel reserves, leaving less net energy for other uses. This diminishing return on energy investments (EROI) undermines economic productivity, particularly in energy-intensive sectors.

Many scholars and bloggers dismiss alternatives to fossil fuels such like biofuels and electric vehicles as insufficient due to their energy intensity, competition with food production, and limited scalability. For example, Richard Heinberg echoes this sentiment in *Restoring Nature Is Our Only*

Climate Solution, arguing that *"predictably, we're looking to alternative technologies to solve what is arguably the biggest dilemma humanity has ever created for itself. But what if that's the wrong approach? What if more technology will worsen the problem in the long run?"* An example of how technology can worsen the problem in the long run is posed by renewable energy technologies, all of which have environmental costs, including resource depletion and habitat loss (Heinberg, 2024b). He therefore advocates for reducing energy demand through population stabilization and economic policies that prioritize well-being over material growth—Degrowth type policies (see also Chap. 7) (Heinberg, 2024b).

Søgaard Jørgensen et al. (2023) have framed the reliance of modern civilization on fossil fuels, which causes climate change, as an "infrastructure lock-in," which is a technology trap where societies become reliant on specific technologies and infrastructures, making it difficult to transition to alternatives. The dependence on fossil fuel-based infrastructure is a prime example of this trap, creating a significant barrier to a sustainable energy transition.

A common fear in the environmental collapse literature is of cascading, mutually reinforcing effects, leading to a series of interconnected crises. Hence the notions of climate tipping points and a polycrisis (Lenton et al., 2019; Tooze, 2022b) are examples. An example of an interconnected crisis is the cost of living crisis, which is connected to diminishing returns on energy production (a declining EROI), combined with the limitations of alternatives (The Honest Sorcerer, 2024b). A second common fear of an interconnected crisis in the environmental collapse literature is of financial collapse, amongst others, due to unsustainable debt levels, money printing, and the decoupling of the financial system from the real economy—which also creates a demand for future energy that ultimately cannot be met (Hagens, 2020; Morgan, 2024; The Honest Sorcerer, 2024a). A third fear of interconnected crises is that resource scarcity and climate change will lead to massive social unrest and political instability due to exacerbated social divisions, declining human security[3] and public dissatisfaction (Clack et al., 2024; Klawans, 2024; The Honest Sorcerer, 2024b).

---

[3] See also: https://www.un.org/en/climatechange/science/climate-issues/human-security

6.3.2 Economic Collapse

Various concerns exist about how economic forces are contributing to the possible collapse of the West. One is a growing and shared concern about the nature of global neoliberal capitalism. The critiques of capitalism have perhaps never been as loud in the West as they were at the time of writing this book. A second concern is that the global order is shifting and that the rise of new powers is eroding Western hegemony. These two concerns are discussed in the rest of this subsection.

Firstly as far as the critiques of neoliberal capitalism—"capitalism on steroids" as Monbiot and Hutchison (2024) described it—are concerned, several recent sources critique the prevailing economic model in the West, described in Chap. 2 of this book as a focus on continuous growth, expansion into new frontiers for exploitation, financialization, and the pursuit of profit above all else. There is a growing realization in the West that neoliberal capitalism is inherently unsustainable and is contributing to a range of economic problems, including rising inequality, declining living standards, and a growing sense of insecurity. Amongst the growing number of authors who have been critical of neoliberal capitalism over the past two decades, a representative sample would include Klein (2008), Piketty (2014), Chomsky (2016), Harvey (2003), Wolf (2023), Zuboff (2019), Mayer (2024), and Streeck (2016). Against these criticisms of capitalism and forewarnings of its collapse, one could read Boldizzoni (2020), who, in his book *Foretelling the End of Capitalism: Intellectual Misadventures since Karl Marx,* speculates on the reasons why, despite the apparent shortcomings and many predictions of its collapse, capitalism has survived so long.

Mayer (2024) levels one of the most often heard criticisms against capitalism, namely that it has become too focused on short-term profit maximization, leading to a disregard for negative externalities and a decline in public trust—see also Wautier's (2024) critical discussion of Mayer (2024) remedies for capitalism—such as prioritizing a "higher purpose over profit" and implementing reforms. Mayer (2024) believes that deep down neoliberal capitalism is good and can be reformed to iron out a few creases.

Morgan (2024) warns about the increasing financialization of the global economy, where financial activity has become detached from the production of actual goods and services. This has resulted in a system driven by speculation, debt, and the pursuit of ever-increasing asset values, creating a "gigantic bubble" vulnerable to collapse (Morgan, 2024).

There seems to be a growing consensus that excessive debt is a major economic problem facing the West (Roubini, 2022). Mounting levels of public and private debt, low interest rates, and quantitative easing measures have created a precarious financial situation that could unravel quickly.

According to Tverberg (2024a, 2024b), the heavy use of debt and leverage in advanced economies makes them particularly susceptible to financial shocks. She argues that the current "bubble of debt" is vulnerable to collapse, potentially leading to a sharp contraction in economic activity. In particular, in economies suffering from a Great Stagnation, as in the West, where economic growth is declining, higher interest rates in the presence of high debt levels can cause a severe economic crisis. As she explains:

> Raising interest rates is thus a way to intentionally slow the economy. If the economy grows too quickly (like a 20-year-old sprinter), then such a change makes sense. But if the economy is behaving like an 80-year-old, hobbling along on a walking stick, it becomes likely the economy will figuratively fall and become severely injured. This is the danger of raising interest rates when the world economy is having difficulty growing at an adequate rate. (Tverberg, 2024a, 2024b)

Historian Niall Ferguson, in his blog article "We're All Soviets Now," draws comparisons between the current state of the US and the late Soviet Union, noting similarities in terms of growing national debt, political polarization, and declining public trust in institutions. In the Soviet Union, government deficits persisted for decades, exceeding 5% of GDP. Similarly, in the US, the Congressional Budget Office projects deficits exceeding 5% of GDP for the foreseeable future, potentially rising to 8.5% by 2054. Ferguson (2024) also compares the US's debt burden to that of Britain after World War I, when its public debt soared to nearly 200% of GDP. The US's current debt exceeds 124% of GDP (Elkhawass, 2024). Ferguson (2024) expresses concerns that rising interest rates could strain the US federal budget and limit its ability to maintain global commitments (Ferguson, 2024; Rich, 2024).

Jones (2023) argues that the economic system in the West, despite promises of freedom and prosperity, is increasingly delivering insecurity, growing inequality, and a decline in well-being. He points to the erosion of secure, well-paid jobs, the weakening of social safety nets, and rising housing and healthcare costs as key factors contributing to this decline.

Joel Kotkin, in "The Road to Neo-feudalism," relatedly expresses concerns about the declining rate of homeownership and despondency, particularly among young adults, and its implications for rising inequality and social mobility. He argues that restrictive urban growth policies and the financialization of housing are driving up prices, making homeownership increasingly unattainable for the middle class and pushing societies towards a neo-feudal system where a small elite controls most of the wealth and property (Kotkin, 2024).

Secondly, many in the West seem concerned that the decline of the West coincides with—and may be the consequence of—the emergence of a multipolar world. They point to China as a new rising economic and military power challenging the West's dominance. Richard D. Wolff argues that China's hybrid economic system, combining state-owned and private capitalist enterprises, is an unprecedented challenge to the US Empire (Wolff, 2024). Wolff (2024) mentions that the rise of China and the BRICS+ comes at a time when the US has experienced military failures in Korea, Vietnam, Afghanistan, and Iraq, and has seen economic sanctions against Russia, Cuba, Iran, and China. Hogue (2021), concerning China's growing economic and military power, draws a parallel to the Roman Senate's famous phrase "*Carthago delenda est*" ("Carthage must be destroyed"), suggesting that there is a similar sentiment towards China within the US.

Wolff (2024), however, also suggests that because China presents a different challenge, and because the world has seen how in the past the declining British Empire eventually avoided attempting to embark on conflict to subdue the rise of the US, that conflict between the declining and rising superpowers might not be inevitable. As he argues,

> In the past, one empire often supplanted another. That may be our future with this century becoming "China's" as previous empires were American, British, and so on. However, China's history includes earlier empires that rose and fell: another unique quality. Might China's past and its present hybrid economy influence China away from becoming another empire and instead toward a genuinely multipolar global organization instead? Might the dreams and hopes behind the League of Nations and the United Nations achieve reality if and when China makes that happen? Or will China become the next global hegemon against heightened resistance from the United States, bringing the risk of nuclear war closer?

In this regard, Tricontinental (2024) describes how, indeed, the unipolar world dominated by the West is giving way to a more multipolar system, driven not just by China but by the Global South's growing economic and political clout and their pursuit of alternatives to Western-dominated institutions and systems. Gerits (2024) describes how the rise of multipolarity in the mid-twentieth century was not just the result of the Cold War, but also the consequence of anticolonial movements. Gerits (2024) argues in this regard that decolonization fostered a "Crowded Safari" of competing ideologies.

This rise of a multipolar world order is manifested in the Global South's increasing reluctance to align with the Global North's geopolitical strategies, their exploration of alternative financial and development models, and the strengthening of regional organizations. According to the analysis in Tricontinental (2024), the US struggles to maintain its grip on the world order amid pushback from the Global South. Tricontinental (2024) highlights several factors contributing to the Global North's anxieties, such as the Global South's reluctance to support the West's stance against Russia regarding the Ukraine conflict, China's impressive economic growth and its efforts to establish alternative financial and development institutions, such as the Belt and Road Initiative and the New Development Bank. On 23 October 2024 the BRICS+ issued the XVI BRICS Summit Kazan Declaration,[4] entitled "*Strengthening Multilateralism for Just Global Development and Security*" wherein it states (p.8):

> We reiterate our grave concern at the deterioration of the situation and humanitarian crisis in the Occupied Palestinian Territory, in particular the unprecedented escalation of violence in the Gaza Strip and in the West Bank as a result of the Israeli military offensive, which led to mass killing and injury of civilians, forced displacement and widespread destruction of civilian infrastructure. We stress the urgent need for an immediate, comprehensive and permanent ceasefire in the Gaza Strip, the immediate and unconditional release of all hostages and detainees from both sides who are being illegally held captive and the unhindered sustainable and at-scale supply of humanitarian aid to the Gaza Strip, and cessation of all aggressive actions. We denounce the Israeli attacks against humanitarian operations, facilities, personnel and distribution points. For this purpose, we call for the

---

[4] See: https://dirco.gov.za/wp-content/uploads/2024/10/XVI-BRICS-Summit-Kazan-Declaration-23-October-2024.pdf

full implementation of resolutions 2712 (2023), 2720 (2023), 2728 (2024) and 2735 (2024) of the United Nations Security Council.

This statement is in contrast with the statements and positions from the US government, who has been providing military and political support to Israel (see Chap. 5). That the rise of China—and more generally the BRICS+ group of countries—undermines the West is thus a common fear. One concrete fear in this regard is that the BRICS+ are working towards de-dollarization and the decline of the US Dollar. These countries are, not surprising in light of the discussions in Chap. 5, seeking to reduce their reliance on the US and are working towards establishing a more equitable global financial system, including, for example, the New Development Bank. The Honest Sorcerer (2024a) argues that this is not necessarily an active attempt by the BRICS+ countries to undermine the West but rather reflects that they are

> now busy building resilience and actively preparing for the West's impending fall. Contrary to what most in European countries believe (or rather have been told), however, the Eurasian powers have not the faintest interest in conquering the old continent [...] Quite the contrary: they are more concerned with containing the crisis than expanding it, trying to prevent WWIII from escalating into a bloodbath all over the world.

The Honest Sorcerer (2024a) argues that the BRICS+ have no interest in controlling Western lands, viewing them as "full of people who hate them" and lacking in valuable resources. This perspective implies that the West is increasingly perceived as a burden rather than a prize, with its internal divisions and declining economic prospects making it unattractive to rising powers.

Nevertheless, by freeing or unshackling the former colonies from Europeans and US control, the rise of the BRICS+ would, as per Vladimir Lenin's recognition that to destroy capitalism in its heartlands, their colonies have to be freed (Darwin, 2007), undermine the fundamental logic of neoliberal capitalism, as explained in Chap. 2.

Fofack (2024) outlines progress made in de-dollarization, as reflected in a decline in the US dollar's share of global reserves from 73% in 2001 to 58% in 2022, a tenfold faster decline than in the previous two decades. According to Fofack (2024), this has been due to increased gold purchases with central banks buying more gold, diversifying their reserves away from the US dollar; increased local currency settlements (LCS), such as India now paying for UAE oil in rupees, and China increasingly using the renminbi for trade; progress in digital payment systems, such as those being introduced in Southeast Asian countries and using a QR-code-based system for cross-border payments, bypassing the US dollar. Fofack (2024) also mentions that one-fifth of global oil trade was settled in non-dollar currencies in 2023, and Saudi Arabia has signed long-term oil contracts in renminbi (petroyuan) with China.

Ironically, it is due to oil that de-dollarization is accelerating. As Fofack (2024) describes, the US shale boom in the mid-2000s transformed the country into a major oil producer, lessening its reliance on foreign oil, including Saudi oil. This diminished dependence reduced the strategic importance of the US-Saudi relationship, which was a cornerstone of the petrodollar system. As the US became more energy independent, the need to protect the flow of oil priced in US dollars decreased, potentially creating space for other currencies to play a larger role in global energy markets.

Historian Alfred W. McCoy predicts that China, with its rapidly growing economy, will surpass the US as the world's leading economic power by 2030. This shift in economic dominance, McCoy argues, will have cascading effects, particularly on the status of the US dollar. McCoy predicts that the US dollar will lose its position as the world's dominant reserve currency by 2030 (Ratner, 2017). This loss of financial dominance, he argues, will lead to increased costs for imports and overseas travel for Americans, a reduction in the US budget, forcing a pullback and shrinking of American military forces. McCoy also predicts a decline in living standards for Americans, characterized by skyrocketing prices and heightened social tensions. This internal turmoil, he argues, will necessitate a "major rewriting of the American social contract" (McCoy, 2024).

6.3.3 Political Collapse

Contemporary commentators describe three dimensions of concern that could herald political collapse in the West, all of which have already been raised in this book as being closely associated with the rise of the oligarchy and the Permanent War Economy. These are internal divisions, political paralysis, and a decline in public trust, of which many see the "Culture Wars" as a symptom; the decline in the US's global image and its ability to inspire others (the loss of soft power); and the rising power of oligarchs and the closely associated Military Industrial Complex (see Chaps. 3 and

5 for more detail). Why and how these could lead to collapse have been made clear in the previous chapters and are summarized in the rest of this subsection with reference to how they have been considered in some of the recent literature.

First, as far as internal divisions are concerned, the West has become a house divided. Many authors stress that internal divisions and dysfunctions are contributing to a decline in the West's global influence, social cohesion, and capacity for effective governance. While many acknowledge external pressures and economic factors, they primarily focus on how political problems are eroding the West's foundations, potentially leading to a loss of its historical dominance and fragmentation of its social and political order.

Central amongst these political problems is the growing crisis of legitimacy in Western political institutions. Citizens are increasingly disillusioned with traditional political parties, bureaucratic structures, and the perceived disconnect between elite decision-making and the needs of ordinary people. This erosion of trust is fuelling political instability, apathy, and susceptibility to populist movements that exploit public discontent.

Bradford DeLong, in "How humanity lost control," argues that complex systems like governments have become increasingly unaccountable and opaque, leading to a sense of powerlessness among citizens Bradford DeLong, 2024). This lack of transparency and responsiveness breeds distrust and cynicism, undermining the legitimacy of democratic institutions. Aurelien. (2023) and others have argued that Western societies suffer from a "*politics of exhaustion*," characterized by a lack of meaningful political discourse, a rejection of traditional history, and a focus on immediate gratification over long-term societal development. This has created a "culture of caricature," where political movements are reduced to superficial slogans and soundbites devoid of any real substance.

Moreover, suffering from a politics of exhaustion, many authors are concerned about a growing sense of nihilism in Western societies. This, coupled with a decline in traditional values and a sense of disillusion with the future, erodes social cohesion and undermines the belief in progress that has long characterized the West (Rich, 2024; Todd, 2024). Rich (2024) also argues that American elites are trapped in a "mental prison" of exceptionalism, much like the Soviet leadership was confined by Leninist ideology. He contends that this "bubble of impunity" prevents them from recognizing the severity of America's decline and taking meaningful action to address it.

Other authors have pointed to the "culture wars" as a symptom of a deeper malaise within Western societies. These conflicts, often centred around issues of identity, values, and the interpretation of history, are exacerbating social and political divisions, making it increasingly difficult to find common ground and address pressing challenges. Paul Kingsnorth, in an essay entitled "The West Must Die," criticizes both sides of the culture wars, arguing that they are ultimately distractions from the more profound issue of cultural decay (Kingsnorth, 2023). He sees the "woke tribe" as superficial and hypocritical, while the "based tribe," often attempting to "defend the West," lacks a cohesive understanding of what they are defending. Kingsnorth (2023) furthermore uses the metaphor of "the Machine" to represent the forces of modernity that have come to define Western society. He argues that "the Machine" is driven by efficiency, control, and the pursuit of material progress, leading to a detachment from nature, a loss of spiritual depth, and an erosion of cultural identity.

Relatedly, Bradford DeLong (2024) highlights the paradox of modern society: despite being significantly wealthier than our ancestors, we are not necessarily happier. This is partly because the pursuit of endless economic growth, a defining feature of complex social systems, has created a treadmill of consumerism and a relentless focus on material acquisition. This materialistic orientation, Bradford DeLong (2024) suggests, ultimately fails to provide lasting fulfilment and may even contribute to anxiety, depression, and a sense of emptiness.

Jones (2023) is not so convinced that the political decline in the West is due to culture wars or issues like moral decay, multiculturalism, and the reassessment of European history. He contends that these are scapegoats for deeper economic problems—as discussed in subsection 6.3.3—that are the true drivers of decline (Jones, 2023). The use of these scapegoats reflects that the West is suffering from a crisis of leadership characterized by a lack of vision, indecisiveness, and accountability. In some cases, this is accompanied by outright corruption. Political leaders are more and more seen as being beholden to the oligarchy.

In addition to these reasons, the reason for the crisis of leadership is, according to Engelhardt (2023), the "Gerontocracy" that heads the US. In this, he refers to the advanced ages of Joseph Biden and Donald Trump as a symbolic representation of America's decline. He argues that their ages highlight a nation clinging to an ageing leadership in a rapidly changing world. Ferguson (2024) concurs and compares the ageing leadership of the late Soviet Union and the 2024 political leadership in the US.

Todd (2024), as has been discussed, argues that a crisis of leadership is driving the decline of the West. He suggests that the West's declining global influence is due to poor leadership, which makes it misguidedly reliant on the Permanent War Economy and makes it unable to adapt to a multipolar world (Ledger-Lomas, 2024).

McCoy (2024) argues that the US is facing a confluence of three major international crises—in Ukraine, Gaza, and Taiwan—due to political leadership failures. As far as Ukraine is concerned, McCoy (2024) argues that the US mishandled its relationship with Ukraine and Russia after the Cold War, particularly regarding NATO expansion. He also attributes the escalating crisis in Gaza to long-standing US policy failures in the Middle East, particularly its inability to achieve a lasting peace agreement between Israel and Palestine. He argues that the US's unwavering support for Israel, even in the face of its actions against Palestinians and the findings of the International Court of Justice (ICJ), has further damaged American diplomatic credibility in the region. Regarding Taiwan, McCoy (2024) argues that China threatens Taiwan, pointing to the country's increasingly assertive actions in the region. He believes that China is strategically manoeuvring to erode Taiwan's sovereignty and that the US would be unlikely to intervene militarily in the event of a Chinese takeover, leading to a humiliating American retreat from the Pacific.

Bardi (2024) points out that the West, while responsible for atrocities like the genocide of Native Americans, aerial bombings in World War II, and other acts of violence, including the catastrophic conflict in Ukraine and the plausible Genocide in Gaza, is not inherently more wicked than previous empires. He contends that all empires, regardless of their specific historical context, tend to engage in similar brutality when motivated by self-interest, expansion, and hubris.

As a result of the above, populism has become a threat to liberal democracy. Populist leaders often exploit public anger and anxieties, offering simplistic solutions and scapegoating minorities or external enemies, further deepening social divisions and eroding faith in democratic processes. Populist leaders are, however, according to several analysts, playing along the script eventually written by the Oligarchs. The latter—as Chap. 3 of this book details—are increasingly being recognized as posing the most significant single threat to democratic processes (Monbiot & Hutchison,

2024). As was discussed in Chap. 3, these oligarchs use their financial power to sway elections, control media narratives, and shape policies in their favour.

6.3.4 Population and Collapse

Traditionally, excess human population has been the reason for societal collapse. For example, in his 1798 *Essay on the Principle of Population*, Thomas Malthus argued that civilization's fixed natural resources, such as land, limit civilization's progress. Because "the power of population is so superior to the power of the earth to produce subsistence for man," it is inevitable, he argued, "that premature death must in some shape or other visit the human race" (Malthus, 1798:44).

In 1960, Von Foerster et al. (1960) in a paper in *Science*, predicted that Doomsday would occur on Friday 13 November 2026, because given up until then super-exponential growth rates in population, extrapolation indicated that global population would approach infinity by 2026. And in 1968 Paul Ehrlich (1968:11) predicted that, as a result of population growth, "In the 1970s hundreds of millions of people will starve to death […] At this late date, nothing can prevent a substantial increase in the world death rate."

People did not starve as predicted—mainly as a result of technological progress (the Green Revolution), which, like economic growth, depended on the use of fossil fuels to enable industrial farming and the provision of sufficient fertilizers.

Today, there is still, on the one hand, a belief that world population is too large and threatening societal collapse through several channels. One channel is that it is driving ecological overshoot and that the extent of the world population is such that high population levels relative to finite fossil fuel resources create a precarious situation. Heinberg (2024a, 2024b) suggests that the unprecedented challenge of transitioning to renewable energy sources given the current size of the human population may require a reduction in overall energy demand, which could necessitate a reassessment of population growth trajectories.

A second channel that connects population size with civilization collapse is the complexity effects that a large population brings with it. Bardi (2011) argues that societies often collapse under the weight of their own intricate structures. While not explicitly linking this to population size, the implication is that larger populations necessitate greater complexity in terms of governance, infrastructure, and resource management, potentially amplifying the risks of systemic failure. Similarly, Bradford DeLong (2024) argues that humanity has created complex systems, such as globalized economies and interconnected technologies, that have unintended consequences and are challenging to manage effectively. Larger populations contribute to the scale and interconnectedness of these systems, potentially making them more prone to unpredictable behaviour and catastrophic failures.

A third channel is that larger political entities are inherently less stable and responsive to the needs of their citizens (Kohr, 1957). Kohr (1957) in his book *The Breakdown of Nations* suggested that smaller, more decentralized political units are better suited to promoting social well-being and avoiding the pitfalls of overexpansion and bureaucratic inefficiency. Kohr's argument implies that larger populations, often concentrated in megacities, contribute to the creation of unwieldy and ultimately unsustainable political structures. Moreover, these lead to large political units and a dangerous aggregation of power. Kohr (1957) contends this concentration of power is inherently destabilizing and increases the likelihood of conflict, oppression, and the erosion of individual liberties. Moreover, as political units grow larger, the distance between the rulers and the ruled increases, leading to a disconnect between the needs of the people and the priorities of the state. This disconnect, he argues, breeds alienation, resentment, and a sense of powerlessness among citizens (Kohr, 1957).

More recently, Brooks and Agosta (2024) have added another elaboration to population size as a threat to collapse, by taking an evolutionary biology lens and arguing that sociopaths gain control of societal institutions when populations grow too large and concentrated, such as in large cities. This is because larger populations make it difficult for people to identify sociopaths before they rise to power, whereas in contrast in more decentralized, less densely populated society would make it harder for sociopaths to take control. In smaller communities, individuals are more likely to know each other and recognize manipulative behaviour.

While the four channels discussed above are concerned about the links between too much population and collapse, a growing number of authors and commentators, on the other hand, argue that declining population growth and changes in population composition, including ageing, are driving Western societies to collapse.

Several authors have argued that the biggest problem facing the West is not too much population growth, but a decline in population. Since the

1970s, fertility rates in the West have fallen below population replacement levels. While in the US, the population growth rate remained positive, largely due to immigration, it has been declining, and by 2021, the US population growth rate was at a historical low (Thompson, 2022a). Since 2010, the US has experienced demographic stagnation, with an annual growth of only 2 million people from 2011 to 2017. In 2020, the population grew by just 1.1 million, and in 2021, only 393,000 people were added to the US population, marking the slowest growth rate in history (Thompson, 2022a, 2022b). An article in *The Atlantic* concluded that the US is in a "demographic danger zone" due to the combination of low birth rates, high death rates, and declining immigration (Thompson, 2022a, 2022b).

Todd (2024), for example, suggests that declining birth rates, particularly in Europe and the US, weaken these societies both economically and militarily, diminishing their ability to project power and maintain global dominance. Ferguson (2024) highlights the decline in US life expectancy and the rise of "deaths of despair" as troubling trends that mirror similar issues in the late Soviet Union. He attributes these issues, in part, to social and economic factors that contribute to a sense of hopelessness and despair among specific segments of the population, potentially exacerbating population decline and further weakening the US. Hanson (2024a, 2024b) explores the potential consequences of declining population growth in the West due to "cultural drift." He suggests that a shrinking population could lead to reduced innovation and economic dynamism, ultimately contributing to a decline in living standards and a loss of global competitiveness.

In the context of the Great Stagnation in the West, the decline in Western population growth, and the ageing of Western society are argued by many to make migration an increasingly sensitive issue in the West, potentially contributing to the instability and decline of Western societies. Aurelien. (2023) argues that Western societies are struggling with a loss of shared identity and purpose and are ill-equipped to handle the social and political challenges associated with large-scale migration and demographic change. Generally, the argument is made that societies struggling with economic insecurity and a lack of social cohesion are more vulnerable to the divisive rhetoric and political opportunism that often exploit anxieties surrounding immigration and cultural change.

Finally, in the analysis and predictions of Genco (2024), eventually, the combination of the outcomes of the above pressures from population dynamics will result in the population itself collapsing. He describes this as widespread death resulting from starvation, dehydration, and heatstroke, all of which will be caused by resource depletion and an increasingly hostile climate. Genco (2024) explains that factors that have traditionally allowed the human population to exceed the carrying capacity, like technological advancements in food production and distribution, will no longer be sufficient as climate change places increasing pressure on food production systems and disrupts supply chains. Although it is difficult to determine precisely how many people the Earth can sustainably support, Genco (2024) suggests that it is likely far lower than the current global population, perhaps in the range of 1 to 3 billion people, significantly less than the projected 10 billion people that are expected to be alive in 2050

6.4 Declinists vs. Optimists

While a growing number of authors and scholars argue that the West is declining due to the four waves or four drivers discussed in Sect. 6.3 and, moreover, facing collapse, there are also dissenting voices. Thus, the debate can be characterized as one between so-called *Declinists and Optimists*.

Those who subscribe to the "Declinist" view argue that the US is experiencing a decline in its global power and influence, potentially leading to its eventual collapse as an empire. Some authors, such as Niall Ferguson and Alfred McCoy, argue that the US is experiencing a significant and potentially irreversible decline. The Declinists' arguments can be summarized as follows, in light of the discussion in Sect. 6.3 of this chapter.

The Declinists point to internal and external factors that are leading to the collapse of the West. Internal factors, as discussed in Sect. 6.3, include economic decline, military overstretch, political dysfunction, and moral decay. External factors include the rise of China, the emergence of a multipolar world order, and the loss of soft power.

The declinists thus typically argued that the US is increasingly unable to effectively project its power and achieve its strategic objectives, as a long list of military failures attests to; that the erosion of democratic institutions weakens the nation's ability to address challenges and maintain its global standing; and that the pursuit of global dominance, often at the expense of other nations and their people, is a betrayal of American ideals and a contributing factor to the empire's decline. They also lament that the US's image has been tarnished by its military interventions, its support for authoritarian regimes, and its perceived hypocrisy on issues such as human rights and democracy.

On the other hand, "optimists" argue that the US remains a powerful force on the world stage and that predictions of its imminent collapse are exaggerated. They acknowledge the challenges the US faces but maintain that it possesses the resources, resilience, and adaptability to overcome these obstacles and maintain its global leadership.

Optimists emphasize the US's unmatched military might, arguing that its global reach and advanced technology provide a decisive advantage in deterring adversaries and shaping the international order. They also point out that despite challenges, the US economy remains amongst the largest in the world, and its global economic influence, particularly through the US dollar's role as the dominant reserve currency, provides a significant advantage.

An optimist such as Peter Zeihan, in his book *The End of the World Is Just the Beginning: Mapping the Collapse of Globalization*, believes that the globalized economy will collapse because of the US's withdrawal from providing military protection over global shipping lanes and that in this post-globalization world, the US will be the best off because of its energy independence, its geographical position surrounded by oceans and friendly neighbours, its favourable demographics, and its access to cheap Mexican labour. Zeihan (2022:3) envisages the collapse of the US Empire, but not the US Empire. As he puts it

> Since 1945, the world has been the best it has ever been. The best it will ever be. This is a poetic way of saying that this era, our world, is doomed. The 2020s will see a collapse of consumption and production and investment and trade almost everywhere. (Zeihan, 2022:3–4)

Note—the collapse will be *almost* everywhere. The US remains exceptional. Indeed the US "will largely escape the carnage to come" according to optimists like Zeihan (2022:5).

Tricontinental (2024) seems to support, to some extent, Zeihan's optimism about the West and the US specifically. It describes five areas of control that the West has traditionally held over the Global South, based on the work of Samir Amin. These include control over natural resources, control over financial flows, control over science and technology, control over military power and control over information. They point out that essentially, the West maintains control in all of these areas, despite facing challenges (stagnation and deglobalization), challengers (The BRICS+), and internal contradictions (collapse or moral integrity).

Ultimately, optimists believe that the US political system, despite its current dysfunction, possesses the capacity for self-correction and renewal. Hunt (2017), for instance, argues that the US has historically demonstrated an ability to adapt to changing circumstances and overcome crises (Hunt, 2017).

In conclusion, it should be noted that the "debate" between Declinists and Optimists is not binary. Many analysts hold nuanced views that fall somewhere between these two poles.

6.5 Concluding Remarks: Ars Moriendi

This chapter explored whether and how the West's economic decline could lead to its eventual collapse. It expanded on the book's central and simple thesis, which is that the West is in economic decline due to the Guns-Oil-Oligarchy nexus. The chapter analysed contemporary debates about the collapse of the West, focusing on the interplay of economic, environmental, political, and population-related pressures.

The chapter started in Sect. 6.1 by defining societal collapse as a significant decline in a society's complexity and ability to function. It then explored various perspectives on collapse in Sect. 6.2. Section 6.3 examined four interconnected patterns or waves that collapse could follow: environmental, economic, political, and population-related collapse.

Section 6.4 pointed out that there is no consensus that the West will collapse despite its problems. Thus, there are not only "declinists" who believe that collapse is inevitable but also "optimists." The latter believe that the West has the resilience to adapt and overcome challenges.

The discussion in Sects. 6.1–6.4 leads to the conclusion that where many of the collapse narratives discussed have a point in common, it is about neoliberal capitalism and its future. There is almost a consensus that the system of capitalism that marks the current empire is rotten. For most of the political Left, it simply means that the time of capitalism and neoliberalism is over and that it has to make place for communism, socialism, and other perturbations of collective management of society. The Degrowth movement is an example of a movement based on a broad basis of ideas, fundamentally Marxian.

For many others, capitalism needs to be reformed. The world needs, so they argue, a capitalism with a human face, a green capitalism, and a not selfish or greedy capitalism. Others, yet more radically, want more of the neoliberalism—the capitalism on steroids—that has marked much of the past seventy years, and for them, the problem is that democracy weakens capitalism too much. This view seems most popular among Silicon Valley CEOs and billionaires—the oligarchy. Some reckon that capitalism has, in any case, already morphed into something even worse—Yanis Varoufakis, for instance, argues that capitalism is already "dead" and has been replaced by Technofeudalism. (while the problems of technofeudalism are real, this book's thesis has been that capitalism is far from dead).

Then there are those who either consider the collapse of the West as a net positive event—with collapse over the chance for transformation of capitalism, or those who see not the West collapsing but rather the geopolitical order, with the US not collapsing as such, but withdrawing as the world's policeman, leaving the rest of the world to fall into states at various levels of development and each seeking its power either through deals or conflict—and ultimately succeeding or failing determined by fundamentals of geography and demography. Peter Zeihan, a proponent of this view, believes the outcome would be a relatively more robust and prosperous US but less interested in being a global hegemon.

Whether or not the West is only declining or even collapsing, perhaps Schneider (2019) has a point in suggesting that the West needs to develop a "politics of decline" that focuses on how to transition gracefully from its position of global dominance. This would require a radical shift from current perspectives that stress American exceptionalism and European moral superiority. Instead of clinging to future greatness, Schneider (2019) argues that a "memento mori culture" would focus on addressing present injustices and inequalities and move away from a mindset of domination and control towards cooperation and shared responsibility on the global stage. Schneider (2019) acknowledges that embracing *Ars Moriendi* in US politics is a challenging endeavour because US politics historically lacks the necessary humility and selflessness.

While there is no consensus on the specific timeline or the inevitability of collapse, there is a growing consensus that the current trajectory is unsustainable and that a fundamental shift in thinking and policy is necessary to avoid collapse. The next chapter explores what such a fundamental shift could entail.

CHAPTER 7

Beyond the Growth Trap

7.1 Introduction

At the start of this final chapter, it is helpful to summarize the arguments from the preceding chapters to draw this book to a close. Chapter 2 introduced the Guns-Oil-Oligarchy nexus as an interconnected set of influences on, and symptoms of, the economic decline of the West. It was argued that the multifaceted relationship between militarization, the need for fossil fuels, and the growing concentration of economic power underpins and accentuates a Grow-or-Die rule (a Growth Trap) in the global economy. Firms and the economy need to grow, or else it will collapse in on itself. This need for evermore economic growth has caused an ecological overshoot of Earth's systems. Biodiversity loss, climate change, and resource depletion are three consequences of this overshoot. Ultimately, ecological overshoot may cause climate tipping points to be breached, with catastrophic consequences. The Growth Trap is also characterized by increased inequality, greater job insecurity, and erosion of the social fabric.

Chapter 3 analysed how a small wealth elite, the oligarchs, threatens Western societies by stifling innovation, undermining democracy, obstructing a collective solution to climate change, and promoting militarism. The chapter discussed the oligarchies in finance, industrial agriculture, the mainstream media, and in the tech industry.

Chapter 4 dealt with oil and Big Oil in the West's economic rise and decline. It was argued that the West is caught in an energy trap, where the dependence on oil hastened the decline, because of its impacts on Earth Systems and the gradual decline in energy availability. In the latter regard, Peak Oil and the increasing energy costs of extracting remaining fossil fuels threaten higher inflation, lower living standards, and geopolitical instability—including resource wars.

Chapter 5 explored "Guns"—the MIC—as a cause of the economic decline of the West. The chapter traced the historical development of the MIC, starting with early twentieth-century interventions and the post-World War II economic boom, to the post-Cold War "projects" of the War on Terror, the militarization of Africa, NATO expansion, the reshaping of the Middle East, and the containment of China. Because of the West's dependence on the military and defence industries for economic growth, it was argued that Western economies are increasingly suffering from the effects of the misallocation of resources, the illusion of job creation, the distortion of market forces, and the perpetuation of conflicts. Moreover, the MIC is undermining Western moral standing.

Chapter 6 explored how the confluence of the MIC the oligarchy, the central but declining role of fossil fuels, and the war economy is reflected in the growing number of articles, books, and blogs that have announced the imminent collapse of the West. This chapter thus puts the contribution of this book into the broader perspective of the "west-is-collapsing" industry. The chapter started by highlighting historical and contemporary arguments by scholars like Spengler, Turchin, and Tainter. Many subsequent scholars and commentators agree that the West is dealing with increasing challenges under which weight it could eventually collapse.

Thus, with Guns, Oil, and Oligarchs driving and reflecting the economic decline of the West, and giving the potential of this economic decline to tip over and cause a broad collapse of the West's "empire"—which would be a more catastrophic event than a slow but steady economic decline—the rest of this chapter examines whether a post-growth society is possible, how it may look like, and what would be its implications. The need to do this, to consider the outlines of a post-growth society, stems from the meta-problem outlined in Chap. 2—the Growth Trap. Cutting away the rot—the embeddedness of the Growth Spiral—will diffuse the cancerous spread of the MIC and the oligarchy and perhaps make the energy transition more manageable. Having noted this, this chapter is only an introductory exploration of the post-growth economy—economics and business studies have severely neglected this topic, which it may be expected will become of more research and policy interest in the future.

The rest of the chapter is organized as follows. Section 7.2 explains the nature of a post-growth society. Section 7.3 discusses a proposal to achieve a post-growth society through Degrowth. Section 7.4 critically examines whether proposals for Degrowth are compatible with the nature of business firms and entrepreneurship as it is currently perceived. Section 7.5 expands on implications for dismantling capitalism's current business and entrepreneurship vision, and Sect. 7.6 discusses what this would mean for business firm accountability in future. Section 7.6 concludes that the fundamental problem that the analysis in this book has raised is one of "damned if you do, damned if you don't": capitalism with economic growth has become dangerous, but capitalism without economic growth is likewise dangerous. In either scenario, the end of the Western Empire is but a question of time. It would be less damaging if the system of neoliberal capitalism would collapse before it does.

7.2 The Nature of a Post-growth Society

Given that economic growth may now impose more costs than benefits on the world [see Chap. 2], but that the embeddedness of the Growth Spiral in neoliberal capitalism obliges firms and countries to pursue it, giving rise to the spectre of the Guns-Oil-Oligarchy nexus (see Chaps. 3–5), the question thus clear is how society can shake off the growth obsession and what to replace it with.

Of course, it may be unlikely that the broad society would ever concur voluntarily with the need to shake off the growth obsession. This is why Reitz et al. (2021) note that in a post-growth society— the one that seems involuntarily to be unfolding, as discussed in Chap. 2—various desperate attempts will be made in the political-economic sphere to stretch out growth as much as possible. They mention that such resistance could manifest in "populist-authoritarian projects of national enrichment" to "elitist-authoritarian projects for securing transnational capital accumulation" and "technological solutionism" (Ibid, p. 256). These forms of resistance can be found in the fractured political discourses in the world in anno 2024, in which the influence of the oligarchy is evident. One also finds the increased militarization of Western economies—its dependence on the Permanent War Economy—a pronounced manifestation of resistance to growing economic stagnation (Naudé, 2024a).

Thus, in the era of the *Ossified Economy* or the *Great Stagnation* as the current era has been labelled, "Visions of growth have become either aggressive (such as economic nationalism) or questionable (such as green growth), and the intensification of distributional struggles engenders a rise of authoritarian political options" (Reitz et al., 2021, pp. 256–257). The spectre of the Guns-Oil-Oligarchy nexus is part of the outcome of desperate attempts in the political-economic sphere to stretch out growth as much as possible.

The question of how to shake off the growth obsession and disassemble the Guns-Oil-Oligarchy nexus has generated several proposals. As discussed by Rätzer et al. (2018), these proposals encompass the so-called *Steady-State Economy* (e.g. Daly (1972), the *Diverse Economies Approach*[1] and the *Degrowth movement* (Kallis & March, 2015). One could also add *Ecosocialism* and *Ecoanarchist* approaches (Banerjee et al., 2021).

A full discussion of all of these post-growth society ideas falls outside the scope of this book. For present purposes, this section focuses on describing the essential conceptualization of a post-growth society and the not uncontroversial claim that Degrowth is necessary to eventually achieve such an economy (Farley et al., 2013).

A definition of post-growth economics is provided by Paech (2017, p. 478), who states that

> in contrast to environmental economics, which aims at the ecological decoupling of the Gross Domestic Product (GDP), post-growth economics focuses on economic systems, subsystems and even lifestyles to reduce the quantities of supply and demand.

The emerging field of post-growth economics studies the limits to growth, the growth compulsion, and the establishment of a post-growth economy (Paech, 2017).

A post-growth society differs from a Steady-State Economy, as envisaged by Daly (1972), or a Doughnut Economy by Raworth (2017). Economic growth is still possible and even somewhat desirable in both of these. In the case of the Steady State, economic growth is welcome but subject to limits. Similarly, in the Doughnut Economy, economic growth is bound from above by planetary boundaries but also bound from below by the need to meet the basic needs of human development—hence, some

---

[1] In this approach, firms and countries' growth orientation is to be replaced by a vitality orientation that seeks to expand marginalized and alternative economic approaches in a post-growth society, see Gibson-Graham (2008).

minimum growth is still vital. In contrast, in a post-growth economy, growth has ceased to be imperative, and the economic-social system aims at "prosperity without growth" (Jackson, 2016).

The challenge for the many firms, entrepreneurs, and households that constitute the economy to contribute to prosperity without growth, that is, to add value to society without contributing to ecological overshoot, is the twofold challenge of operating and surviving in an increasingly resource-scarce economy, with "peak everything" (Heinberg, 2007) as well as in an economy that is not expanding (Cyron & Zoellick, 2018). Here, the concern is indeed that if post-growth would come to characterize the current neoliberal capitalist system, where it is either growth or collapse, under post-growth, the world economy would become inflexible, transaction costs would increase, and there would be overall stagnation, with all the social and political consequences that would entail (Cyron & Zoellick, 2018).

7.3 Achieving Post-Growth via Degrowth

Hug et al. (2022) refer to the changes required to move the economy and society from dependence on and obsession with firm growth and economic growth as a sustainability transformation. Such a sustainability transformation would entail, in their words, going beyond green growth and decoupling and involve fundamental changes on the industry and firm level. The enterprises that will characterize this transformation have been labelled growth-neutral enterprises, post-growth businesses, degrowth companies, common- good-oriented companies, or transformative enterprises (Hug et al. (2022).

The Degrowth Movement, and the idea of Degrowth, is a proposal for achieving this sustainable transformation to a stable society without growth. Degrowth is an "equitable downscaling of production and consumption that increases human wellbeing and enhances ecological conditions at the local and global level, in the short and long term" (Schneider et al., 2010, p. 511). As explained by Banerjee et al. (2021, pp. 342–343), Degrowth is based on the recognition that capitalism and neoliberalism "in their current forms have created the social-ecological crises we now face."

Degrowth's anti-capitalism and anti-neoliberalism stance is Marxist. The French Marxist philosopher André Gorz indeed provided Degrowth's intellectual raison d'être. Saito (2023, p. 171) has described Karl Marx as a "degrowth communist." Hence, Degrowth wants to abolish capitalism. The burden of Degrowth should fall on the affluent West—to allow some growth to enrich the Global South. Degrowth is thus not wholly anti-growth. The West should also pay the Global South climate reparations for misappropriating more than its fair share of carbon emissions (Schmelzer & Nowshin, 2023). These reparations could stimulate economic growth in the Global South by raising aggregate demand and consumption, which is also no problem for advocates of Degrowth as long as this growth is not excessive. In this regard, Cuba has been described as a role model for Degrowth, a country that degrowth advocates consider to be appropriately developed (Hickel, 2015).

7.4 Business, Entrepreneurship, and Degrowth: Compatible?

Global economic growth is driven through business firms created and financed and often run by entrepreneurs—many of whom become oligarchs, as explained in Chaps. 2 and 3. The question is what to do with oligarchs specifically and, more generally, with entrepreneurial-driven firm creation and growth. While degrowth scholars, as well as a broad range of economic and business scholars and policymakers, have argued for the stricter regulation of monopolistic and oligopolistic behaviour, for much higher taxation of billionaires and their multinational corporations, and for closing the revolving door between politics and business, the general question about whether entrepreneurship and Degrowth are compatible is neglected. Hug et al. (2022) and Leonhardt et al. (2017) point out that more scholarly studies are needed to help clarify how entrepreneurs can participate in and collaborate in Degrowth. One requirement is that entrepreneurs must divorce their entrepreneurial ambitions from firm growth or economic growth and, indeed, be able to function within a zero-growth context and possibly during a transition in a degrowth context. Gebauer (2018) refers to this as growth-independent and post-growth-oriented entrepreneurship.

Johanisova et al. (2013), Rätzer et al. (2018), and Wirtz (2013) argue that "social" entrepreneurship can help facilitate Degrowth. This is because social entrepreneurs have different goals than profit maximization, although they can be very profitable, as many entrepreneurs in the micro-finance industry have experienced, and having a social mission may often be chosen to obtain a competitive advantage (Muñoz & Kimmitt, 2019). Nevertheless, in principle, social entrepreneurs can promote Degrowth (and thus ultimately a post-growth society) by not requiring economic growth as necessary for profits, by potentially having a reduced impact on the environment and a smaller carbon footprint because most social enterprises tend to be embedded in a local context (few scales), and by being able to contribute to alleviating the consequences of both market and government failures, for instance, in areas central to human well-being such as education and healthcare. Muñoz and Cohen (2017) do not consider Degrowth. Nevertheless, they argue for an approach to sustainable entrepreneurship, which they call "entrepreneurial synchronicity," that would be partly consistent with Degrowth. By entrepreneurial synchronicity with nature, they call on a slower, less urgent form of entrepreneurship such as that which characterizes the dynamics of HGFs and scale-ups. They fail, however, to consider the rebound (Jevons paradox) effects that this could have if, for instance, better synchronicity increases firm productivity and efficiency.

Another category of entrepreneurship that could facilitate Degrowth is lifestyle entrepreneurship. Lundmark et al. (2023) argue that more and more firms should be based on lifestyle entrepreneurship because such entrepreneurship operates "outside of the hegemonic growth paradigm" (p. 42). They provide, for example, the experience of lifestyle tourism entrepreneurs in Scandinavia. Whether their findings can be generalized is, however, doubtful—recent studies have been critical, for instance, at so-called sustainable or environmental tourism approaches elsewhere—see, for instance, the papers in Thakholi et al. (2024).

Some entrepreneurs could thus contribute, in principle, towards promoting Degrowth, although the evidence is scant and the literature thin. It is more likely that instead of contributing, entrepreneurship could detract from Degrowth. Hinderer and Kuckertz (2024) state that the central down-scaling aim of Degrowth is "at odds with conventional wisdom about entrepreneurship" (Hinderer & Kuckertz, 2024, p. 1). They note in particular that so-called sustainable entrepreneurs face a dilemma in that their enterprises can only have a significant impact if scaled, but that the process of scaling will require growth, which will put further pressure on natural resources and the environment.

Despite these examples, whether entrepreneurship is compatible with Degrowth and post-growth has not yet been studied sufficiently. Despite this, an argument can be made that Degrowth is incompatible with modern notions of entrepreneurship. One of the critical aspects of Degrowth that makes it incompatible is not as much the decline in economic growth or economic stagnation which a downsizing of the global economy will require (entrepreneurship may, for instance, as social, sustainable, and lifestyle entrepreneurs survive this), but the potential incompatibility of Degrowth with the type of freedom which is a *sine qua non* of entrepreneurship.

One of today's most fundamental freedoms is spending their money as they wish (Douthwaite, 1992). However, as stressed by Windegger and Spash (2022), given that degrowth and post-growth call for radical limits on consumption, it seems impossible to achieve significant reductions in such consumption except by limiting people's freedom in this regard. Degrowth, for instance, variously proposes that consumption be curtailed, that in order to do this, advertising be banned, and that caps be put on specific resource uses. It proposes reductions in the workweek, limits on the wealth and incomes of the rich, cooperative ownership of capital, and changes in people's values—amongst others. The questions that proposals for limits on consumption raise are, how much should a person be allowed to consume a particular product? Who decides? Who enforces this? Rightly so, Spash (2015, p. 374) has pointed out that the problem this poses is to "square this circle with non-coercion."

Audretsch and Fiedler (2022) investigated why entrepreneurship flourished in Vietnam despite a relative lack of freedom. Their conclusion has stark implications for Degrowth and its accompanying zero-sum politics. They conclude that the case of Vietnam shows that "When it comes to entrepreneurship, democracy and economic freedom matter relative to a country's past and expected future, and not necessarily in absolute terms." They found that "even minor and incremental advances of economic freedom in the context of Vietnam can significantly enhance entrepreneurial activity" (Audretsch & Fiedler, 2022, p. 1181). The implication is that the converse would be true for entrepreneurship in Western liberal democracies: even minor setbacks in economic freedom could significantly reduce entrepreneurial activity.

7.5 Dismantling the Entrepreneurial Ecosystem

In light of the Growth Spiral into which modern economies are locked and in light of the restrictions of individual behaviour implied by a move to post-growth via Degrowth, Paech (2017, p. 484) comes to a damning indictment of entrepreneurship: he in effect, calls for the entire dismantling of the entrepreneurial ecosystem during Degrowth:

> An ecologically and socially sustainable economy must therefore be free from all dependency on growth and subsequent pressure for growth, including the innovation orientation of modern market economies, the present monetary and interest-earning system, expectations of high profit, external supplies of resources based on a model of global division of labour, and a culture of unquestioning pursuit of material self-actualization.

This quote refers to virtually all the growth-causing imperatives in modern neoliberal capitalism, hence all the mechanisms that need to be rooted out in order to establish a post-growth society.

All these mechanisms are linked to entrepreneurship. It is, therefore, useful to briefly discuss their role in growth and what their absence in a post-growth society will mean for.

7.5.1 Free from Innovation

The first growth-imperative cause mentioned in the above quote is "the innovation orientation." In Chap. 2, where the Growth Spiral was discussed, it was pointed out that innovation is ultimately driven by entrepreneurs' quest for consumer markets—to offer new goods and services to avoid satiating consumer demand. This encourages marketing and the promotion of consumption for consumption's sake. Innovation and overconsumption results in waste, pollution, and puts pressure on natural resources and ecosystems. This may especially be the case for innovations that are more energy-intensive—such as innovations in artificial intelligence have shown to be.

7.5.2 Free from Finance

The second growth-imperative cause mentioned is the "monetary and interest-earning system." Chapter 2 mentioned how modern monetary creation occurs when banks lend to entrepreneurs, expecting interest to be paid out of profits. The money/debt created in this way can be seen as a claim on future resources (when it is to be repaid) and, hence, future energy (Hagens, 2020, p. 7). This implies that the modern monetary and financial system is not linked to the biophysical reality and limits of the planet (Farley et al., 2013).

As such, proponents of post-growth and Degrowth see the reform of the financial system necessary for post-growth, although as Olk et al. (2023) point out, proposals for Degrowth have so far neglected monetary and financial considerations. Existing proposals have mainly been for a 100% reserve banking system, that is, in which private banks cannot create money (Dittmer, 2015) and for combining Degrowth with Modern Monetary Theory (MMT)—where governments essentially print money to pay their debt, thus not needing tax revenues from future growth (Olk et al., 2023). One can note that both these proposals are likely to generate macro-economic instability: a 100% banking system would generate interest rate instability, and MMT broader financial instability, similar to the more than 120 financial crises the world has seen since abandoning the Bretton Woods system.

7.5.3 Free from Profits

The third growth-imperative cause is the need for high profits, explained in Chap. 2 as necessary not only to qualify for bank lending but also to raise private equity capital. Such investors, including venture capitalists, expect rapid firm growth—preferably scaling up —to earn dividends.

A main objective of firm and industry restructuring during Degrowth would be to remove the profit motive. One way would be to dismantle the financial system, particularly the power of commercial banks to create money. It could also be done by prohibiting the levying of interest (Douthwaite, 1992). Another way would be to break up large firms and ensure the small firms that remain are locally oriented and democratically run, without a profit motive (Duprez, 2024). If this fails to result in a livable wage for the owners and workers, then the government should provide all people with basic income grants—funded by the government creating money (Olk et al., 2023).

7.5.4 Free from Globalization

The fourth growth-imperative cause in the above quote is "external supplies of resources based on a model of global division of labour." This refers to the global expansionism—often de facto imperialism—of modern corporations seeking to secure access to resources, including cheap labour and markets. Corporations need to grow to access capital to expand globally and to expand globally to earn the profit prospects with which to attract capital (Luxemburg, 1913). This results in a spiral of growth.

Thus, according to the degrowth movement, Degrowth of the economy requires immediate de-globalization (Decker, 2018). How to do this, what alternatives should be replacing the current global order is, however, very insufficiently explored in the degrowth literature, as Frame (2023) points out.

7.5.5 Free from Material Pursuits

Finally, the quote above mentions the "culture of unquestioning pursuit of material self-actualization" as a cause of the growth imperative. This refers to the dominant entrepreneurship culture, where billionaire, unicorn-creating entrepreneurs who pursue high-growth ventures are the heroes of modern society—the ones to be emulated.

In contrast, Degrowth envisages a Utopian alternative: where competition makes way for cooperation, and where limits become meaningful. For advocates of Degrowth, replacing the pursuit of material goods by self-imposed limits can be, paradoxically, a source of freedom. In the words of Kallis (2021, p. 2),

> Liberation and freedom, I argue in my book, require limits, like a pianist needs a finite keyboard to make music. Adventure without limit, without an Ithaca to return to, is no adventure. This classical ideal of limited worlds is in direct contrast to the Western-frontier fiction of liberation from all limits (at the expense of the colonized 'other'), mythologized by Hollywood movies in which the hero beats death, the ultimate limit.

7.6 Holding Business Firms Fully Accountable

If the causes of the growth imperative discussed in Chap. 2 were to be dismantled in the process of Degrowth towards a post-growth economy, as described in subsection 7.5, it would result in an economy in which key aspects of modern entrepreneurship—the search for innovative new products and production methods, access to finance and debt, profit-orientation, international expansion and trade, firm growth, and entrepreneurial ambition tied to personal wealth—would cease to be dimensions of entrepreneurship.

But wait, there is more. Dismantling these dimensions of entrepreneurship and entrepreneurial ecosystems is necessary but, however, not sufficient for a post-growth society. As Douthwaite (1992) argues, one would also have to establish a new moral-cultural system wherein the business firms and entrepreneurs are held firmly accountable for their actions. Douthwaite (1992, pp. 315–316) describes what will await business firms under a post-growth moral-cultural system:

> the entrepreneur should be responsible for the consequences of his actions. Thus, if he puts someone out of work, at home or abroad, in his firm or another, he should support them until there is something else suitable for them to do [...]Similarly, if the entrepreneur is involved in something like the destruction of the sea-trout, he should do the equivalent of compensating the game fishery owners for the loss of their fish. [...] we should no longer give new projects automatic economic and social approval, assuming that if the entrepreneur finds the venture worthwhile, the community will do so too. Henceforward, just as we insist on environmental impact assessments for new developments, we must demand economic and social impact assessments for projects and technologies.

If this could scare anyone out of business, this may precisely be the point of Degrowth: Nesterova et al. (2020) declared that "degrowth should scare business" calling for a fundamental transformation of society that would be "so radical that businesses as we know them will cease to be businesses."

7.7 Will Rosa Luxemburg Have the Last Word?

We are destined to conquer space after all! How could we do that with a stone ax?' —B, 2024a

Is it possible, then, to imagine the West's powerful and oligarchic business- and entrepreneurship-driven economies, with its dependence on oil and war, in such a post-growth context?

This is difficult—but not impossible. The biggest challenge—a zero-sum game—can be pictured. It paints a picture of a reversal into a medieval economy or even, as B (2024d) does, of a reversal into a Second Stone Age:

We are heading towards another stone age - at least from a purely technical perspective. After the easy-to-get parts of fossil fuels and rich deposits of minerals (all mined and processed by burning coal, oil and gas) deplete, we won't be able to maintain a high-tech civilization and are bound to relive our history in reverse.

In a degrowth or post-growth context, where the economy does not grow, any business firm that requires profit to repay a loan and its interest can only earn such profits at the expense of another entrepreneur. Inevitably, conflict would result—including outright violence, as one most often encounters in countries where economic prospects have deteriorated (Naudé & Power, 2024). While capitalism with growth is destructive, it is also the case that "capitalism without growth is destructive" (Blauwhof, 2012, p. 255).

In her magnum opus, Rosa Luxemburg alluded to the post-growth world resembling the pre-growth world, a simple, circular, self-sufficient, no-growth economy marked by "general economic and cultural stagnation." It is worth quoting in full of Luxemburg (1913, p. 41):

> In the ancient agrarian and communist village communities, for instance, increase in population did not lead to a gradual expansion of production, but rather to the new generation being expelled and the subsequent founding of equally small and self-sufficient colonies. The old small handicraft units of India and China provide similar instances of a traditional repetition of production in the same forms and on the same scale, handed down from generation to generation. But simple reproduction is, in all these cases, the source and unmistakable sign of a general economic and cultural stagnation. No important forward step in production, no memorial of civilization, such as the great waterworks of the East, the pyramids of Egypt, the military roads of Rome, the Arts and Sciences of Greece, or the development of craftsmanship and towns in the Middle Ages would have been possible without expanding reproduction; for the basis and also the social incentive for a decisive advancement of civilization lies solely in the gradual expansion of production beyond immediate requirements, and in continual growth of the population itself as well as of its demands.

In the coming Second Stone Age, there will be no "decisive advancement of civilization" as a "gradual expansion of production beyond immediate requirements, and in a continual growth of the population itself as well as of its demands" will not be possible. For some, like B (2024d), this is perhaps the best outcome achievable:

After examining our biophysical realities - the coming decline in net energy production, the loss of biodiversity, climate change, resource depletion etc. - we must say: becoming hunter-gatherers (again) would be the best possible outcome. In fact, that would be quite a feat, even as sea levels rise, species go extinct and pollution reigns supreme... All this against the backdrop of an accelerating civilizational collapse (with nukes to boot).

7.8 Conclusion: Damned If You Do, Damned If You Don't

This book has argued that the rise of the West as the world's current hegemon has resulted in an ecological overshoot, the rise of neoliberalism and its slash-and-burn model of continuous growth, extraction, expansion, and conquest. With this model pushing against planetary boundaries, threatening ecological disaster, and depleting many resources, including increasingly fossil fuels, the growth compulsion has been driving the emergence of the Guns-Oil-Oligarchy nexus. The Guns-Oil-Oligarchy nexus is, however, an adverse coping mechanism—it is hastening the economic decline of the West.

The obvious first line of response is to try and address the symptoms—which the Guns-Oil-Oligarchy nexus partly is. Indeed, many scholars, politicians, and social movements struggle to counter militarism, conflict, and dependence on fossil fuels and strive to break up and regulate the oligarchy. Ultimately, however, this first line of response will not succeed as long as the underlying cause—the growth-dependent neoliberal system of capitalism—remains intact. Moreover, most first-line responses remain piecemeal and ad hoc, with little coordination between those who oppose militarism and those attempting the breakup and restraint of oligarchies. Most often, those who take on the oligarchies and the concentration of business are oblivious to the growing interweaving of the tech industry and military industry, or those who campaign for peace are unaware of the role of fossil fuels in economic growth.

Therefore, addressing the deep cause is necessary. Because of the interdependent nature of the Guns-Oil-Oligarchy nexus, an appropriate response requires an encompassing, not piecemeal, approach. The end goal must be a post-growth society. If neither perpetual firm growth nor perpetual economic growth is possible nor desirable, and given that at least the Western world has, despite the attempts of the guns-oil-oligarchy nexus, been slowing but surely edging towards a post-growth society, then it is necessary to consider what a post-growth society could entail. Hence, this chapter critically discussed visions of post-growth and Degrowth. The conclusion is that, in essence, a post-growth society with modern notions of business and freedom seems inconceivable. All the aspects of ecosystems and support and understanding how the nature of business firms and entrepreneurship leads to growth through good institutions will need to be undermined/dismantled to ensure Degrowth and, eventually, post-growth. Indeed, as some degrowth advocates have put it, "degrowth should scare business."

It is not uncontroversial to state that no government, nor its business and entrepreneurial class, will endorse Degrowth, except to the extent that it can be turned into an opportunity, which has led Alexander and Gleeson (2019) to remark that the only prospect of the degrowth path to a post-growth society ever being followed would only be if sufficient grassroots (household and community level) pressure can be mobilized, which, however, they admit is unlikely ever to be the case.

Hence, this chapter has ended up describing an unstoppable object (ecological, social, and economic decline) heading towards an apparently unmovable object (the Growth Spiral of neoliberal capitalism).

The fundamental problem is one of "damned if you do, damned if you don't": capitalism with economic growth has become dangerous, but capitalism without economic growth is likewise dangerous. Neither the post-growth nor Degrowth literature has presented a convincing alternative to a post-growth and degrowth society. Just stopping growth as an ideology and obsession, as Degrowth aims to do, but without fundamentally dismantling the neoliberal agenda ("capitalism on steroids") that constitutes the modern global economic system, will worsen all crises. It may trigger an earlier societal collapse than with continued (but stuttering) growth.

In this respect, a sober reminder is that, historically, the only example of a thriving stationary (non-growing) society was Japan during the Edo (Tokugawa) period (1603–1868). It was "a brutal dictatorship" (Bardi, 2020, p. 221). Moreover, it was stable but stagnating. Rosa Luxemburg (1913:41), who was deeply critical of capitalism, has nevertheless warned that without growth, the incentives for the "decisive advancement of civilization" may fall away.

References

Abraham, Y. (2024a, April 3). Lavender: The AI machine directing Israel's bombing spree in Gaza. *+972 Magazine*.

Abraham, Y. (2024b, August 4). Order from Amazon: How tech giants are storing mass data for Israel's war. *+972 Magazine*.

Acemoglu, D., & Robinson, J. (2011). *Why nations fail. The origins of power, prosperity, and poverty*. Penguin.

Acs, Z. (2006). How is entrepreneurship good for economic growth? *Innovations, 1*(Winter), 97–107.

Acs, Z. J., Braunjerhjelm, P., Audretsch, D., & Carlsson, B. (2009). The knowledge spillover theory of entrepreneurship. *Small Business Economics, 32*(1), 15–30.

Acs, Z., Astebro, T., Audretsch, D., & Robinson, D. T. (2016a). Public policy to promote entrepreneurship: A call to arms. *Small Business Economics Journal, 47*, 35–51.

Acs, Z., Szerb, L., & Autio, E. (2016b). *Global entrepreneurial index 2016*. GEDI Institute.

Afoaku, O. G. (1997). The US and Mobuto Sese Seko: Waiting on disaster. *Journal of Third World Studies, 14*(1), 65–90.

Akcigit, U., & Ates, S. (2019a). Ten facts on declining business dynamism and lessons from endogenous growth theory. In *CEPR Discussion Paper no. 13668*. Centre for Economic Policy Research.

Akcigit, U., & Ates, S. (2019b). What happened to U.S. business dynamics? *CEPR Discussion Paper no. 13669*. Centre for Economic Policy Research.

Akkerman, M., Bhriain, N. N., & Valeske, J. (2022a). *Smoke screen: How states are using the war in Ukraine to drive a new arms race*. TNI and Stop Wapenhandel.

Akkerman, R., van Apeldoorn, B., & de Vries, N. (2022b). Militarising the EU: The convergence of economic and security agendas. *Journal of Common Market Studies, 60*(5), 1217–1235.

Aldrich, H., & Ruef, M. (2018). Unicorns, Gazelles, and other distractions on the way to understanding real entrepreneurship in the United States. *Academy of Management Perspectives, 32*(4), 458–472.

Alexander, S., & Gleeson, B. (2019, February 21). *Post-capitalism: Life within environmental limits*. Blog, University of Melbourne.

Allison, G. (2017). *Destined for war: Can America and China escape thucydides's trap?* Houghton Mifflin Harcourt.

Almeida, D. V., Kolinjivadi, V., Ferrando, T., Roy, B., Herrera, H., Gonçalves, M. V., & Van Hecken, G. (2023). The "greening" of empire: The European Green Deal as the EU first agenda. *Political Geography, 105*, 102925.

Almeida, D., Naudé, W., & Sequeira, T. (2024a). Artificial Intelligence and the discovery of new ideas: Is an economic growth explosion imminent? In *IZA Discussion Paper No. 16766*. IZA Institute of Labour Economics.

Almeida, V., Azoulay, P., Celik, E., & Zivin, J. S. (2024b). *Artificial intelligence and scientific discovery: A skeptical view*. (Working Paper No. w31631). National Bureau of Economic Research. https://doi.org/10.3386/w31631

Amnesty International. (2000, June). NATO/Federal Republic of Yugoslavia: Collateral damage or unlawful killings? Violations of the laws of war by NATO during operation allied force. https://www.amnesty.org/en/wp-content/uploads/2021/06/eur700182000en.pdf

Amnesty International. (2022). *Israel's apartheid against Palestinians: A look into decades of oppression and domination*. Amnesty International. https://www.amnesty.org/en/documents/mde15/5141/2022/en/

Anand, A., Argade, P., Barkemeyer, R., & Salignac, F. (2021). Trends and patterns in sustainable entrepreneurship research: A bibliometric review and research agenda. *Journal of Business Venturing, 36*(3), 106092.

Andrews, D., Criscuolo, C., & Gal, P. (2016). The best versus the rest: The global productivity slowdown, divergence across firms and the role of public policy. In *OECD Productivity Working Papers no. 5*. OECD.

Anghel, V., & Stolle, D. (2022, June 28). In praise of reality, not realism: An answer to Mearsheimer. *EUIdeas*.

Anthony, A. (2024, April 28). Eugenics on steroids: The toxic and contested legacy of Oxford's Future of Humanity Institute. *The Guardian*.

Archer, E. (2020, January 29). *The intellectual and moral decline in academic research*. James G. Martin Center for Academic Renewal.

Arnoux, L. (2022, January 19). The tooth fairy versus thermodynamics. *Medium*. https://medium.com/@louis.arnoux/the-tooth-fairy-versus-thermodynamics-8b43917e26a8

Arrow, K. (1962). Economic welfare and the allocation of resources for invention. In *The rate and direction of inventive activity: Economic and social factors, Universities-National Bureau Committee for Economic Research, Committee on Economic Growth of the Social Science Research Council.* Princeton University Press.

Aschenbrenner, L. (2020). *Existential Risk and Growth.* Working Paper, Oxford: Future of Humanity Institute.

Assaad, M., Bloem, A., Bribosia, A., Chatila, R., Cornu, A. L., Djeffal, C., Feldstein, S., Flanagan, M., Garcia, D., Gil, C., et al. (2024a). Mapping responsible AI principles for the military domain. *Nature Machine Intelligence, 6*(6), 603–613.

Assaad, Z., Sanders, L., & Liivoja, R. (2024b, September 16). Global powers are grappling with responsible use of military AI. What would that look like? *The Conversation.*

Atkinson, A., Piketty, T., & Saez, E. (2011). Top incomes in the long run of history. *Journal of Economic Literature, 49*(1), 3–7.

Audretsch, D., & Fiedler, A. (2022). The Vietnamese entrepreneurship paradox: How can entrepreneurs thrive without political and economic freedom? *The Journal of Technology Transfer, 47*(4), 1179–1197.

Audretsch, D., & Thurik, A. (2000). Capitalism and democracy in the 21st century: From the managed to the entrepreneurial economy. *Journal of Evolutionary Economics, 10*(1–2), 17–34.

Audretsch, D., & Thurik, R. (2004). *A model of the entrepreneurial economy.* Discussion Paper on Entrepreneurship, Growth and Public Policy, Max Planck Institute.

Auffhammer, M. (2018). Quantifying Economic Damages from Climate Change. *Journal of Economic Perspectives, 32*(4), 33–52.

Aurelien. (2023, July 3). *The politics of exhaustion.* Trying to understand the world. Retrieved October 27.

Autor, D., Dorn, D., Katz, L. F., Patterson, C., & Van Reenen, J. (2017a). The fall of the labor share and the rise of superstar firms. *The Quarterly Journal of Economics, 132*(4), 1473–1544.

Autor, D., Dorn, D., Katz, L., Patterson, C., & Reenen, J. V. (2017b). The fall of the labour share and the rise of superstar firms. In *Working Paper no. 23396.* National Bureau of Economic Research.

Ayyagari, M., Beck, T., & Demirguc-Kunt, A. (2007). Small and medium enterprises across the globe. *Small Business Economics, 29*, 415–434.

Ayyagari, M., Demirguc-Kunt, A., & Maksimovic, V. (2011). Small vs young firms across the world: Contribution to employment, job creation and growth. In *Policy Research Working Paper 5631.* The World Bank.

Ayyagari, M., Demirguc-Kunt, A., & Maksimovic, V. (2014). Who creates jobs in developing countries? *Small Business Economics Journal, 43*, 75–99.

Azoulay, P., Fuchs, E., Goldstein, A., & Kearney, M. (2018). Funding breakthrough research: Promises and challenges of the ARPA model. *Innovation Policy and the Economy, 19*, 69–96.

B. (2024a, June 19). The energy transition story has become self-defeating. *Medium* (at: https://medium.com/@username/the-energy-transition-story-has-become-self-defeating-e17e64d139f4).

B. (2024b, August 2). Downslope. The Fossil Fuel bonanza is slowly... *Medium* (at https://medium.com/@HonestSorcerer/downslope-the-fossil-fuel-bonanza-is-slowly-7b32ac9726d6).

B. (2024c, August 5). Deep sea delusions. *Medium* (at https://medium.com/@sorcerer28/deep-sea-delusions-c760a9c6829f).

B. (2024d, October 14). Will there be a second stone age? *Medium*.

BailoutWatch and Friends of the Earth. (2022, March 10). All-American Oligarchs: The big oil CEOs profiting from war in Ukraine [Analysis]. *BailoutWatch*.

Baily, M. (2003). The source of economic growth in OECD countries: A review article. *International Productivity Monitor, 7*, 66–70.

Baissa, L. (1989). United States Military Assistance to Ethiopia, 1953-1974: A reappraisal of a difficult patron-client relationship. *Northeast African Studies, 11*(3), 51–70.

Bajgar, M., Beraja, M., Crouzet, N., & Cunningham, C. (2023a). *Falling stars or supernovas? The effects of US antirust investigations on innovation*. Working Paper No. w31387. National Bureau of Economic Research. https://doi.org/10.3386/w31387

Bajgar, M., Berlingieri, G., Calligaris, S., Criscuolo, C., & Timmis, J. (2023b). Industry concentration in Europe and North America. *Industrial and Corporate Change*, dtac059.

Baker, M. (2016). 1,500 scientists lift the lid on reproducibility. *Nature, 533*, 452–454.

Baldwin, R., & Harrigan, J. (2011). Zeros, quality, and space: Trade theory and trade evidence. *American Economic Journal: Microeconomics, 3*, 60–88.

Banerjee, S., Jermier, J., Peredo, A., Perey, R., & Reichel, A. (2021). Theoretical perspectives on organizations and organizing in a post-growth era. *Organization, 28*(3), 337–357.

Barak, G. (2024, January 2). American oligarchy: The fight for democracy is just the first step. *Salon*.

Bardi, U. (2011, March 27). Tainter's law: Where is the physics? [Blog post]. *Cassandra's Legacy* (at https://cassandralegacy.blogspot.com/2011/03/tainters-law-where-is-physics.html).

Bardi, U. (2020). *Before the collapse: A guide to the other side of growth*. Springer Nature Switzerland.

Bardi, U. (2024, May 12). A concise history of the global empire. *The Seneca Effect*.

Barnosky, A., Matzke, N., & Tomiya, S., et al. (2011). Has the earth's sixth mass extinction already arrived? *Nature, 471*, 51–57.

Barrabi, T. (2024, July 25). Open AI may reportedly lose $5b this year alone on massive ChatGPT costs. *New York Post*.

Barrow, J. D. (1998). *Impossibility: The limits of science and the science of limits*. Oxford University Press.

Barry, J. (2020). Planning in and for a post-growth and post-carbon economy. In S. Davoudi, R. Cowell, I. White, & H. Blanco (Eds.), *The Routledge companion to environmental planning* (1st ed., pp. 120–129). Routledge.

Barth, J. R. (2008, June 25). *US subprime mortgage meltdown*. Paper presented at the 14th Dubrovnik Economic Conference. Dubrovnik Available at www.hnb.hr/dub-konf/14-konferencija/barth.ppt

Barthe, B., & Rémy, J-P. (2024, October 2). How Israel is trying to impose a new regional order in the Middle East. *Le Monde*.

Basedau, M., & Richter, T. (2014). Why do some oil exporters experience civil war but others do not?: Investigating the conditional effects of oil. *European Political Science Review, 6*(4), 549–574.

Bastos, P., & Silva, J. (2010). The quality of a firm's exports: Where you export to matters. *Journal of International Economics, 82*(2), 99–111.

Baumol, W. (1990). Entrepreneurship: Productive, unproductive and destructive. *The Journal of Political Economy, 98*, 893–921.

Baumol, W. J. (2008). Entrepreneurs, inventors and the growth of the economy, part of the supplemental materials for innovation and U.S. competitiveness. *The Conference Board Report #R-1441-09-RR*.

Baumol, W. J., & Strom, R. J. (2007). Entrepreneurship and economic growth. *Strategic Entrepreneurship Journal, 1*, 233–237.

Becker, B. (2015). Public R&D policies and private R&D investment: A survey of the empirical evidence. *Journal of Economic Surveys, 29*, 917–942.

Beek, L. van Hajer, M., Pelzer, P., van Vuuren, D., & Cassen, C. (2020). Anticipating futures through models: The rise of Integrated Assessment Modelling in the climate science-policy interface since 1970. *Global Environmental Change, 65*, 102191.

Beddoes, Z. M. (2023, November 13). 2024 will be stressful for those who care about liberal democracy. *The Economist*.

Belitski, M., Stettler, T., Wales, W., & Martin, J. (2023). Speed and scaling: An investigation of accelerated firm growth. *Journal of Management Studies, 60*(3), 639687.

Bello, W. (2024). *China ascendant: The collapse of American global power*. Transnational Institute. https://www.tni.org/en/article/china-ascendant

Benjamin, M., & Davies, N. J. S. (2024a, July 3). We need to challenge NATO's insidious war summit in Washington. *Fair Observer*.

Benjamin, M., & Davies, N. J. S. (2024b). Ukraine: The west is running out of time - and options. *The Guardian*. https://www.theguardian.com/world/2024/feb/03/ukraine-the-west-is-running-out-of-time-and-options.

Bennett, F., Lederman, D., Pienknagura, S., & Rojas, D. (2019). The volatility of world trade in the 21st century: Whose fault is it anyway? *The World Economy, 42*(9), 2508–2545.

Bergengruen, V. (2024, February 8). How tech giants turned Ukraine into an AI war lab. *Time Magazine*.

Bessen, J., Denk, E., Kim, J., & Righi, C. (2020). *Declining industrial disruption*. Boston University Law School Working Paper.

Bettencourt, L. M., & West, G. (2010). A unified theory of urban living. *Nature, 467*(7318), 912–913.

Bhaskar, M. (2021). *Human frontiers: The future of big ideas in an age of small thinking*. The Bridge Street Press.

Bijnens, G., & Konings, J. (2020). Declining business dynamism in Belgium. *Small Business Economics, 54*, 1201–1239.

Bilmes, L., Hartung, W. D., & Semler, S. (2024). *United States spending on Israel's military operations and related U.S. operations in the region*, October 7, 2023–September 30, 2024. Brown University.

Binswanger, H. (2013). *The growth spiral: Money, energy, and imagination in the dynamics of the market process*. Springer.

Blakeley, G. (2024, May 2). How today's American Capitalism undermines democracy. *Next Big Idea Club Magazine*.

Blanchflower, D. (2004). *Self-employment: More may not be better*. NBER Working Paper no. 10286. The National Bureau for Economic Research.

Blauwhof, F. (2012). Overcoming accumulation: Is a capitalist steady-state economy possible? *Ecological Economics, 84*, 254–261.

Bloom, N., Jones, C. I., Van Reenen, J., & Webb, M. (2020). Are ideas getting harder to find? *American Economic Review, 110*(4), 1104–1144.

Bloom, N., van Reenen, J., & Williams, H. (2019). A toolkit of policies to promote innovation. *Journal of Economic Perspectives, 33*(3), 163–184.

Boccia, R., & Lett, D. (2024, April 4). The threat of fiscal dominance: Will the US resort to money-printing to finance the rising debt challenge? *Cato at Liberty Blog*.

Boettke, P. J. (2020). *The future of liberalism*. Working Paper No. 24–20. George Mason University, Department of Economics. https://papers.ssrn.com/sol3/papers.cfm?abstract_id=4768017

Boland, P. (2014). The relationship between spatial planning and economic competitiveness: The path to economic nirvana or a dangerous obsession? *Environment and Planning A, 46*(4), 770–787.

Boldizzoni, F. (2020). *Foretelling the end of capitalism: Intellectual misadventures since Karl Marx*. Harvard University Press.

Bonaiuti, C., Maranzano, P., Pianta, M., & Stamegna, M. (2023a). *Arming Europe: Military expenditures and their economic impact in Germany, Italy and Spain*. Greenpeace.

Bonaiuti, M., Cartosio, C., & Truger, A. (2023b). The militarisation of the European Union: A critical political economy perspective. *European Journal of Economics and Economic Policies: Intervention, 20*(1), 1–18. https://doi.org/10.4337/ejeep.2023.0001

Bonatti, L. (2023). *The epistemic vices of democracies in the age of populism*. CESifo Working Paper 10569.

Borenstein, S., & Saloner, G. (2001). Economics and electronic commerce. *Journal of Economic Perspectives, 15*(1), 3–12.

Bostrom, N. (2002). Existential risks: Analyzing human extinction scenarios and related hazards. *Journal of Evolution and Technology, 9*(1).

Bostrom, N. (2013). Existential risk prevention as global priority. *Global Policy, 4*, 15–31.

Boudry, M. (2021). *Why Relativism is the Worst Idea Ever*. Blog, 30 July at https://maartenboudry.be/2021/07/whyrelativism-is-the-worst-idea-ever.html

Bradford DeLong, J. (2022). *Slouching towards Utopia: An economic history of the twentieth century*. Basic Books.

Bradford, A. (2023a). The battle for technological supremacy: The US-China Tech War. In *Digital empires: The global battle to regulate technology*. Oxford Academic.

Bradford, S. C. (2023b). Decoupling or recoupling? Global value chain reconfiguration in the US-China trade war. *Cambridge Journal of Economics, 47*(4), 937–963. https://doi.org/10.1093/cje/bead012

Bradshaw, C. J. A., Ehrlich, P. R., Beattie, A., Ceballos, G., Crist, E., Diamond, J., et al. (2021). Underestimating the challenges of avoiding a ghastly future. *Frontiers in Conservation Science, 1*, 615419. https://doi.org/10.3389/fcosc.2020.615419

Brenner, R. (2024). Gaza: The rest rejects the West. *CounterPunch*. https://www.counterpunch.org/2024/01/26/gaza-the-rest-rejects-the-west/

Bris, A. (2023, June 30). *We're entering a zero-sum economy. Let's not pretend otherwise*. IMD.

Brooks, D., & Agosta, S. (2024). *A Darwinian survival guide: Hope for the twenty-first century*. The MIT Press.

Brown, J. H., Burnside, W. R., Davidson, A. D., DeLong, J. P., Dunn, W. C., Hamilton, M. J., et al. (2011). Energetic limits to economic growth. *BioScience, 61*(1), 19–26. https://doi.org/10.1525/bio.2011.61.1.7

Brüggemann, B. (2021). Higher taxes at the top: The role of entrepreneurs. *American Economic Journal: Macroeconomics, 13*(3), 1–36.

Brunk, I., & Hakimi, M. (2022). Russia, Ukraine, and the Future World Order. *American Journal of International Law, 116*(4), 687–697.
Bryant, K. (2018, October 11). How we create and destroy growth: The 2018 Nobel laureates. VOX EU/CEPR.
Brzezinski, Z. (1997). The grand chessboard: American primacy and its geostrategic.
Brzezinski, Z. (2003). Hegemonic quicksand. *The National Interests, 4,* 5–16.
Bufacchi, V. (2021). Truth, lies and tweets: A consensus theory of post-truth. *Philosophy & Social Criticism, 47*(3), 347–361.
Bulter, S. D. (1935). *War is a racket.* Round Table Press.
Burja, S. (2020). *Why Civilizations Collapse.* The Side View, 19 Aug.
Burke, J. (2023, October 5). France's departure from Niger reflects years of failure in its former colonies. *The Guardian.*
Cairncross, F. (2014). *The legacy of the golden age: The 1960s and their economic consequences.* Routledge.
Cairo, I., Hyatt, H., & Zhao, N. (2015). *The U.S. job ladder in the new millennium,* Meeting papers 893, Stonybrook, NY, Society for Economic Dynamics.
Calligaris, S., Criscuolo, C., & Marcolin, L. (2018). *Mark-ups in the digital era.* OECD Working Paper no. 2018-10. OECD.
Campbell, C., & Laherrere, J. (1998). The End of Cheap Oil. *Scientific American, 278*(3), 80–86.
Candelon, B., Lemaire, A., & Stahnke, P. (2021a). Artificial intelligence in finance. *Journal of Banking & Finance, 131,* 106245.
Candelon, F., di Carlo, R., Bondt, M. D., & Evgeniou, T. (2021b, September/October). AI regulation is coming: How to prepare for the inevitable. *Harvard Business Review.*
Carpenter, A. (2020, June 29). Vienna, Schoenberg and the advent of musical modernism. *Aeon.*
Cassidy, C. (2024, February 23). We landed on the moon again. *The Morning Brew.*
Caverley, Z.R. (2023, November 4). Who should fund science? *Quillette.*
Cercone, J. (2023, January 27). Factcheck: The amount the U.S. has spent in Ukraine is "double the U.S. expenditure for its own war in Afghanistan". *Politifact.* Poynter Institute.
Chan, C. L. (2015a). Fallen behind: Science, technology and Soviet Statism. *Intersect: The Stanford Journal of Science, Technology and Society, 8*(3).
Chan, H., Griffin, J., Lim, J., Zeng, F., & Chiu, A. (2018). The impact of 3D printing technology on the supply chain: Manufacturing and legal perspectives. *International Journal of Production Economics, 205,* 156–162.
Chan, N. T. L. (2011, December 9). *Excessive leverage root cause of financial crisis.* Speech at the Economic Summit 2012 Roadmap to Hong Kong Success, Hong Kong.
Chan, S. (2015b). *The end of the American century: US hegemony and the rise of East Asia.* Brookings Institution Press.

Chancel, L. (2022). Global carbon inequality over 1990–2019. *Nature Sustainability, 5*, 931–938.

Chancel, L., & Piketty, T. (2021). Global income inequality, 1820-2020: The persistence and mutation of extreme inequality. *HAL Id. halshs-03321887.*

Cheong, M., & Shin, W. (2024, September 16). The Internet is worse than it used to be. How did we get here, and can we go back? *The Conversation.*

Chiang, T. (2017, December 18). Silicon valley is turning into its own worst fear. *BuzzFeed News.*

Chivvis, C.S., & Keating, J. (2024, October 8). Cooperation between China, Iran, North Korea, and Russia: Current and potential future threats to America. *The Carnegie Endowment for International Peace.*

Cho, D. (2009, August 28). Banks too big to fail have grown even bigger. *The Washington Post.*

Choi, S., Lee, J., & Lee, S.-H. (2024). Cryptocurrency Ponzi schemes and their modus operandi in South Korea. *Security Journal, 37*, 1285.

Chomsky, N. (2016). *Profit over people: Neoliberalism & global order.* Audible Studios on Brilliance.

Chomsky, N. (2017). *Requiem for the American Dream: The 10 principles of concentration of wealth and power.* Seven Stories Press.

Chu, J. S. G., & Evans, J. A. (2021). Slowed canonical progress in large fields of science. *PNAS, 118*(41), e2021636118.

Chui, M., & Yee, L. (2023, July 7). AI could increase corporate profits by $4.4 trillion a year, according to new research. *Fast Company.*

Clack, T., Meral, Z., & Selisny, L. (2024). *Climate change, conflict and (in)security hot war.* Routledge.

Coad, A., & Binder, M. (2014). Causal linkages between work and life satisfaction and their determinants in a structural VAR approach. *Economics Letters, 124*, 263–268.

Coad, A., Bornhäll, A., Daunfeldt, S., & McKelvie, A. (2024). *Scale-ups and high-growth firms?: Theory, definitions, and measurement* (1st ed.). Springer Nature.

Coase, R. (1937). The nature of the firm. *Economica, 4*(16), 386–405.

Cobaugh, P. (2024, April 19). Big oil, oligarchy, and the threat they pose to US and global security. *Truth about Threats.*

Colgan, J. (2013). *Oil, conflict, and U.S. national interests.* Policy Brief, Harvard Kennedy School Belfer Center for Science and International Affairs.

Collins, C., Flannery, H., Fitzgerald, J., Ocampo, O., Paslaski, S., & Thomhave, K. (2021). *Silver Spoon Oligarchs: How America's 50 Largest Inherited-Wealth Dynasties Accelerate Inequality.* IPS report, 16 June.

Conant, M. A. (1992). Middle East stability: A view from the USA. *Energy Policy, 20*(11), 1027–1031.

Cooke, P. (2019). World turned upside down: Entrepreneurial decline, its reluctant myths and troubling realities. *Journal of Open Innovation: Technology, Market, and Complexity, 5*(2), 22.

Corbin, M. (2024, June 3). BRICS and de-dollarization, how far can it go? *Responsible Statecraft*.

Coskun, A. (2024, July 11). AI supercharges data center energy use straining the grid and slowing sustainability efforts. *The Conversation*.

Covarrubias, M., Gutierrez, G., & Philippon, T. (2019). From good to bad concentration? U.S. industries over the past 30 years. NBER Working Paper no. 25983, National Bureau of Economic Research.

Cowen, T. (2010). *The great stagnation: How America ate all the low-hanging fruit of modern history, got sick, and will (eventually) feel better*. Penguin (Dutton).

Cowie, R. H., Bouchet, P., and Fontaine, B. (2022). The Sixth Mass Extinction: Fact, Fiction or Speculation? *Biological Reviews, 97*(2), 640–663.

Cowls, J., Tsamados, A., Taddeo, M., et al. (2023). The AI Gambit: Leveraging artificial intelligence to combat climate change-opportunities, challenges, and recommendations. *AI & Society, 38*, 283–307.

Crouzet, N., & Eberly, J. (2018). Understanding weak capital investment: The role of market concentration and intangibles. *Technical Report, Jackson Hole Economic Policy Symposium*. Federal Reserve Bank of Kansas City, August 23–25, 2018.

Curtis, M. (2024, February 9). Gaza shows Britain is an oligarchy: Let's stop pretending it isn't. *Declassified UK*.

Cyron, T., & Zoellick, J. (2018). Business development in post-growth economies: Challenging assumptions in the existing business growth literature. *Management Revue, 29*(3), 206–229.

Czarnitzki, D., & Thorwarth, S. (2012). Productivity effects of basic research in low-tech and high-tech industries. *Research Policy, 41*(9), 1555–1564.

Daepp, M., Hamilton, M., West, G., & Bettencourt, L. (2015). The mortality of companies. *Journal of the Royal Society Interface, 12*, 20150120.

Daly, H. (1972). In defense of a steady-state economy. *American Journal of Agricultural Economics, 54*(5), 945–954.

Darwin, J. (2007). *After tamerlane: The rise and fall of global empires, 1400–2000*. Penguin.

Dattani, S. (2022, July 21). Real peer review has never been tried. *Works in Progress*.

Davidsson, P., & Wiklund, J. (2000). Conceptual and empirical challenges in the study of firm growth. In D. Sexton & H. Landstrom (Eds.), *The Blackwell handbook of entrepreneurship* (pp. 26–44). Blackwell.

Davidsson, P., Achtenhagen, L., & Naldi, L. (2010). Small firm growth. *Foundations and Trends in Entrepreneurship, 6*(2), 69–166.

Davies, N.J.S. (2020, July 6). Key US ally indicted for organ trade murder scheme. *Common Dreams*.

Davis, S. (2015). *Regulatory complexity and policy uncertainty: Headwinds of our own making*. Economics Working Paper 15118. Hoover Institution, Stanford, Stanford University.

De Souza, R., & Seifert, R. (2018). Understanding the alternative of not growing for small mature businesses. *Management Revue, 29*(4), 333–348.

Dearing, J., Cooper, G., & Willcock, S. (2023, June 25). Ecological doom-loops: Why ecosystem collapses may occur much sooner than expected. *The Conversation.*

Deaton, A., & Case, A. (2021). *Deaths of despair and the future of capitalism.* Princeton University Press.

Decker, R., Haltiwanger, J., Jarmin, R., & Miranda, J. (2014). The role of entrepreneurship in U.S. job creation and dynamics. *Journal of Economic Perspectives, 28*(3), 3–24.

Decker, R., Haltiwanger, J., Jarmin, R., & Miranda, J. (2017). Declining dynamism, allocative efficiency, and the productivity slowdown. *American Economic Review, Papers and Proceedings, 107*(5), 322–326.

Decker, S. (2018, January 23). From degrowth to de-globalization. *Degrowth Blog.*

DeLay, V. (2024). *Future of denial.* Verso Books.

BradfordDeLong, J. (2024, July 2). How humanity lost control. *Project Syndicate* (at https://www.project-syndicate.org/commentary/how-humanity-lost-control-by-j-bradford-delong-2024-07).

Demaria, F., Schneider, F., Sekulova, F., & Martinez-Alier, J. (2016). What is degrowth? From an activist slogan to a social movement. In N. Haenn, A. Harnish, & R. Wilk (Eds.), *The environment in anthropology: A reader in ecology, culture, and sustainable living* (pp. 390–400). New York University Press.

Denamiel, T., Schleich, M., Reinsch, W. A., & Todman, W. (2024, January 22). *The global economic consequences of the attacks on red sea shipping lanes.* Center for Strategic and International Studies (CSIS).

Denton, S. (2022, January 11). Why is so little known about the 1930s coup attempt against FDR? *The Guardian.*

Derbyshire, J. (2012). High-growth firms: A new policy paradigm or a need for caution? *Local Economy, 27*(4), 326–328.

Dickson, P. (2007). *Sputnik: The Shock of the Century.* New York: Walker Books.

Di Placido, D. (2024a, October 26). The AI bubble is bursting and Sam Altman knows it. *The Guardian.*

Di Placido, D. (2024b, March 28). AI is generating online backlash and mockery. *Forbes.*

Diamond, J. (1997). *Guns, germs, and steel: The fates of human societies.* W.W. Norton.

Diamond, J. (2005). *Collapse: How societies choose to fail or succeed.* Viking Press.

Diaye, M., Ho, S., & Oueghlissi, R. (2022). ESG performance and economic growth: A panel co-integration analysis. *Empirica, 49,* 99–122.

Dittmer, K. (2015). 100 per cent reserve banking: A critical review of green perspectives. *Ecological Economics, 109,* 9–16.

Dirzo, R., Ceballos, G., & Ehrlich, P. (2022). Circling the drain: The extinction crisis and the future of humanity. *Philosophical Transactions of the Royal Society of London Biological Sciences, 377*(1857), 20210378.

Dobbins, J., Cohen, R. S., Chandler, N., Frederick, B., Geist, E., DeLuca, P., Morgan, F. E., Shatz, H. J., & Williams, B. (2019). *Overextending and unbalancing Russia: Assessing the impact of cost-imposing options.* RB-10014. RAND Corporation. https://www.rand.org/pubs/research_briefs/RB10014.html

Dolby, N. (2023, September 11). Artificial intelligence can make companies greener, but it also guzzles energy. *The Wall Street Journal.*

Doomberg. (2024, July 31). Eating their own: NATO and the EU put the screws to two of its members.

Dou, S., Xu, D., Zhu, Y., & Keenan, R. (2023). Critical mineral sustainable supply: Challenges and governance. *Futures, 146*, 103101.

Douthwaite, R. (1992). *The growth illusion: How economic growth enriched the few, impoverished the many and endangered the planet.* Green Books.

Duflo, E. (2017). The economist as plumber. *American Economic Review, 107*(5), 1–26.

Duncan, C. P. (2022a). The economics of US militarism. *Monthly Review: An Independent Socialist Magazine, 73*(8), 1–14.

Duncan, C. P., & Coyne, C. J. (2013a). The overlooked costs of the permanent war economy: A market process approach. *The Independent Review, 18*(1), 111–125.

Duncan, T. (2022b). The continuing costs of the permanent war economy. *SSRN.*

Duncan, T., & Coyne, C. (2013b). The origins of the permanent war economy. *The Independent Review, 18*(2), 219–240.

Dunn, W. (2022, July 1). The end of the long boom. *The New Statesman.*

Dunne J. P., & Sköns, E. (2009). *The Military industrial complex.* Working Paper 0907, Department of Accounting, Economics and Finance, Bristol Business School, University of the West of England.

Duprez, C. (2024, May 13). Can businesses get beyond profit and growth? *Network for Business Sustainability.*

Eckhardt, W. (1990). Civilizations, empires, and wars. *Journal of Peace Research, 27*(1), 9–24.

Eden, M., & Kuruc, K. (2023). *The long-run relationship between per capita incomes and population size.* Mimeo, Global Priorities Institute.

Editorial. (2019, July 10). Cancer, climate, plastics: why 'earthshots' are harder than moonshots. *Nature.*

EEA. (2020). *Growth without economic growth.* Briefing no. 28/2020, European Environmental Agency.

Ehrenreich, B. (2020). How do you know when society is about to fall apart? *New York Times Magazine*, 4 Nov.

Ehrlich, P. (1968). *The population bomb.* Ballantine Books.

Ehteshami, A., & Horesh, N. (2020). *How China's rise is changing the Middle East* (Vol. 1, 1st ed.). Routledge.

Eisinger, J., Ernsthausen, J., & Kiel, P. (2021, June 8). The secret IRS files: Trove of never-before-seen records reveal how the wealthiest avoid income tax. *ProPublica*.

Elkhawass, N. (2024, July 22). *Are we witnessing the decline of the American empire?* UW Economics Society.

Ely, B. (2009). Bad rules produce bad outcomes: Underlying public-policy causes of the U.S. financial crisis. *Cato Journal, 29*(1), 93–114.

Engelhardt, T. (2023, December 13). American decline and fall: A tale of two elections. *TomDispatch*.

Erixon, F., & Weigl, B. (2016). *The innovation illusion*. Yale University Press.

Evans, B. (2024a, November 11). Why AI has flopped so far - and how it can still win. *Benedict Evans (blog)*.

Evans, B. (2024b, July 9). The AI summer. *Benedict Evans Blog*.

Faber, D. (2023). American oil-igarchy: How the corporate assault on liberal democracy and the climate are connected. *Capitalism Nature Socialism, 34*(3), 1–21.

Faggionato, G. (2024, September 9). Draghi demands €800B cash boost to stem Europe's rapid decline. *POLITICO*.

Fanning, A., O'Neill, D., Hickel, J., & Roux, N. (2022). The social shortfall and ecological overshoot of nations. *Nature Sustainability, 5*, 26–36.

Farley, J., Burke, M., Flomenhoft, G., Kelly, B., Forrest Murray, D., Posner, S., Putnam, M., Scanlan, A., & Witham, A. (2013). Monetary and fiscal policies for a finite planet. *Sustainability, 5*, 2802–2826.

Farnia, F. (2022). Confronting the legacies of US imperialism in The Philippines. *Monthly Review: An Independent Socialist Magazine, 74*(5), 30–40.

Farnia, F. (2024). Sanctions as a tool of white supremacy. *Al Jazeera*. https://www.aljazeera.com/opinions/2024/4/10/sanctions-as-a-tool-of-white-supremacy

Ferguson, N. (2021, August 20). Niall Ferguson on why the end of America's empire won't be peaceful. *The Economist*.

Ferguson, N. (2024, June 18). *Niall Ferguson: We're all Soviets now*. The Free Press. https://www.thefp.com/p/niall-ferguson-were-all-soviets-now

Fernald, J., & Wang, B. (2015, February 9). The recent rise and fall of rapid productivity growth. *FRBSF Economic Letter, 2015-04*.

Fetzer, T., & Schwarz, C. (2021). Tariffs and politics: Evidence from trumps trade wars. *The Economic Journal, 31*(636), 1717–1741.

Fichtner, J., Heemskerk, E., & Garcia-Bernardo, G. (2017, May 10). These three firms own corporate America. *The Conversation*.

Fischer, J. (2024). The dangerous new dimension of the Middle East conflict. *Project Syndicate*. https://www.project-syndicate.org/commentary/israel-hamas-war-global-economic-crisis-by-joschka-fischer-2024-10

Fishback, P. (2020a). The Second World War in America: Spending, deficits, multipliers, and sacrifice. In S. Broadberry & M. Harrison (Eds.), *The economics of the second world war: Seventy-five years on*.

Fishback, P. V. (2020b). *How did World War II affect the US economy?* Oxford Research Encyclopedia of American History. https://doi.org/10.1093/acrefore/9780199329175.001.0001

Fishkin, J., & Forbath, W. E. (2024). *Anti-oligarchy constitution reconstructing the economic foundations of american democracy*. Harvard University Press.

Fix, B. (2020a, July 11). Why America won't be 'great' again. *Economics from the Top Down*.

Fix, B. (2020b, November 16). Peak oil never went away. *Economics from the Top Down*.

Flôres, R. G. (2022). The China-US relationship. In *The world corona changed* (1st ed., pp. 11–22). Routledge.

Floyd, J., Alexander, S., Lenzen, M., Moriarty, P., Palmer, G., Chandra-Shekeran, S., Foran, B., & Keysser, L. (2020). Energy descent as a post-carbon transition scenario: How 'knowledge humility' reshapes energy futures for post-normal times. *Futures, 122*, 102565.

Fofack, H. (2024, June 27). The eclipse of the petrodollar. *Project Syndicate*.

Formisano, R. P. (2015). *Plutocracy in America: How increasing inequality destroys the middle class and exploits the poor*. Johns Hopkins University Press.

Foster, J., & McChesney, R. (2014). Surveillance capitalism: Monopoly finance capital, the military-industrial complex, and the digital age. *Monthly Review, 66*(3), 1–31.

Fouse, S., Cross, S., & Lapin, Z. (2020). DARPA's impact on artificial intelligence. *AI Magazine*, Summer, 3–9.

Frame, M. (2023). Integrating degrowth and world-systems theory: Toward a research agenda. *Perspectives on Global Development and Technology, 21*(5–6), 426–448.

Frankel, J. A., & Romer, D. (1999). Does trade cause growth? *American Economic Review, 89*(3), 379–399.

Frey, C. (2015, January 1). How to prevent the end of economic growth. *SciAm*.

Freynman, N. (2024, February 18). Ukraine aid lifts the US economy, backers say. *The Morning Brew*.

Friedemann, A. J. (2021). *Life after fossil fuels: A reality check on alternative energy*. Springer.

Frye, N. (1974). The decline of the west by Oswald Spengler. *Daedalus, 103*(1), 1–13.

Fuchs, R., Herold, M., Verburg, P., & Clevers, J. (2013). A high-resolution and harmonized model approach for reconstructing and analysing historic land changes in Europe. *Biogeosciences, 10*, 15431559.

Fuentes, M. (2023, July 28). Noam Chomsky versus collapse theory - A new "debate of the century". *Dialektika*.
Fukuyama, F. (1992). *The end of history and the last man*. Polity Press.
Funk, J., & Smith, G. (2022, October 4). The hyper-specialization of university researchers. *Mind Matters*.
G&R. (2023, June 30). The Permian Basin is depleting faster than we thought. *Goehring & Rozencwajg*.
Galvin, R., Dütschke, E., & Weiss, J. (2021). A conceptual framework for understanding rebound effects with renewable electricity: A new challenge for decarbonizing the electricity sector. *Renewable Energy, 176*, 423–432.
Gebauer, J. (2018). Towards growth-independent and post-growth-oriented entrepreneurship in the SME sector. *Management Revue, 29*(3), 230–256.
Gelvin, L. (2024). *The new Middle East: What everyone needs to know* (2nd ed.). Oxford University Press.
Genco, S. (2024, June 25). What are we talking about when we talk about collapse? *Medium*.
Gerges, F. A. (2024). The war in Gaza: How America lost the Middle East. *Foreign Affairs*. https://www.foreignaffairs.com/articles/middle-east/2024-10-27/war-gaza-how-america-lost-middle-east.
Gerits, F. (2024). The route to progress. AEON, 27 June.
Geroski, P. (1990). Innovation, technological opportunity, and market structure. *Oxford Economic Papers, 42*, 586–602.
Gewin, V. (2023, November 6). How five researchers fared after their 'great resignation' from academia. *Nature*.
Ghosh, J. (2021, January 19). Lessons from the Moonshot for fixing global problems, *Nature*.
Gibson-Graham, J. (2008). Diverse economies: Performative practices for 'other worlds'. *Progress in Human Geography, 32*(5), 613–632.
Gilbert, N. (2023, July 14). Deep-sea mining could soon be approved - How bad is it? *Nature*.
Giljum, S., Bruckner, M., & Martinez, A. (2015). Material footprint assessment in a global input-output framework. *Journal of Industrial Ecology, 19*, 792–804.
Gledhill, R. (2024). The US prepares for permanent war. *The Nation*. https://www.thenation.com/article/world/us-permanent-war-ukraine/
Gliesen, D. (2024). *The Ukraine war and the Eurasian world order*. Clarity Press.
Global South Insights. (2024). *The Bretton Woods system: A legacy of inequality*. https://globalsouthinsights.org/bretton-woods-system
Global Witness. (2024, February 19). US & European big oil profits top a quarter of a trillion dollars since the invasion of Ukraine (at: https://www.globalwitness.org/en/press-releases/us-european-big-oil-profits-top-quarter-trillion-dollars-invasion-ukraine).

Glubb, J. (1976). *The fate of empires and search for survival.* William Blackwood & Sons Ltd.

Gnana, J., Norways, K., & Al-Ansare, M. (2023, December 15). Global trade at risk as shippers shun Red Sea over Houthis attacks. *S&P Global.*

Goldgeier, J., & Shifrinson, J. R. I. (2023). *Evaluating NATO enlargement: From cold war victory to the Russia-Ukraine War.* Palgrave Macmillan.

Goldman Sachs. (2024a, June 25). Gen AI: Too much spend, too little benefit?. *Goldman Sachs Global Macro Research Issue, 129.*

Goldman Sachs. (2024b). *United States: GenAI - Early days, but potential is significant.* Global Investment Research.

Goldschlag, N., & Tabarrok, A. (2018). Is regulation to blame for the decline in American entrepreneurship? *Economic Policy, 33*(93), 5–44.

Goldstein, A. (2021, July 30). Interest rates haven't been this low in 5,000 years. *Market Watch.*

González, R. J. (2024). *Venture capital and the militarization of Silicon Valley.* Cato Institute. https://www.cato.org/policy-analysis/venture-capital-militarization-silicon-valley

Goodman, P. (2022). *Davos man: How the billionaires devoured the world.* Custom House.

Gordon, C. (2024, March 7). AI is accelerating the loss of our scarcest natural resource: Water. *Forbes.*

Gordon, M., & Rosenthal, J. (2003). Capitalism's growth imperative. *Cambridge Journal of Economics, 27,* 25–48.

Gordon, R. (2012). *Is U.S. economic growth over? Faltering innovation confronts the six headwinds,* NBER Working Paper No. 18315. National Bureau for Economic Research.

Gordon, R. (2016). *The rise and fall of American growth: The U.S. standard of living since the civil war.* Princeton University Press.

Gordon, R. (2018). *Why has economic growth slowed when innovation appears to be accelerating?* NBER Working Paper 24554. National Bureau for Economic Research.

Görg, H., & Strobl, E. (2007). The effect of R&D subsidies on private R&D. *Economica, 74*(294), 215–234.

Gould, E. (2023, December 4). Bombenomics: How the Biden administration is using Ukraine aid to boost defense spending. *Salon.*

Gowdy, J. (2020). Our hunter-gatherer future: Climate change, agriculture and uncivilization. *Futures, 115,* 102488.

Graeber, D. (2019). *Bullshit jobs: A theory.* Simon and Schuster.

Grantham, J. (2011, April). Time to wake up: Days of abundant resources and falling prices are over forever. *GMO Quarterly.*

Grasso, M., & Heede, R. (2023). Time to pay the piper: Fossil fuel companies' reparations for climate damages. *One Earth, 6*(5), 459–463.

Gratale, J. M. (2012). Geir Lundestad. The rise and decline of the American "empire": Power and its limits in comparative perspective. *European Journal of American Studies, Comptes-rendus, 4.* https://doi.org/10.4000/ejas.9853

Greenpeace International. (2024). *Fossil fuels are fuelling war.* [Brochure]. Greenpeace International.

Greer, J. M. (2005). *How civilizations fall: A theory of catabolic collapse.* https://www.ecoshock.org/transcripts/greer_on_collapse.pdf

Grewal, D. (2024, September 27). How wealth reduces compassion. *Scientific American.*

Gries, T., & Naudé, W. (2011). Entrepreneurship, structural change and a global economic crisis. *Entrepreneurship Research Journal, 1*(3), article 4.

Griffen, P. (2017). The Carbon Majors Database. CDP Carbon Majors Report 2017.

Gross, S. (2020, June). Why are fossil fuels so hard to quit? *Brookings.*

Grossman, G. M., & Helpman, E. (2015). Globalization and growth. *American Economic Review, Papers and Proceedings, 105*(5), 100–104.

Grover Goswami, A., Medvedev, D., & Olafsen, E. (2019). *High-growth firms?: Facts, fiction, and policy options for emerging economies.* International Bank for Reconstruction and Development / The World Bank.

Grullon, G., Larkin, Y., & Michaely, R. (2019). Are U.S. industries becoming more concentrated? *Review of Finance, 23*(4), 697–743.

Grunberg, A. (2023, November 15). Der Fall Lohengrin. *NRC.*

Guo, D., Huang, H., Jiang, K., et al. (2021). Disruptive innovation and R&D ownership structures. *Public Choice, 187*, 143–163.

Gupta, J., et al. (2024). A just world on a safe planet: A Lancet Planetary Health–Earth Commission report on Earth-system boundaries, translations, and transformations. *The Lancet Planetary Health, 0*(0).

Gutiérrez, G., & Philippon, T. (2020). *Some facts about dominant firms.* NBER Working Paper No. 27985. National Bureau of Economic Research.

Guzman, J., & Stern, S. (2020). The state of American entrepreneurship: New estimates of the quality and quantity of entrepreneurship for 32 U.S. States, 1988–2014. *American Economic Journal: Economic Policy, 12*(4), 212–243.

Haapanen, L., & Tapio, P. (2016). Economic growth as phenomenon, institution and ideology: A qualitative content analysis of the 21st century growth critique. *Journal of Cleaner Production, 112*(4), 3492–3503.

Habashi, F. (2000). The first oil well in the world. *Bulletin for History of Chemistry, 25*(1), 64–66.

Haberl, H., Wiedenhofer, D., Virág, D., Kalt, G., Plank, B., Brockway, P., Fishman, T., Hausknost, D., Krausmann, F., Leon-Gruchalski, B., et al. (2020). A systematic review of the evidence on decoupling of GDP, resource use and GHG emissions, Part II: Synthesizing the insights. *Environmental Research Letters, 15*, 065003.

Hagemejer, J., & Mućk, J. (2019). Export-led growth and its determinants: Evidence from Central and Eastern European countries. *The World Economy, 42*(7), 1994–2025.

Hagens, N. (2018, April 23). Where are we going? *Resilience.*

Hagens, N. (2020). Economics for the future—Beyond the superorganism. *Ecological Economics, 169,* 106520.

Hahn, P. L. (2006). Securing the Middle East: The Eisenhower Doctrine of 1957. *Presidential Studies Quarterly, 36*(1), 38–47.

Hall, C. (2017). Will EROI be the primary determinant of our economic future? The view of the natural scientist versus the economist. *Joule, 1,* 635–638.

Hallock, J. L., Wu, W., Hall, C. A. S., & Jefferson, M. (2014). Forecasting the limits to the availability and diversity of global conventional oil supply: Validation. *Energy, 64,* 130–153.

Haltiwanger, J. (2022). Entrepreneurship in the twenty-first century. *Small Business Economics, 58,* 27–40.

Hamilton, B. A. (2000). Does entrepreneurship pay? An empirical analysis of the returns to self-employment. *Journal of Political Economy, 108*(3), 604–631.

Hannesson, R. (2021). Are we seeing dematerialization of world GDP? *Biophysical Economics and Sustainability, 6*(4).

Hanson, R. (2024a, February 12). Our tenured civ. *Overcoming Bias Blog.*

Hanson, R. (2024b, August 18). How far might we fall? *Overcoming Bias Blog.*

Hansen, J. Sato, M., Kharecha, P., Beerling, D., Berner, R., Masson-Delmotte, V., Pagani, M., Raymo, M., Royer, D. L., & Zachos, J. C. (2008). Target atmospheric CO_2: Where should humanity aim? *The Open Atmospheric Science Journal, 2,* 217–231.

Hare, B. (2024, August 11). Dug up in Australia, burned around the world—Exporting fossil fuels undermines climate targets. *The Conversation.*

Harford, T. (2006). *The undercover economist.* Oxford University Press.

Harrington, B. (2024). The broligarchs are trying to have their way: The anti-democratic politics of having it all. *The Atlantic.*

Hart, S., & Milstein, M. (1999). Global sustainability and the creative destruction of industries. *MIT Sloan Management Review, 41*(1), 23.

Hartmann, T. (2021). *The hidden history of American oligarchy: Reclaiming our democracy from the ruling class.* Berrett-Koehler Publishers.

Hartmann, T. (2023). The American oligarchs have arrived to destroy US democracy. *Common Dreams.*

Hartmann, T. (2024). *The Hidden History of the American Dream: The Demise of the Middle Class—and How to Rescue Our Future.* Berrett-Koehler Publishers.

Hartung, W., & Freeman, B. (2023a, May 9). The military industrial complex is more powerful than ever. *The Nation.*

Hartung, W. D. (2023, December 11). The military-industrial complex is more powerful than ever. *The Nation.*

Hartung, W. D., & Freeman, M. (2023b). *U.S. weapons to Ukraine: A boon for the military-industrial complex.* Quincy Institute for Responsible Statecraft. https://quincyinst.org/report/us-weapons-to-ukraine-a-boon-for-the-military-industrial-complex/

Hartung, W. D., & Moix, B. (2000, February 3). *Deadly legacy: U.S. Arms to Africa and The Congo War.* World Policy Institute.

Harvey, F. (2022, August 23). Record profits for grain firms amid food crisis prompt calls for windfall tax. *The Guardian.*

Harvey, D. (2003). *The new imperialism.* Oxford University Press.

Hathaway, J., & Litan, R. (2014, May). *Declining business dynamism in the United States: A look at states and metros.* Economic Studies at Brookings.

Hatton, M., & Webb, W. (2020). The Internet of things myth. *Transforma Insights, UK.*

Hausfather, Z., Drake, H. F., Abbott, T., & Schmidt, G. A. (2020). Evaluating the performance of past climate model projections. *Geophysical Research Letters, 47*, e2019GL085378.

Hausfather, Z., Marvel, K., Schmidt, G. A., Nielsen-Gammon, J. W., & Zelinka, M. (2022). Climate simulations: Recognize the 'hot model' problem. *Nature, 605,* 26–20.

Hausmann, R., & Rodrik, D. (2003). Economic development as self-discovery. *Journal of Development Economics, 72*(2), 603–633.

Hausmann, R., Hwang, J., & Rodrik, D. (2007). What you export matters. *Journal of Economic Growth, 12*(1), 1–25.

Hayek, F. (1944). *The road to serfdom.* Routledge.

Hayek, F. (1960). The constitution of liberty. University of Chicago Press.

Head, M. J., Steffen, W., Fagerlind, D., Waters, C. N., Poirier, C., et al. (2021). The Great Acceleration is real and provides a quantitative basis for the proposed Anthropocene. *Journal of International Geoscience.* https://doi.org/10.18814/epiiugs/2021/021031

Heckelman, J. C. (2007). Explaining the rain: "The rise and decline of nations" after 25 years. *Southern Economic Journal, 74*(1), 1833.

Hedges, C. (2003, July 6). What every person should know about war. *The New York Times.*

Heinberg, R. (2007). *Peak everything: Waking up to the century of declines.* New Society Publishers.

Heinberg, R. (2024a, August 22). What would a real renewable energy transition look like? *Resilience.*

Heinberg, R. (2024b, July 1). Restoring nature is our only climate solution. *Resilience.*

Hern, A. (2023, May 21). Mark Zuckerberg's Metaverse vision is over. Can apple save it? *The Guardian.*

Hessels, J., & Naudé, W. (2019). The intersection of the fields of entrepreneurship and development economics: A review towards a new view. *Journal of Economic Surveys, 33*(2), 389–403.

Hiatt, R. A., & Beyeler, N. (2020). Cancer and climate change. *The Lancet Oncology, 21*, e519–e527.

Hickel, J. (2015, September 23). Forget developing poor countries, it's time to de-develop rich countries. *The Guardian*.

Hickel, J. (2021). What does degrowth mean? A few points of clarification. *Globalizations, 18*(7), 1105–1111.

Hickel, J. (2023). Why growth can't be green: New data proves you can support capitalism or the environment—But it's hard to do both. *Foreign Policy, 50*(2), 40–45.

Hidalgo, C., & Hausmann, R. (2009). The building blocks of economic complexity. *PNAS, 106*(26), 10570–10575.

Hidalgo, C. A., Klinger, B., Barabasi, A.-L., & Hausmann, R. (2007). The product space conditions the development of nations. *Science, 317*(5837), 482–487.

High, J. (2011). Economic theory and the rise of big business in America, 18701910. *Business History Review, 85*(1), 85–112.

Hinderer, S., & Kuckertz, A. (2024). Degrowth attitudes among entrepreneurs hinder fast venture scaling. *Business Strategy and the Environment, 33*, 4990. https://doi.org/10.1002/bse.3735

Hirsch, F. (1977). *Social limits to growth*. MA Harvard University Press.

Hoekstra, A., & Wiedmann, T. (2014). Humanity's unsustainable environmental foot-print. *Science, 344*(6188), 1114–1117.

Hogue, C. (2021, January 12). Empires come and go. Has the decline of the American empire begun? *Pearls and Irritations*.

Homer, S., & Sylla, R. (2005). *A history of interest rates* (4th ed.). Wiley Finance.

Hopenhayn, H., Neira, J., & Singhania, R. (2018). *From population growth to firm demographics: Implications from concentration, entrepreneurship and the labor share*. NBER Working Paper no. 25382.

Horgan, J. (1996). *The end of science: Facing the limits of knowledge in the twilight of the scientific age*. Basic Books.

Hossenfelder, S. (2024). I looked at what quantum computing companies make money with. *Science without the gobbledygook*. https://youtu.be/RtDwpOIRHZM

Hotez, P. J. (2020). Combating antiscience: Are we preparing for the 2020s? *PLoS Biology, 18*(3), e3000683.

Hotez, P. J. (2021, March 29). The antiscience movement is escalating, going global and killing thousands. *Scientific American*.

Hotez, P. J. (2023). *The deadly rise of anti-science: A scientist's warning*. John Hopkins University Press.

Howard, M. W. (1895). *The American plutocracy*. Holland Publishing Company.

Howell, J., & Mwai, P., & Atanesian, G. (2023, April 24). Wagner in Sudan: What have Russian mercenaries been up to? *BBC News*.

Hoyos, C. (2007, March 12). The new Seven Sisters: Oil and gas giants dwarf western rivals. *Financial Times*.

Hubbert, M. (1956). Nuclear Energy and the Fossil Fuels. Presented before the Spring Meeting of the Southern District, American Petroleum Institute, Plaza Hotel, San Antonio, Texas, March 7–9.

Hug, M., Mayer, H., & Seidl, I. (2022). Transformative enterprises: Characteristics and a definition. *Geography Compass, 16*(12).

Huggel, C., Bouwer, L., Juhola, S., & et al. (2022). The existential risk space of climate change. *Climatic Change, 174*(8).

Hummels, D. L., & Klenow, P. J. (2005). The variety and quality of a nation's exports. *American Economic Review, 95*(3), 704–723.

Hunt, E. (2017). *The American Empire Isn't in Decline*. Jacobin, 13 March.

Hurst, S. (2022). Introduction. In *The United States and Iraq since 1979* (pp. 1–23). Edinburgh University Press.

Hutton, W. (2024, October 20). Britain's wealth gap is growing. Its malign effects seep into all aspects of life. It's a national disaster. *The Observer*.

Hutton, W. (2023, November 31). Britain is stuck in a doom loop: the system is rigged against growth. That needs to change. *The Guardian*.

Institute for Economics and Peace. (2012). Economic Consequences of War on the US economy.

Ioannidis, J. P. A. (2005). Why most published research findings are false. *PLoS Medicine, 2*(8), e124.

IPCC. (2021). Intergovernmental Panel on Climate Change. *Climate Change 2021: The physical science basis*. Sixth assessment report. https://www.ipcc.ch/report/sixth-assessment-report-working-group-i/

IRENA. (2024). *Geopolitics of the energy transition: Energy security*. International Renewable Energy Agency.

Isenberg, D. (2014, March 10). Entrepreneurship always leads to inequality. *Harvard Business Review*.

Jackson, A., & Jackson, T. (2021). Modelling energy transition risk: The impact of declining energy return on investment (EROI). *Ecological Economics, 185*, 107023. https://doi.org/10.1016/j.ecolecon.2021.107023

Jackson, T. (2016). *Prosperity without growth*. Routledge.

Jackson, T., & Victor, P. (2015). Does credit create a growth imperative? A quasi-stationary economy with interest-bearing debt. *Ecological Economics, 120*, 32–48.

Jackson, T., & Victor, P. (2019). Unraveling the claims for (and against) green growth. *Science, 366*(6468), 950–951.

Jacobs, L. R., & Page, B. I. (2005). Who influences US foreign policy? *American Political Science Review, 99*(1), 107–123.

James, H. (2020, July 1). Late Soviet America. *Project Syndicate.*
Janeway, W. (2018). *Doing capitalism in the innovation economy: Reconfiguring the three-player game between markets, speculators and the state* (2nd ed.). Cambridge University Press.
Jarzebski, M. P., Elmqvist, T., Gasparatos, A., et al. (2021). Ageing and population shrinking implications for sustainability in the urban century. *NPJ Urban Sustainability, 1.*
Jenkins, P. (2024). Ukraine war: The dangerous pursuit of total victory. *The Guardian.* https://www.theguardian.com/commentisfree/2024/jan/27/ukraine-war-total-victory-russia-peace-talks
Johanisova, N., Crabtree, T., & Franková, E. (2013). Social enterprises and non-market capitals: A path to degrowth? *Journal of Cleaner Production, 38,* 7–16.
Johnson, J. (2024, May 3). 'Absurd!': US billionaires pay lower tax rate than working class for first time. *Common Dreams.*
Johnson, L. (2023, October 11). Greenwashing growing in frequency and complexity. *Report, ESGDIVE.*
Johnson, S. (2009, May). The quiet coup. *The Atlantic.*
Johnson, S., & Kwak, J. (2011). *13 bankers: The Wall Street takeover and the next financial meltdown.* Random House.
Johnstone, C. (2023). What Dystopia looks like. *Peace & Planet News,* Spring.
Jones, A. L. (2020, June 1). An 'excess of democracy': How corporations killed the campus. *Independent Australia.*
Jones, C. (2019). Paul Romer: Ideas, nonrivalry, and endogenous growth. *Scandinavian Journal of Economics, 121,* 859–883.
Jones, C. (2022). The end of economic growth? Unintended consequences of a declining population. *American Economic Review, 112*(11), 3489–3527.
Jones, O. (2023). *Politicians are right about the 'decline of the west' – but so wrong about the causes.* The Guardian, 5 Apr.
Jones, T. C. (2012). America, oil, and war in the Middle East. *Journal of American History, 99*(1), 208–218.
Jorgenson, A. K., Clark, B., & Kentor, J. (2023a). The environmental impacts of militarism. *Annual Review of Sociology, 49*(1), 225–248.
Jorgenson, A. K., Clark, B., Thombs, R. P., Kentor, J., Givens, J. E., Huang, X., El Tinay, H., Auerbach, D., & Mahutga, M. C. (2023b). Guns versus climate: How militarization amplifies the effect of economic growth on carbon emissions. *American Sociological Review, 88*(3), 418–453.
Kaiho, K. (2022). Relationship between extinction magnitude and climate change during major marine and terrestrial animal crises. *Biogeosciences, 19*(14), 3369–2022.
Kaldor, M., Karl, T. L., & Said, Y. (Eds.). (2007). *Oil wars.* Pluto Press.
Kallis, G. (2021). Limits, ecomodernism and degrowth. *Political Geography, 87,* 102367.

Kallis, G., & March, H. (2015). Imaginaries of hope: The utopianism of degrowth. *Annals of the Association of American Geographers, 105*(2), 360–336.

Kamepalli, S. K., Rajan, R., & Zingales, L. (2020). *Kill zone*. BER Working Paper No. 27146.

Kampmark, B. (2020). The UK's military spending spree: A dangerous and unnecessary escalation. *CounterPunch*. https://www.counterpunch.org/2020/11/20/the-uks-military-spending-spree-a-dangerous-and-unnecessary-escalation/

Kapoor, R., & Murmann, J. P. (2023). The Organizational and Technological Origins of the U.S. Shale Gas Revolution, 1947 to 2012, Industrial and Corporate Change, dtad021.

Karahan, F., Pugsley, B., & Şahin, A. (2019). *Demographic origins of the startup deficit (no. 888)*. Federal Reserve Bank of New York Staff Reports.

Kass, H. (2004). Against the militarisation of Europe. *Medicine, Conflict and Survival, 20*(2), 166–168.

Katz, J. M. (2022). *Gangsters of capitalism: Smedley Butler, the marines, and the making and breaking of America's empire*. St. Martin's Press.

Kauppi, P. E., Ausubel, J., Fang, J., Mather, A., Sedjo, R., & Waggoner, P. (2006). Returning forests analyzed with the forest identity. *PNAS, 103*(46), 17574–17579.

Keiser, M. (2008). Who could have predicted revolution in Iceland? *HuffPost Business*.

Kelly, L. (2024, October 10). Israel seeks to reshape Middle East, with force and US backing. *The Hill*.

Kemp, L., Xu, C., Depledge, J., Ebi, K., Gibbins, G., Kohler, T., Rockström, J., Scheffer, M., Schellnhuber, H., Steffen, W., & Lenton, T. (2022). Climate endgame: Exploring catastrophic climate change scenarios. *Proceedings of the National Academy of Sciences, 119*(34), e2108146119.

Keohane, R. O. (1983). Review of the rise and decline of nations: Economic growth, stagflation, and social rigidities, by M. Olson. *Journal of Economic Literature, 21*(2), 558–560.

Kennedy, P. (1987). *The rise and fall of the great powers*. Random House.

Kerschner, C., & Capellán-Pérez, I. (2017). Peak-oil and ecological economics. In C. Spash (Ed.), *Handbook of ecological economics* (pp. 425–437). Routledge.

King, R. S., & Rudy, S. (2023, September 29). The ends of knowledge. *Aeon*.

Kingsnorth, P. (2023). *The West Must Die: Beyond the Revolution*. Substack, 31 May.

Kirzner, I. M. (1979). *Perception, opportunity, and profit*. University of Chicago Press.

Kish, K., & Quilley, S. (2017). Wicked dilemmas of scale and complexity in the politics of degrowth. *Ecological Economics, 142*, 306–317.

Klawans, J. (2024, March 19). How climate change is contributing to global unrest. *The Week*.

Klein, N. (2008). *The Shock Doctrine: The rise of disaster capitalism.* Macmillan.

Klimm, F. (2022). Quantifying the 'end of history' through a Bayesian Markov-Chain approach. *Royal Society Open Science, 9*(11), 221131.

Klüppel, L., & Knott, A. (2023). Are ideas being fished out? *Research Policy, 52*(2), 104665.

Koetsier, J. (2021, January 30). The stock exchange of nature? A startup is tokenizing the planet to save it. *Forbes.*

Kohli, A. (2021, July 6). American oligarchs: Report details how the wealthiest US dynasties hoard their fortunes - And accelerate inequality. *International Consortium of Investigative Journalists.*

Kohr, L. (1957). *The breakdown of nations.* Green Books.

Kolbert, E. (2014). *The Sixth Extinction: An Unnatural History.* Henry Holt and Company. New York.

Kornai, J. (2013). *Dynamism, rivalry, and the surplus economy: Two essays on the nature of capitalism.* Oxford University Press.

Kose, M. A., & Ohnsorge, F. (2024). *Falling Long-Term Growth Prospects: Trends, Expectations, and Policies.* World Bank: Washington, DC. http://hdl.handle.net/10986/39497

Kotkin, J. (2020). *The coming of neo feudalism: A warning to the global middle class.* Encounter Books.

Kotkin, J. (2024). *The road to neo-feudalism.* Quilette, 19 June.

Kotkin, S. (2008). *Armageddon averted: The Soviet Collapse, 1970–2000.* Oxford University Press.

Kotter, J. (2013, April 3). Disrupt or be disrupted. *Forbes.*

Kozeniauskas, N. (2018). *Whats Driving the Decline in Entrepreneurship?.* Mimeo.

Kraus, S., Mahto, R. V., & Walsh, S. (2023). The importance of literature reviews in small business and entrepreneurship research. *Journal of Small Business Management, 61*(3), 1095–1106.

Kremer, M. (1993). Population growth and technological change: One million B.C. to 1990. *The Quarterly Journal of Economics, 108*(3), 681–716.

Krugman, P. (2014, March 14). Notes on Piketty (Wonkish). *The New York Times.*

Kühne, K., Bartsch, N., Tate, R. D., Higson, J., & Habet, A. (2022). "Carbon bombs" - Mapping key fossil fuel projects. *Energy Policy, 166,* 112950. https://doi.org/10.1016/j.enpol.2022.112950

Kuhner, T. K. (2015). American plutocracy. *King's Law Journal, 26*(1), 44–75.

Kuntz, M. (2012). The postmodern assault on science. If all truths are equal, who cares what science has to say? *EMBO Reports, 13*(10), 885–889.

Kuratko, D. F., & Audretsch, D. (2022). The future of entrepreneurship: The few or the many? *Small Business Economics, 59,* 269–278.

Kwon, S. Y., Ma, Y., & Zimmermann, K. (2024). 100 years of rising corporate concentration. *American Economic Review, 114*(7), 2111–2140.

Lac, J. (2024, January 26). The century of humiliation and the century after. *Brown Political Review.*

Lähde, V. (2023, September 23). The polycrisis. *Aeon*.
Laherrère, J., Hall, C. A. S., & Bentley, R. (2022). How much oil remains for the world to produce? Comparing assessment methods, and separating fact from fiction. *Current Research in Environmental Sustainability*, *4*, 100174.
Lakhani, N. (2024, July 24). Revealed: Wealthy western countries lead in global oil and gas expansion. *The Guardian*. https://www.theguardian.com/environment/2024/jul/24/revealed-wealthy-western-countries-lead-in-global-oil-and-gas-expansion
Lakwete, A. (2003). *Inventing the cotton gin: Machine and myth in Antebellum America*. Johns Hopkins University Press.
Lal, V. (2009). Gandhi's West, the West's Gandhi. *New Literary History*, *40*(2), 281–313.
Lamoreaux, N. (2019). The problem of bigness: From standard oil to Google. *The Journal of Economic Perspectives*, *33*(3), 94117.
Landes, D. S., Mokyr, J., & Baumol, W. J. (2010). *The invention of enterprise: Entrepreneurship from ancient Mesopotamia to modern times*. Princeton University Press.
Landström, H., Parhankangas, A., Fayolle, A., & Riot, P. (2019). *Challenging entrepreneurship research*. Routledge.
Lang, G. (2009). Measuring the Returns of R&D: An Empirical Study of the German Manufacturing Sector over 45 Years. *Research Policy*, *38*(9), 1438–1445.
Lang, M., Manahan, M. A., & Bringel, B. (Eds.). (2024). *The geopolitics of green colonialism: Global justice and ecosocial transitions* (1st ed.). Pluto Press.
Lawrence, M., Homer-Dixon, T., Janzwood, S., Rockström, J., Renn, O., & Donges, J. F. (2024). Global polycrisis: The causal mechanisms of crisis entanglement. *Global Sustainability*, *7*, 1–36.
Layton, B. (2008). A comparison of energy densities of prevalent energy sources in units of joules per cubic meter. *International Journal of Green Energy*, *5*, 438–455.
Ledger-Lomas, M. (2024). *Emmanuel Todd Prophesies the Defeat of the West*. Jacobin, 3 October.
Lee, C. (2018). Oil and terrorism: Uncovering the mechanisms. *The Journal of Conflict Resolution*, *62*(5), 903–928.
Lee, J. (2024a). Sixty countries endorse 'blueprint' for AI use in military; China opts out. *Reuters*.
Lee, M. Y. (2024b, September 14). *Countries endorse AI military blueprint as critics warn of loopholes*. Associated Press. https://apnews.com/article/artificial-intelligence-military-weapons-blueprint-summit-4c21b0107c303432edc5d309b95482ab
Lee, S. M. (2021, October 19). A data sleuth challenged a powerful COVID scientist. Then he came after her. *Buzzfeed News*.

Leendertse, J., Schrijvers, M., & Stam, E. (2022). Measure twice, cut once: Entrepreneurial ecosystem metrics. *Research Policy, 51*(9), 104336.

Leiva, B., & Schramski, J. R. (2022). On the rules of life and Kleiber's law: The macroscopic relationship between materials and energy. *Heliyon, 8*(5), e09647.

Lenderink, B., Johannes, I., & Voordijk, H. (2019). Innovation and public procurement: From fragmentation to synthesis on concepts, rationales and approaches. *Innovation: The European Journal of Social Science Research, 35*, 650.

Lent, J. (2019, Winter). The next civilization. *Conversation Worldview*.

Lenton, T. M., Held, H., Kriegler, E., & Schellnhuber, H. (2008). Tipping elements in the earth's climate system. *PNAS, 105*(6), 1786–1793.

Lenton, T. M., Rockström, J., Gaffney, O., Rahmstorf, S., Richardson, K., Steffen, W., & Schellnhuber, H. J. (2019). Climate tipping points - Too risky to bet against. *Nature, 575*(7784), 592–595. https://doi.org/10.1038/d41586-019-03595-0

Lenton, T.M., Xu, C., Abrams, J.F. et al. (2023, May 22). Quantifying the human cost of global warming. *Nature Sustainability*.

Léon, F. (2022). The elusive quest for high-growth firms in Africa: When other metrics of performance say nothing. *Small Business Economics, 58*(1), 225–246.

Leonhardt, H., Juschten, M., & Spash, C. (2017). To grow or not to grow? That is the question: Lessons for social ecological transformation from small-medium enterprises. *GAIA, 26*(3), 269–276.

Leopold, L. (2024, June 24). Pillaging by the super-rich will continue until the working class revolts. *Common Dreams*.

Lewis, T. (2023, October 5). Vaccine scientist warns antiscience conspiracies have become a deadly, organized movement. *Scientific American*.

Liboreiro, J. (2022, October 19). Josep Borrell apologises for controversial 'garden vs jungle' metaphor but defends speech. *Euro News*.

Lieven, A. (2020, August 31). How the west lost. *Prospect Magazine*.

Light, S. (2014). The military-environmental complex. *Boston College Law Review, 55*(3), 879–946.

Lin, J. Y. (2008). *The impact of the financial crisis on developing countries*. Paper presented at the Korea Development Institute, 31 October, Seoul.

Lin, K.-H., & Tomaskovic-Devey, D. (2013). Financialization and U.S. income inequality, 1970–2008. *American Journal of Sociology, 118*(5), 1284–1329.

Lingelbach, D., & Guerra, V. (2023). *The oligarchs grip: Fusing wealth and power*. De Gruyter.

Livingstone, J. (2024, February 16). What was capitalism? *Project Syndicate*.

Lomborg, B. (2020). Welfare in the 21st century: Increasing development, reducing inequality, the impact of climate change, and the cost of climate policies. *Technological Forecasting and Social Change, 156*.

Longpre, S., Elazar, Y., Shavit, Y., Kemper, J., Kiela, D., Prabhu, A., Schoenick, C., & Levy, O. (2024a). *The disappearing web: A study of the implications of robots.txt and Terms of Service on web data availability.* arXiv preprint arXiv:2404.09709.

Longpre, S., Mahari, R. A., Lund, C., Oderinwale, H., Brannon, W., et al. (2024b). Consent in crisis: The rapid decline of the AI data commons. *arXiv preprint arXiv:2407.14933.*

Lu, M. (2023, October 27). Ranked: The world's top 25 defense companies by revenue. *Visual Capitalist.*

Lucas, R. (1990). Why doesn't capital flow from rich to poor countries? *American Economic Review, 80*(2), 92–96.

Lundmark, L., Hall, C., & Zhang, J. (2023). Part 1 Degrowth and tourism entrepreneurship. In *Degrowth and tourism.* Taylor and Francis Group.

Luxemburg, R. (1913). *The Accumulation of Capital.* 1951 Translation published by London: Routledge and Kegan Paul Ltd.

Lynas, M. (2024, January 24). Viewpoint: Nobel laureates and 1,000 other scientists plead with European parliamentarians to 'reject the darkness of anti-science fearmongering' over gene editing. *Genetic Literacy Project.*

Mackinder, S. H. (1943). The round war and the winning of peace. *Foreign Affairs, 21*(4), 595–605.

Mahbubani, K. (2022). Can America escape plutocracy? In *The Asian 21st century. China and globalization.* Springer.

Mainela, T., Puhakka, V., & Sipola, S. (2018). International entrepreneurship beyond individuals and firms: On the systemic nature of international opportunities. *Journal of Business Venturing, 33*(4), 534–550.

Malthus, T. (1798). *An Essay on the Principle of Population.* London: Printed for J. Johnson, in St. Paul's Churchyard.

Mandel, M. (2001). Politics and human rights in international criminal law: Our case against NATO and the lessons to be learned from it. *Fordham International Law Journal, 25*(1), article 4.

Marangos, J. (2008). The evolution of the anti-Washington consensus debate: From post-Washington consensus' to after the Washington Consensus. *Competition & change, 12*(3), 227–244.

Mark, S., Holder, S., Hoyer, D., Schoonover, R., & Aldrich, D. P. (2023). Understanding polycrisis: Definitions, applications, and responses.

Markus, S., & Charnysh, V. (2017). The flexible few: Oligarchs and wealth defense in developing democracies. *Comparative Political Studies, 50*(12), 1632–1665.

Marx, K. (1867). *Das Kapital. Kritik der politischen Oekonomie.* Verlag von Otto Meisner.

Mason, R. (2008, October 19). Iceland falls out of love with its billionaires. *The Telegraph.*

Masters, J., & Merrow, A. (2023). *U.S. nuclear weapons in Europe.* Council on Foreign Relations. https://www.cfr.org/backgrounder/us-nuclear-weapons-europe

Mayer, C. (2024). *Capitalism and crises: How to fix them.* Oxford University Press.

Mazzucato, M. (2011). *The entrepreneurial state.* Penguin.
Mazzucato, M. (2021). *Mission economy: A moonshot guide to changing capitalism.* Allen Lane.
McAnany, P. A., & Yoffee, N. (2010). *Questioning collapse: Human resilience, ecological vulnerability, and the aftermath of empire.* Cambridge University Press.
McCallum, M. (2015). Vertebrate biodiversity losses point to a sixth mass extinction. *Biodiversity and Conservation, 24,* 2497–2519.
McCauley, R.N., Chinn, M.D., & Ito, H. (2024, July 29). The Russian sanctions and dollar foreign exchange reserves. *VOXEU/CEPR.*
McCloskey, D. N. (2016). *Bourgeois equality: How ideas, not capital or institutions, enriched the world.* University of Chicago Press.
McCoy, A. W. (2024, March 13). Facing three global crises, the American empire may be nearing final collapse. *Salon.com.*
McCulloch, W., & Pitts, W. (1943). A logical calculus of the ideas immanent in nervous activity. *Bulletin of Mathematical Biophysics, 5,* 115–133.
McGoey, L. (2023, January 19). Elite universities gave us effective altruism, the dumbest idea of the century. *Jacobin.*
McGowan, M., Andrews, D., & Millot, V. (2017). *The walking dead? Zombie firms and productivity performance in OECD countries.* Working Paper no. 1372. OECD.
McKern, S. (2024). The Gaza conflict: How the West lost the narrative. *The Diplomat.* https://thediplomat.com/2024/10/the-gaza-conflict-how-the-west-lost-the-narrative/
McKie, R. (2024, February 3). The situation has become appalling': Fake scientific papers push research credibility to crisis point.
McMichael, P. (1991). Slavery in capitalism: The rise and demise of the U. S. Ante-Bellum cotton culture. *Theory and Society, 20*(3), 321–349.
McPhetres, J., & Zuckerman, M. (2018). Religiosity predicts negative attitudes towards science and lower levels of science literacy, *Plos One.* https://doi.org/10.1371/journal.pone.0207125
McWilliams, B., Sgaravatti, G., Tagliapietra, S., & Zachmann, G. (2024, February 22). The European Union-Russia energy divorce: State of play. *Brueghel.*
Meadows, D., Meadows, D., Randers, J., & a. W. B. (1971). *The limits to growth; A report for the club of Romes project on the predicament of mankind.* Universe Books.
Meaker, M. (2023, September 5). Welcome to the age of Technofeudalism. *WIRED.*
Mearsheimer, J. J. (2014). Why the Ukraine crisis is the west's fault: The liberal delusions that provoked Putin. *Foreign Affairs, 93,* 1–12.
Mechanic, M. (2021, April 4). Does wealth rob the brain of compassion? *The Atlantic.*
Meho, L. I. (2007). The rise and rise of citation analysis. *Physics World, 20*(1), 32.

Menon, R., & Ruger, W. (2023). NATO enlargement and US grand strategy: A net assessment. In J. Goldgeier & J. R. I. Shifrinson (Eds.), *Evaluating NATO enlargement*. Palgrave Macmillan.

Michaelides, M. (2024, July 4). Nature's value: How to make biodiversity conservation profitable and scalable? *Illuminem*.

Michaux, S. (2021, September 1). A bottom-up insight reveals: Replacing fossil fuels is even more enormous task than thought. *Geological Survey of Finland (GTK)*.

Mier, M. (2023). *European electricity prices in times of multiple crises*. IFO Working Paper no. 394.

Milanović, B. (2024, July 28). Branko Milanović—Living through another great transformation... *Brave New Europe*. https://braveneweurope.com/branko-milanovic-living-through-another-great-transformation/

Mills, C. W. (1956). *The power elite*. Oxford University Press.

Milman, O. (2024, July 24). 'This used to be a beautiful place': How the US became the world's biggest fossil fuel state. *The Guardian*.

Milman, O., Lakhani, N., & Witherspoon, A. (2024, July 24). Revealed: Wealthy western countries lead in global oil and gas expansion. *The Guardian*.

Minniti, M., Naudé, W., & Stam, E. (2023). *Is productive entrepreneurship getting scarcer? A reflection on the contemporary relevance of Baumol's typology*, IZA DP No. 16408. IZA Institute for Labor Economics.

Minter, W. (1991). The US and the war in Angola. *Review of African Political Economy, 50*, 135–144.

Mirković, D. (2001). NATO's genocidal war to prevent genocide: A critique. *Peace Research, 33*(1), 69–77.

Mirrlees, J. A. (2021a). *Tax by design*. Oxford University Press.

Mirrlees, T. (2021b). Sanctioning China's tech industry to secure Silicon Valley's global dominance. In S. Davis & I. Ness (Eds.), *Sanctions as war: Anti-imperialist perspectives on american geo-economic strategy*.

Moeini, S. A. (2022). From "noble lie" to "fake news": A genealogy of truth and power in the "war on terror". *Globalizations, 19*(4), 664–679.

Mohr, S., Wang, J., Ellem, G., Ward, J., & Giurco, D. (2015). Projection of world fossil fuels by country. *Fuel, 1*, 120–135.

Mok, A. (2023, May 18). Trump supporters and Christians are the most worried that AI is an existential threat to humanity, poll says. *Business Insider*.

Mokyr, J. (2003). Why was the industrial revolution a European phenomenon? *Supreme Court Economic Review, 10*, 27–63.

Mokyr, J. (2007). The power of ideas. *World Economics, 8*(3), 53–110.

Mokyr, J. (2014, April 28). Growth and technology: The wild ride ahead. *Milken Institute Review*.

Mokyr, J. (2016). *A culture of growth: The origins of the modern economy*. Princeton University Press.

Moloney, E. (2022, March 10). Call to restart Irish peat harvesting amid energy crisis and Russia's war on Ukraine. *Independent.Ie*.
Monbiot, G. (2016, April 15). Neoliberalism the ideology at the root of all our problems. *The Guardian*.
Monbiot, G. (2022a, May 19). The banks collapsed in 2008 and our foodsystem is about to do the same. *The Guardian*.
Monbiot, G. (2022b, October 30). The oligarch's oligarch. https://www.monbiot.com/2022/10/30/the-oligarchs-oligarch/
Monbiot, G. (2024, June 27). Things are not going to get better as long as oligarchs rule the roost in our democracies. *The Guardian*.
Monbiot, G., & Hutchison, P. (2024). *Invisible doctrine: The secret history of neoliberalism*. Crown.
Moorsom, R., & Raber, J. (2024). AFRICOM: The US military's expanding footprint in Africa. *Review of African Political Economy, 51*(180), 296–312.
Morgan, T. (2024, July 15). #283: The seductive risk of financialization. *Surplus Energy Economics Blog*.
Morris, I. (2010). *Why the west rules - For now: The patterns of history and what they reveal about the future*. Profile Books.
Morris, I. (2015). *Foragers, farmers, and fossil fuels: How human values evolve*. Princeton University Press.
Mortazavi, A. (2022, January 21). Cryptocurrency is a Giant Ponzi scheme. *Jacobin*.
Moskovitz, T. J., & Vissing-Jørgensen, A. (2002). The returns to entrepreneurial investment: A private equity premium puzzle? *American Economic Review, 92*, 745–778.
Muñoz, P., & Cohen, B. (2017). Towards a social-ecological understanding of sustainable venturing. *Journal of Business Venturing Insights, 7*, 1–8.
Muñoz, P., & Cohen, B. (2018). Sustainable entrepreneurship research: Taking stock and looking ahead. *Business Strategy and the Environment, 27*(3), 300–322.
Muñoz, P., & Kimmitt, J. (2019). Social mission as competitive advantage: A configurational analysis of the strategic conditions of social entrepreneurship. *Journal of Business Research, 101*, 854–861.
Murphy, D., Raugei, M., Carbajales-Dale, M., & Estrada, B. R. (2022). Energy return on investment of major energy carriers: Review and harmonization. *Sustainability, 14*(12), 7098.
Murphy, K., Schleifer, A., & Vishny, R. (1991). The allocation of talent: Implications for growth. *Quarterly Journal of Economics, 106*(2), 503–530.
Murphy, S., & Burch, D. (2012). *Cereal secrets: The world's largest grain traders and global agriculture* (Oxfam Research Reports). Oxfam GB for Oxfam International.
Murphy, T. (2011a, January 11). Peak oil perspective. *Do The Math Blog*.
Murphy, T. (2011b, October 18). The energy trap. *Do The Math Blog*.
Murphy, T. (2022). Limits to economic growth. *Nature Physics, 18*, 844–847.

Murphy, T., Murphy, D., Love, T., LeHew, M., & McCall, B. (2021). Modernity is incompatible with planetary limits: Developing a PLAN for the future. *Energy Research & Social Science*, *81*, 102239.

Murray, J., & King, D. (2012). Oil's tipping point has passed. *Nature*, *481*, 433–435.

Mutschler, M. M., & Bales, M. (2020). *Global Militarisation Index 2020*. Bonn International Center for Conversion (BICC).

Naím, M. (2016, August 17). The six political events that have "distorted" the world of oil. *About Oil*.

Naudé, W., & Nagler, P. (2022). *The ossified economy: The case of Germany, 1870–2020*, IZA DP No. 15607. IZA Institute of Labor Economics.

Naudé, W. (Ed.). (2010a). *Entrepreneurship and economic development*. Palgrave Macmillan.

Naudé, W. (2010b). The global economic crisis and developing countries: Impacts, responses and options for sustainable recovery. *Poverty and Public Policy*, *2*(2), article 8.

Naudé, W. (2011). Global finance after the crisis: Reform imperatives and vested interests. *Global Economy Journal*, *11*(2), article 6.

Naudé, W. (2016). *Is European entrepreneurship in crisis?* IZA DP No. 9817. IZA Institute for Labor Economics.

Naudé, W. (2020). *Industrialization under medieval conditions? Global development after COVID-19*, IZA Discussion Paper No. 13829. IZA Institute of Labor Economics.

Naudé, W. (2022a). From the entrepreneurial to the ossified economy. *Cambridge Journal of Economics*, *46*(1), 105–131.

Naudé, W. (2022b, November 21). "Longtermism" and AI: How our billionaire overlords want to live forever. *Medium*.

Naudé, W. (2023b). *Destructive digital entrepreneurship*. IZA DP No. 16483. IZA Institute of Labor Economics.

Naudé, W. (2023a). *Economic growth and societal collapse: Beyond green growth and degrowth fairy tales*. Palgrave Macmillan.

Naudé, W. (2023c). Late industrialisation and global value chains under platform capitalism. *Journal of Industrial and Business Economics*, *50*, 91–119.

Naudé, W. (2023d, March 8). The stop button society: Longing for the end of capitalism? *Medium*.

Naudé, W. (2023e). *We already live in a degrowth world, and we do not like it*. IZA Discussion Paper No. 16191. IZA Institute for Labour Economics.

Naudé, W. (2023f, July 31). Degrowth: Slowing down rich economies to deal with climate change is a flawed idea. *The Conversation*.

Naudé, W. (2023g, April 4). Airstrikes on rogue AI datacenters? Fears that artificial intelligence pose an existential risk has reached new heights of hysteria. *Medium*.

Naudé, W. (2023h). No, degrowth won't save us. *BMJ (British Medical Journal), 382*, 2245.

Naudé, W. (2023i, February 26). Degrowth's radical political project to de-develop the world. *Medium*.

Naudé, W. (2024a). The end of the empire that entrepreneurship built: How seven sources of rot will undo the west. *Foundations and Trends in Entrepreneurship, 2092*(5), 400–492.

Naudé, W., & Cameron, M. J. (2021). Export-led growth after COVID-19: The case of Portugal. *Notas Económicas, 52*(1), 7–53.

Naudé, W., & Dimitri, N. (2019). *Public procurement and innovation for human-centered artificial intelligence*, IZA DP No. 14021. IZA Institute for Labour Economics.

Naudé, W., & Power, B. (2024). *Handbook of research on entrepreneurship and conflict*. Edward Elgar Publishers.

Naudé, W., Amorós, J., & Cristi, O. (2014). Surfeiting, the appetite may sicken: Entrepreneurship and happiness. *Small Business Economics Journal, 42*(1), 523–540.

Naudé, W., Gries, T., & Dimitri, N. (2024). *Artificial intelligence: Economic perspectives and models*. Cambridge University Press.

Naudé, W. (2024b). *Is the scholarly field of entrepreneurship at its end?* IZA Discussion Paper no. 16916. IZA Institute of Labor Economics.

Nayak, B.S. (2020). Oligarchs of mainstream mass media in service of capitalism.

Neate, R. (2023, July 6). World's 722 biggest companies 'making $1tn' in windfall profits. *The Guardian*.

Nerlinger, M., & Utz, S. (2022). The impact of the Russia-Ukraine conflict on energy firms: A capital market perspective. *Finance Research Letters, 50*, 103243.

Nesterova, I., Maier, F., Robra, B., & Parker, S. (2020). Why degrowth should scare business. *Degrowth Blog*.

Newlove-Eriksson, L., & Eriksson, J. (2023). Conceptualizing the European military-civilian-industrial complex: The need for a helicopter perspective. *Defence Studies, 23*(4), 561–588.

Nichols, J. (2022, September 29). It's official: America is an oligarchy. *The Nation*.

Norrlöf, C. (2024, July 5). The decline and fall of the petrodollar? *Project Syndicate*.

Notes on Progress. (2023, May 15). Degrowth and the monkey's paw. *Works in Progress*.

Nowogrodzki, A. (2022, September 21). Most US professors are trained at same few elite universities. *Nature*.

Nunn, N. (2008). The long-term effects of Africa's slave trades. *The Quarterly Journal of Economics, 123*(1), 139–176.

O'Brien, I. (2024, September 15). Data Center Emissions probably 662% Higher than Big Tech claims. can it keep up the ruse? *The Guardian*.

O'Rourke, K. H., & Williamson, J. G. (2000). *When did globalization begin?* NBER Working Paper No. 7632. National Bureau of Economic Research.
Oakes, J. (2016). Capitalism and slavery and the civil war. *International Labor and Working-Class History, 89*, 195–220.
Oakes, W. (1944, February). Toward a permanent war economy? In E. Haberkern (Ed.), *Politics*. Center for Socialist History.
Oberg, J. (2023). *The West's last resort: Militarism and the decline of empire.* Transnational Institute. https://www.tni.org/en/article/the-wests-last-resort
Odum, H., & Odum, E. (2001). *A prosperous way down: Principles and policies.* University Press of Colorado.
OECD. (2011). *Fostering innovation for green growth*. OECD.
Office of the Historian. (n.d.). *The Suez crisis, 1956, milestones in the history of U.S. foreign relations.* Foreign Service Institute, US Department of State. Online at: https://history.state.gov/milestones/1953-1960/suez
Olk, C., Schneider, C., & Hickel, J. (2023). How to pay for saving the world: Modern monetary theory for a degrowth transition. *Ecological Economics, 214*, 107968.
Olson, M. (1982). *The rise and decline of nations: Economic growth, stagflation, and social rigidities*. Yale University Press.
Olumba, E. E. (2024). The necropolitics of drone bases and use in the African context. *Critical Studies on Terrorism*, 1–23.
Ord, T. (2020). *The precipice: Existential risk and the future of humanity.* Hachette Books.
Oreskes, N. (2004). The scientific consensus on climate change. *Science, 30*, 1686–1686.
Osman, M. B., Tierney J., Zhu, J., Tardif, R., Hakim, G. J., King, J., & Poulsen, C. J. (2021). Globally resolved surface temperatures since the Last Glacial Maximum. *Nature, 599*(7884), 239–244.
Ottenberg, E. (2024, March 15). The evil of a permanent war economy. *Global South Colloquy.*
Paech, N. (2017). Post-growth economics. In *Routledge handbook of ecological economics* (Vol. 1, 1st ed., pp. 477–486).
Panetta, F. (2023, June 23). Paradise lost? How crypto failed to deliver on its promises and what to do about it. *European Central Bank: Speech by Fabio Panetta, Member of the Executive Board of the ECB, at a panel on the future of crypto at the 22nd BIS Annual Conference.*
Park, M., Leahey, E., & Funk, R. (2023). Papers and patents are becoming less disruptive over time. *Nature, 613*, 138–144.
Patnaik, U., & Patnaik, P. (2021). *Capital and imperialism: Theory, history, and the present.* Monthly Review Press.
Peltier, R. (2023). *The opportunity costs of military spending.* Center for American Progress. https://www.americanprogress.org/article/opportunity-costs-military-spending/

Perez-Orive, A., & Timmer, Y. (2023, June 23). Distressed firms and the large effects of monetary policy tightenings. *FEDS Notes*.

Perret, B. (2017). The economy as the opium of the people. In J. Alison & W. Palaver (Eds.), *The Palgrave handbook of mimetic theory and religion (Chapter 38)* (pp. 287–294).

Philipp-Muller, A., Lee, S. W. S., & Petty, R. E. (2022). Why are people anti-science, and what can we do about it? *PNAS, 119*(30), e2120755119.

Piaskowska, D., Tippmann, E., & Monaghan, S. (2021). Scale-up modes: Profiling activity configurations in scaling strategies. *Long Range Planning, 54*, 102101.

Pielke, R., Burgess, M. G., & Ritchie, J. (2022). Plausible 2005–2050 emissions scenarios project between 2 °C and 3 °C of warming by 2100. *Environmental Research Letters, 17*, 024027.

Pigeaud, F., & Sylla, N. S. (2021). *Africa's last colonial currency: The CFA Franc story*. Pluto Press.

Piketty, T. (2014). *Capital in the twenty-first century*. Harvard University Press.

Pillay, K. (2024, July 31). Trump and the Tech Bros: A threat to democracy. *Campaign on Digital Ethics*.

Pinker, S. (2018). *Enlightenment now: The case for reason, science, humanism and progress*. Viking.

Pluckrose, H. (2017, March 27). How French "intellectuals" ruined the west: Postmodernism and its impact, explained. *Langaa*.

Plunk, D. (1986, December 5). *Strengthening the U.S.-Zaire relationship*. The Heritage Foundation.

Polanyi, K. (1944). *The great transformation*. Farrar & Rinehart.

Polonsky, M. (2024). Defeat of the West? *Emmanuel Todd and the Russo-Ukrainian War*. The Article, March 26.

Polychroniou, C.J. (2022, August 4). 21st-century US foreign policy is shaped by fears of China's rise, Chomsky Says. *TruthOut*.

Polychroniou, C.J. (2023, May 26). Interview with Noam Chomsky on the state of the world. *Global Policy*.

Pomeranz, K. (2021). *The great divergence: China, Europe, and the making of the modern world economy*. Princeton University Press.

Porter, P. (2015). Was Paul Kennedy Right? *War on the Rocks*, 17 June.

Prifti, B. (2017). *US foreign policy in the Middle East: The case for continuity* (1st ed.). Springer International Publishing.

Qureshi, I. (2023a). Superstar firms and the digital economy. In *The Routledge companion to the digital economy* (pp. 117–131). Routledge.

Qureshi, Z. (2023b, May 16). Rising inequality: A major issue of our time. *Brookings*.

Radley, B. (2023). Green imperialism, sovereignty, and the quest for national development in The Congo. *Review of African Political Economy, 50*(177–178), 322–339.

Radtke, K. W. (2007). China and the Greater Middle East: Globalization no longer equals westernization. *Perspectives on Global Development and Technology, 6*, 389–341.

Rammer, C., & Schubert, T. (2018). Concentration on the few: Mechanisms behind a falling share of innovative firms in Germany. *Research Policy, 47*(2), 379–389.

Rasler, K., & Thompson, W. R. (1985). War and state making: The shaping of the global powers. *Unwin Hyman*.

Ratner, P. (2017). *Why the fall of the American empire will happen by 2030*. Big Think, 29 July.

Rätzer, M., Hartz, R., & Winkler, I. (2018). Editorial: Post-growth organizations. *Management Revue, 29*(3), 193–205.

Raworth, K. (2017). *Doughnut economics: Seven ways to think like a 21st-century economist*. Random House Business.

Razom We Stand. (2023). Fossil fuel dictatorships and petrostates: How oil and gas revenues fund wars and violate human rights. https://razomwestand.org/en/article/how-oil-and-gas-revenues-fund-wars-and-violate-human-rights-new-report

Rees, M. (2021a, October 18). Seti: Why extraterrestrial intelligence is more likely to be artificial than biological. *The Conversation*.

Rees, W. E. (2021b). A note of climate change and cultural denial. *Population Matters*.

Rees, W. E. (2022). Why large cities won't survive the twenty-first century. In R. Brears (Ed.), *The Palgrave encyclopedia of urban and regional futures*. Palgrave Macmillan.

Reitz, T., Schulz, P., Schütt, M., & Seyd, B. (2021). Democracy in post-growth societies: A zero-sum game? *Anthropological Theory, 21*(3), 251–259.

Rich, J. (2024. After Kabul, Ukraine, Africa, and West Asia: US defeats continue. *CounterPunch*. https://www.counterpunch.org/2024/02/02/after-kabul-ukraine-africa-and-west-asia-us-defeats-continue/

Richards, C., Lupton, R., & Allwood, J. (2021). Re-Framing the threat of global warming: An empirical causal loop diagram of climate change, food insecurity and societal collapse. *Climatic Change, 164*(49).

Richbourg, R. (2018a). *Deep learning: Measure twice, cut once*. Institute for Defense Analyses.

Richbourg, R. (2018b). Is artificial intelligence perpetually on the verge of another AI winter? *Journal of Business Strategy, 39*(6), 10–15.

Ridley, M. (2011). *The rational optimist*. 4th Estate.

Ridley, M. (2020). *How innovation works*. 4th Estate.

Ritchie, P., Clarke, J., Cox, P., & Huntingford, C. (2021). Overshooting tipping point thresholds in a changing climate. *Nature, 592*, 517523.

Roberts, A. (2024). The decline of American empire: A Kübler-Ross cycle analysis. *Quillette*.

Roberts, P. (2023, October 24). New report details the €3 trillion cost of Europe saying 'no to science' on gene editing. *Alliance for Science*.

Robins-Early, N. (2024). Oxford shuts down institute run by Elon Musk-backed philosopher.

Robinson, J.A. (2009). *Industrial policy and development: A political economy perspective*. Paper presented at the 2009 World Bank ABCDE conference, 22–24 June, Seoul.

Rockström, J., Gupta, J., Qin, D., et al. (2023). Safe and just earth system boundaries. *Nature, 619*, 102–111.

Rockström, J., Steffen, W., Noone, K., Persson, A., Chapin, F., Lambin, E., Lenton, T., et al. (2009). Planetary boundaries: Exploring the safe operating space for humanity. *Ecology and Society, 14*(2).

Roeder, K. (2024, May 3). Tech companies spent over $342m on lobbying while laying down stakes in DC. *TECHNICAL.LY*.

Romer, P. (1993). Idea gaps and object gaps in economic development. *Journal of Monetary Economics, 32*(3), 543–573.

Romer, P. (2016, April 13). The deep structure of economic growth. *Paul Romer Blog* at https://paulromer.net/economic-growth/

Romer, P. M. (1986). Increasing returns and long-run growth. *Journal of Political Economy, 94*(5), 1002–1037.

Romer, P. M. (1990). Endogenous technological change. *Journal of Political Economy, 98*(5), S71–S102.

Rosenberg, N. (1990). Why do firms do basic research (with their own money)? *Research Policy, 19*, 165–174.

Rosenberg, A. (2012). *The atheist's guide to reality: Enjoying life without illusions*. WW Norton & Co.

Ross, M. L. (2012). *The oil curse: How petroleum wealth shapes the development of Princeton*. Princeton University Press.

Roubini, N. (2022). *Megathreats: Ten dangerous trends that imperil our future, and how to survive them*. Little Brown & Co.

Rubin, B. (1990). *Reshaping the Middle East* (Vol. 69). Council on Foreign Relations.

Ruiz, A., Vranken, B., Vignarca, F., Calvo, J., Sédou, L., & de Vries, W. (2021a). *A Militarised Union: Understanding and confronting the militarisation*. Rosa-Luxemburg-Stiftung.

Ruiz, C. F., Smith, D., & Perlo-Freeman, S. (2021b). *Militarising the EU: The security-industrial complex pushes for deeper integration*. Rosa Luxemburg Stiftung. https://www.rosalux.de/en/publication/id/45557/militarising-the-eu

Rushkoff, D. (2020, September 24). The violence of growth-obsessed capitalism: Corporate progress almost always comes at a cost to the most vulnerable. *Medium*.

Rushkoff, D. (2022a, January 9). Silicon Valley's elite prize data over reality, and it's hurting us all. *Fast Company.*

Rushkoff, D. (2022b, November 28). What's a meta for? Part two. *Medium.*

Rushkoff, D. (2023). *Survival of the richest: Escape fantasies of the tech billionaires.* W.W. Norton.

Sachs, J. D. (2022). Ukraine is the latest neocon disaster. *The Nation.* https://www.thenation.com/article/world/ukraine-russia-us-nato/

Sachs, J. D. (2018, October 23). America's plutocrats are winning, *Project Syndicate.*

Sachs, J.D. (2023, May 23). The war in Ukraine was provoked- and why that matters to achieve peace. *Common Dreams.*

Sachs, J.D. (2024, June 19). Why won't the US help negotiate a peaceful end to the war in Ukraine? *Common Dreams.*

Sadowski, J. (2020a). *Too smart: How digital capitalism is extracting data, controlling our lives, and undermining democracy.* The MIT Press.

Sadowski, L. (2020b). The internet of landlords: Digital platforms and new mechanisms of rentier capitalism. *Antipode, 52*(2), 562–580.

Saito, K. (2023). *Marx in the anthropocene: Towards the idea of degrowth communism.* Cambridge University Press.

Sample, I. (2024, January 12). Why landing on the moon is proving more difficult today than 50 years ago. *The Guardian.*

Sampson, A. (1991). *The seven sisters: The great oil companies and the world they shaped.* Bantam Books.

Sarkar, B. K. (1919). The reshaping of the Middle East. *Journal of Race Development, 9*(4), 332–343.

Satyadini, A., & Song, L. (2023). Modern entrepreneurship and the doughnut: Productive or destructive? *Asian-Pacific Economic Literature, 37*(2), 119–141.

Scanlan, A., & Witham, A. (2013). Monetary and fiscal policies for a finite planet. *Sustainability, 5,* 2802–2826.

Scharfman, J. (2023). *The cryptocurrency and digital asset fraud casebook.* Springer International Publishing.

Schmelzer, M., Nowshin, T. (2023, June 27). Ecological reparations and degrowth: Towards a convergence of alternatives around world-making after growth. *Development.*

Schmidt, E. (2023, January 22). US policy toward Ethiopia is a story of cynicism and self-interest. *Jacobin.*

Schneider, F., Kallis, G., & Martinez-Alier, J. (2010). Crisis or opportunity? Economic degrowth for social equity and ecological sustainability. Introduction to this special issue. *Journal of Cleaner Production, 18*(6), 511–518.

Schneider, N. (2019). The American empire is in decline—and we're not ready for what comes next, America - The Jesuit Review. 5 Nov.

Schneider, N. (2024, June 19). The American empire is in decline. *America Magazine.*

Schönholzer, D. (2023). The entrepreneurial state. *Works in Progress, 21.* https://static1.squarespace.com/static/61319a7079d26a721c1829db/t/648a068b2a78827a89a007a7/1686724459668/The+entrepreneurial+state+-+Works+in+Progress.pdf

Schramm, C. (2004). Building entrepreneurial economies. *Foreign Affairs, 83*, 104–115.

Schumpeter, J. A. (1943). *Capitalism, socialism, and democracy* (6th ed.). George Allen & Unwin.

Schwab, K. (2016). The Fourth Industrial Revolution: What it means, how to respond.

Schwartz, P., & Leiden, P. (1997, July 1). The long boom: A history of the future, 1980–2020. *WIRED Magazine.*

Schwartzman, D. (2022, January 5). A critique of degrowth. *Climate & Capitalism.*

Schwarz, B. (2022). The war in Ukraine: A geopolitical catastrophe. *Jacobin.* https://jacobin.com/2022/02/ukraine-war-russia-nato-putin-us-foreign-policy

Scoles, S. (2024, May 8). In the race for space metals, companies hope to cash in. *Undark.*

Serge, B. (2024). *NATO at the Crossroads Incoherent Security Architecture and the Problem of Grand Strategy.* Medium, 19 July.

Sédou, L. (2023a, January 8). War in Ukraine, cover for EU's all-out Militarisation. *Stop Wapenhandel Blog.*

Sédou, T. (2023b). EU sustainable finance taxonomy: Opening the door to the arms lobby. *Observatoire des armements.* https://www.observatoiredesarmements.fr/en/eu-sustainable-finance-taxonomy-opening-the-door-to-the-arms-lobby/

Shalf, J. M. (2020). The future of computing: From Moore's law to the end of silicon. *Philosophical Transactions of the Royal Society A: Mathematical, Physical and Engineering Sciences, 378*(2168), 20190061.

Shane, S. (2009). Why encouraging more people to become entrepreneurs is bad public policy. *Small Business Economics Journal, 33*, 141–149.

Shannon, C. (1948). A mathematical theory of communication. *The Bell System Technical Journal, 27*, 379–423.

Shepherd, D., & Patzelt, H. (2011). The new field of sustainable entrepreneurship: Studying entrepreneurial action linking what is to be sustained with what is to be developed. *Entrepreneurship: Theory and Practice, 35*(1), 137–163.

Shields, P. (2024, July 29). Tech bytes: OpenAI tipped to lose $5 billion, may be bankrupt within a year. *Proactive.*

Shilov, A. (2024, July 5). AI industry needs to earn $600 billion per year to pay for massive hardware spend. *Yahoo Finance.*

Shulman, C., & Bostrom, N. (2021). Sharing the world with digital minds. In S. Clarke, H. Zohny, & J. Savulescu (Eds.), *Rethinking moral status.* Oxford Academic.

SIC. (2010). Report of the Special Investigation Commission.
Sinclair, I. (2022, November 17). Did the UK torpedo peace talks on Ukraine? *Stop the war Coalition*.
Skujins A. (2024, October 17). NATO secretary-general says Ukraine will join alliance 'in the future'. *Euronews*.
Smil, V. (2018). *Energy and civilization: A history*. The MIT Press.
Smil, V. (2019). *Growth: From microorganisms to megacities*. The MIT Press.
Smith, C. (2015, February 4). War-for-oil conspiracy theories may be right. *Our World*.
Smith, M., Yagan, D., Zidar, O., & Zwick, E. (2019). Capitalists in the twenty-first century. *The Quarterly Journal of Economics, 134*(4), 1675–1745.
Søgaard Jørgensen, P., Jansen, R. E. V., Avila Ortega, D. I., Wang-Erlandsson, L., Donges, J. F., Österblom, H., et al. (2023). Evolution of the polycrisis: Anthropocene traps that challenge global sustainability. *Philosophical Transactions of the Royal Society B, 379*(1886), 20220261. https://doi.org/10.1098/rstb.2022.0261
Sokal, A., & Bricmont, J. (1998). *Fashionable nonsense*. Picador.
Solow, R. (1956). A contribution to the theory of economic growth. *Quarterly Journal of Economics, 70*, 65–94.
Song, H., Kemp, D., Tian, L., Chu, D., Song, H., & Dai, X. (2021). Thresholds of temperature change for mass extinctions. *Nature Communications, 12*(4694).
Sorokin, P. A. (1957). *Social and cultural dynamics*. Porter Sargent.
South, N. (2022a). The business plot: How a group of millionaires tried to overthrow FDR. *Jacobin*. https://jacobin.com/2022/01/business-plot-coup-roosevelt-butler-smedley
South, T. (2022b, September 27). Smedley Butler, American empire & war profiteering subject of new book. *Marine Corps Times*.
Sovacool, B. K., Martiskainen, M., Hook, A., & Baker, L. (2019). Decarbonization and its discontents: A critical energy justice perspective on four low-carbon transitions. *Climatic Change, 155*(3–4), 581–619. https://doi.org/10.1007/s10584-019-02521-7
Spash, C. (2015). The future post-growth society. *Development and Change, 46*(2), 366–380.
Spengler, O. (1918). *The decline of the west*. Allen & Unwin.
Srnicek, N. (2016). *Platform capitalism*. Polity.
Stam, E., & Spigel, B. (2018). Entrepreneurial ecosystems. In R. Blackburn, D. De Clercq, & J. Heinonen (Eds.), *The Sage handbook of small business and entrepreneurship* (pp. 407–422). SAGE.
Staples, S. (2000). The relationship between globalization and militarism. *Social Justice, 27*(4 (82)), 18–22.
Steffen, W., Broadgate, W., Deutsch, L., Gaffney, O., & Ludwig, C. (2015a). The trajectory of the anthropocene: The great acceleration. *The Anthropocene Review, 2*(1), 81–98.

Steffen, W., Richardson, K., Rockström, J., Cornell, S., Fetzer, I., et al. (2015b). Planetary boundaries: Guiding human development on a changing planet. *Science, 347*(6223), 1259855.

Stein, J., & Cocco, F. (2024a, July 25). How four U.S. presidents unleashed economic warfare across the globe. *The Washington Post.*

Stein, J., & Cocco, D. (2024b, April 1). The US has sanctioned a third of the world. Here's what you need to know. *The Washington Post.*

Stiglitz, J. (2015, September 12). Why the us could soon be the worlds first former middle class society. *Huff Post Business.*

Stiglitz, J. E. (2009). The anatomy of a murder: Who killed America's economy? *Critical Review, 21*(2–3), 329–339.

Stinchcombe, A. L. (1984). Review of the rise and decline of nations: Economic growth, stagflation, and social rigidities, by M. Olson. *Theory and Society, 13*(4), 613–617.

Stokstad, E. (2024, February 7). European Parliament votes to ease regulation of gene-edited crops. *Science.*

Stone, R. W. (1995). *Satellites and commissars: Strategy and conflict in the politics of soviet-bloc trade.* Princeton University Press.

Streeck, W. (2016). *How will capitalism end? Essays on a failing system.* Verso Books.

Strubell, E., Ganesh, A., & McCallum, A. (2019). Energy and policy considerations for modern deep learning research. *Proceedings of the AAAI conference on artificial intelligence, 34*(9), 13693–13696.

Strunz, S., & Bartkowski, B. (2018). Degrowth, the project of modernity, and liberal democracy. *Journal of Cleaner Production, 196*, 1158–1168.

Sun, Y., Farnsworth, A., Joachimski, M. M., & Wignall, P. B., et al. (2024). Mega El Niño instigated the end-Permian mass extinction. *Science, 385*, 1189–1195.

Supran, G., & Oreskes, N. (2021). Rhetoric and frame analysis of ExxonMobil's climate change communications. *One Earth, 4*(5), 696–719.

Sveikauskas, L. (2007). *R&D and productivity growth: A review of the literature.* Bureau of Labor Statistics Working Paper 408. Bureau of Labor Statistics.

Syvitski, J., Waters, C., Day, J., et al. (2020). Extraordinary human energy consumption and resultant geological impacts beginning around 1950 CE initiated the proposed anthropocene epoch. *Communications Earth and Environment, 1*, 32.

Szirmai, A., Naudé, W., & Goedhuys, M. (2011). *Entrepreneurship, innovation, and economic development.* Oxford University Press.

Taibbi, M. (2009, April 2). How Wall Street is using the bailout to stage a revolution. *Rolling Stone.*

Tainter, J. (1988). *The collapse of complex societies.* Cambridge University Press.

Taplin, J. (2017). *Move fast and break things: How Facebook, Google, and Amazon cornered culture and undermined democracy. Little Brown and Co.*

Tapscott, D. (1995). *The digital economy: Promise and peril in the age of networked intelligence*. McGraw-Hill.

Taylor, M. (2024, September 10). Rich countries silencing climate protest while preaching about rights elsewhere, says study. *The Guardian*.

Tenreyro, S. (2018, January 15). The fall in productivity growth: causes and implications. *Bank of England*.

Terry, P. C. (2015). The Libya intervention (2011): Neither lawful, nor successful. *The Comparative and International Law Journal of Southern Africa, 48*(2), 162–182.

Thakholi, L., Koot, S., & Büscher, B. (2024). Introduction: Fallen from grace? The legacy and state of Southern African Conservation. *Environment and Planning E: Nature and Space, 7*(1), 3–21.

The Economist. (2014, May 15). Planet plutocrat: The countries where politically connected businessmen are most likely to prosper. *The Economist Magazine*.

The Economist. (2023, May 2). The 2023 crony-capitalism index.

The Honest Sorcerer. (2023, May 21). The final countdown: Peak oil is coming fast, and it won't be nice. *Substack* at https://thehonestsorcerer.substack.com

The Honest Sorcerer. (2024, August 26). Downslope. *Medium*.

The Honest Sorcerer. (2024a, July 23). Time of troubles, *Medium*.

The Honest Sorcerer. (2024b, July 2). 2019: Peak (western) civilization. *Medium*.

Theodoraki, C. (2024). Building entrepreneurial ecosystems sustainably. *Foundations and Trends in Entrepreneurship, 20*(4), 384–480.

Thierer, A. (2016). *Permissionless innovation and public policy: A 10-point blueprint*. Mercatus Centre, George Mason University.

Thompson, D. (2022a, March 28). Why U.S. population growth is collapsing. *The Atlantic*.

Thompson, H. (2022b). The geopolitics of energy is reshaping the world again. *Nature, 603*, 364.

Thomson, A. (2008). *U.S. foreign policy towards apartheid South Africa, 1948–1994*. Palgrave Macmillan.

Thurik, A. (2011). From the managed to the entrepreneurial economy: Considerations for developing and emerging economies. In W. Naudé (Ed.), *Entrepreneurship and economic development*. Palgrave Macmillan.

Thurik, A., Stam, E., & Audretsch, D. (2013). The rise of the entrepreneurial economy and the future of dynamic capitalism. *Technovation, 33*(8–9), 302–310.

Tirole, J. (2021). Digital dystopia. *American Economic Review, 111*(6), 2007–2048.

Todd, E. (2024). *La Défaite de l'Occident*. Gallimard.

Toft, M. D. (2018a). Kinetic diplomacy: Covert operations as a tool of US foreign policy. *Security Studies, 27*(1), 139–165.

Toft, M.D. (2018b, May 14). The dangerous rise of kinetic diplomacy. *War on the Rocks*.

Tollefson, J. (2023, October 6). US science agencies on track to hit 25-year funding low. *Nature*.
Tooze, A. (2022a). Chartbook #94: Ukraine and the shock doctrine. *Chartbook*. https://adamtooze.substack.com/p/chartbook-94-ukraine-and-the-shock
Tooze, A. (2022b, October 28). Welcome to the world of the polycrisis. *Financial Times*.
Torres, E.P. (2021a, October 19). Against longtermism, *Aeon*.
Torres, E.P. (2021b, July 28). The dangerous ideas of "longtermism" and "existential risk". *Current Affairs*.
Tory, M. (2023). Britain PLC in liquidation, 2006-? *ONDRA*. Available at: https://www.ondra.com/assets/pdfs/Britainplc_131023.pdf
Toynbee, A. J. (1948). *Civilization on trial*. Oxford University Press.
Tricontinental. (2024, June). *The Congolese fight for their own wealth* [Dossier no. 77]. https://thetricontinental.org/dossier-77-congolese-fight-for-wealth/
Tricontinental. (2023). US military presence in Africa: AFRICOM's objectives and neo-colonial ambitions. https://www.thetricontinental.org/studies/dossier-53-africom/
Trincado, E. (2010). The current relevance of Rosa Luxemburg's thought. *Socialist Studies, 6*(2), 141–159.
Truscello, M. (2018). Catastrophism and Its Critics: On the New Genre of Environmentalist Documentary Film. In J. Jagodzinski (Ed.), *Interrogating the Anthropocene. Palgrave Studies in Educational Futures*. Palgrave Macmillan, Cham.
Turchin, A., & Denkenberger, D. (2020). Classification of global catastrophic risks connected with artificial intelligence. *AI & Society, 35*, 147–163.
Turchin, P., & Gavrilets, S. (2009). Evolution of complex hierarchical societies. *Social Evolution & History, 8*(2), 167–198.
Turchin, P. (2023). *End times: Elites, counter-elites, and the path of political disintegration*. Penguin.
Turing, A. M. (1936). On computable numbers, with an application to the Entscheidungsproblem. *Proceedings of the London Mathematical Society, 2*(1), 230–265.
Türk, V. (2023, November 1). Protect the 'right to science' for people and the planet. *Nature*.
Turley, J. (2014, January 11). Big money behind war: the military-industrial complex. *AlJazeera*.
Turner, G. (2014). *Is global collapse imminent? An updated comparison of the limits to growth with historical data*. (MSSI Research Paper No. 4). Melbourne Sustainable Society Institute, The University of Melbourne. https://www.researchgate.net/publication/267751719
Turse, N. (2008). *The complex: How the military invades our everyday lives*. Henry Holt and Company.

Tverberg, G. (2024a, January 15). 2024: Too many things going wrong. *Blog: Our Finite World.*
Tverberg, G. (2024b, July 22). How does the economy really work? *Our Finite World.*
Ulfstein, G., & Christiansen, H. F. (2013). The legality of the NATO bombing in Libya. *International and Comparative Law Quarterly, 62*(1), 159–171.
Umbrello, S. (2021a). AI Winter. In M. Klein & P. Frana (Eds.), *Encyclopedia of artificial intelligence: The past, present, and future of AI* (pp. 7–8).
Umbrello, S. (2021b). *Why and how we should regulate generative AI.* The Gradient.
UNCTAD. (2021). *Digital economy report 2021: Cross-border data flows and development: For whom the data flow.* United Nations Conference on Trade and Development.
Urbano, D., Aparici, S., & Audretsch, D. (2019). Twenty-five years of research on institutions, entrepreneurship, and economic growth: What has been learned? *Small Business Economics, 53*(1), 21–49.
Vakulchuk, R., Overland, I., & Scholten, D. (2020). Renewable energy and geopolitics: A review. *Renewable and Sustainable Energy Reviews, 122,* 109547.
Vakulenko, S. (2024, May 16). *Russia has the resources for a long war in Ukraine.* Carnegie Russia Eurasia Center, Carnegie Endowment for International Peace.
Valdespino, G. (2023, March 12). How France has continued exploiting its former African colonies. *Jacobin.*
Van Nieuwkoop, M. (2019, June 17). Do the costs of the global food system outweigh its monetary value? *World Bank Blog.*
Van Noorden, R. (2023, November 6). How big is science's fake-paper problem? *Nature.*
Vance, Z. (1951). A statement on Korea. *Congressional Record, 97*(Appendix, Part 10), A4058–A4061.
Varoufakis, Y. (2021, June 28). Techno-Feudalism is taking over. *Project Syndicate.*
Varoufakis, Y. (2023). *Technofeudalism: What killed capitalism.* Penguin.
Varoufakis, Y. (2024a). The EU is becoming an authoritarian superstate. *Project Syndicate.* https://www.project-syndicate.org/commentary/european-union-becoming-authoritarian-by-yanis-varoufakis-2024-03
Varoufakis, Y. (2024b, January 3). What is the point of NATO? *DiEM25.*
Velez-Ginorio, J. (2019, October 5). Artificial intelligence isn't very intelligent and won't be any time soon. *Salon.*
Verso Books. (2024). Enshittification: The 2023 digital word of the year. *Verso Books Blog.*
Vietor, R., Rivkin, J., & Seminerio, J. (2008). *The offshoring of America.* Harvard Business School Working Paper 9–708-030.
Vollset, S. E., et al. (2020). Fertility, mortality, migration, and population scenarios for 195 countries and territories from 2017 to 2100: a forecasting analysis for the Global Burden of Disease Study. *The Lancet, 396,* 1285–1306.

Von Foerster, H., Mora, P. M., & Amio, L. (1960). Doomsday: Friday, 13 November A. D. 2026. *Science, 132*(3436), 1291–1295.

Wagner, J. (2007). Exports and productivity: A survey of the evidence from firm-level data. *The World Economy, 30*(1), 60–82.

Wagner, K. (2023, August 7/14). Lessons from the catastrophic failure of the metaverse. *The Nation.*

Wallis, J. J. (1983). Review of the rise and decline of nations: Economic growth, stagflation, and social rigidities, by M. Olson. *The Journal of Business, 56*(4), 566–568.

Wang, H., Fu, T., Du, Y., et al. (2023). Scientific discovery in the age of artificial intelligence. *Nature, 620,* 47–60.

Ward, J., Sutton, P., Werner, A., Costanza, R., Mohr, S., & Simmons, C. (2016). Is decoupling GDP growth from environmental impact possible? *PLoS One, 11*(10), e0164733.

Watkins, T. (2024, May 18). Killing St. George. *Blog: The Consciousness of Sheep.*

Watts, J. (2024, April 4). Just 57 companies linked to 80% of greenhouse gas emissions since 2016. *The Guardian.*

Wautier, J.-B. (2024). The Profit Trap. *Project Syndicate.* June 28.

Weinzierl, M. (2023). Expanding economic activity in space may offer a solution to secular stagnation. *Proc Natl Acad Sci USA, 120*(43), e2221347120.

Weitzman, M. (1998). Recombinant growth. *Quarterly Journal of Economics, 113,* 331–360.

Wennekers, S., Uhlaner, L. M., & Thurik, R. (2002). Entrepreneurship and its conditions: A macro perspective. *International Journal of Entrepreneurship Education, 1*(1), 25–64.

West, G. (2017). *Scale: The universal laws of life and death in organisms, cities and companies.* Weidenfeld and Nicolson.

Wezeman, P. D., Djokic, K., George, M., Hussain, Z., & Wezeman, S. T. (2024, March). Trends in international arms transfers, 2023. *SIPRI Factsheet.*

Wheeler, R. (1952a, August). A life of disagreement. *The Atlantic.*

Wheeler, S. (Ed.). (1952b). *The impact of science on society.* Columbia University Press.

Wiblin, R., & Harris, S. (2023). The most important century: Guest: Ian Morris. *80,000 Hours (blog).* https://80000hours.org/podcast/episodes/ian-morris-the-most-important-century/

Wiedmann, T., et al. (2020). Scientists warning on affluence. *Nature Communications, 11*(1), 3107.

Wiedmann, T., Schandl, H., Lenzen, M., Moran, D., Suh, S., West, J., & Kanemoto, K. (2015). The material footprint of nations. *PNAS, 112*(20), 6271–6276.

Wiklund, J., & Shepherd, D. (2003). Aspiring for and achieving growth: The moderating role of resources and opportunities. *Journal of Management Studies, 40,* 1919–1941.

Willcock, S., Cooper, G. S., Addy, J., & Dearing, J. A. (2023). *Earlier Collapse of Anthropocene Ecosystems driven by Multiple Faster and Noisier Drivers*. Nature Sustainability, June.

Wilbert, M. (2022, August 1). That era is over! This is our reality. In *Noam Chomsky versus collapse theory - A new "debate of the century"*. Dialektika.

Williams, M. J. (2024). *From Kabul to Kyiv: The long shadow of NATO's war in Afghanistan, CSDS Policy Brief, 13/2024*. Centre for Security, Diplomacy and Strategy.

Williamson, A. (2007a, June 28). The Hobbled Hegemon. *The Economist*.

Williamson, D. (2007b). The age of the warfare state. *Review of Radical Political Economics, 39*(4), 501–520.

Windegger, F., & Spash, C. (2022). Reconceptualising freedom in the 21st century: Neoliberalism vs degrowth. *New Political Economy, 28*(4), 554–573.

Winters, J. A., & Page, B. I. (2009). Oligarchy in the United States? *Perspectives on Politics, 7*(04), 731–751.

Wirtz, M. (2013). The role of social entrepreneurship in a degrowth economy. *Sozialwissenschaften und Berufspraxis, 36*(1), 68–74.

Witze, A. (2024, March 6). Geologists reject the Anthropocene as Earth's new epoch - After 15 years of debate. *Nature*.

WMO (2023). *WMO Global Annual to Decadal Climate Update* (Target years: 2023–2027). World Meteorological Society.

Wolf, R. (2023). *The crisis of democratic capitalism*. Penguin.

Wolff, R. (2022, April 13). The role of capitalism in the war in Ukraine. *Brave New Europe*.

Wolff, R. D. (2024, September 9). The decline of the U.S. Empire: Where is it taking us all? *CounterPunch*.

Wong, E., & Ismay, J. (2022, March 8). US speeds up weapons for Taiwan as hopes for 'porcupine' strategy grow. *The New York Times*.

Wong, J., & Cantor, M. (2019, June 27). How to speak Silicon Valley: 53 essential tech-bro terms explained. *The Guardian*.

Wong, M. (2023, June 2). AI Doomerism is a Decoy. *The Atlantic*.

Wood, P. (2024, October 5). Israel is reshaping the Middle East in its favour. *The Spectator*.

Woolf, S. (2023). Falling behind: The growing gap in life expectancy between the United States and other countries. *American Journal of Public Health, 113*, 970–980.

Wright, Q. (1965). *A study of war*. University of Chicago Press.

Wright, R. (2024). Alex Karp and the militarization of tech. *Nonzero Newsletter*. https://nonzero.substack.com/

Wrigley, E. (2013). Energy and the English industrial revolution. *Philosophical Transactions of the Royal Society A, 371*, 20110568.

Yergin, D. (1990). *The prize: The epic quest for oil, money, and power*. Simon & Schuster.

Yermakov, V. (2024). *Follow the Money: Understanding Russia's oil and gas revenues*. Oxford Institute for Energy Studies, March.

Yong, E. (2022). America was in an early-death crisis long before COVID. *The Atlantic, 21*.

Young, A. A. (1928). Increasing returns and economic progress. *The Economic Journal, 38*(12), 527–542.

Yu, E., Luu, B. V., & Chen, C. H. (2020). Greenwashing in environmental, social and governance disclosures. *Research in International Business and Finance, 52*, 101192.

Yudkowski, E. (2023, March 29). Pausing AI developments isn't enough. We need to shut it all down. *Time Magazine*.

Zabala-Iturriagagoitia, J., Aparicio, J., Ortiz, L., Carayannis, E., & Grigoroudis, E. (2021). The productivity of national innovation systems in Europe: Catching up or falling behind? *Technovation, 102*, 102215.

Zeihan, P. (2022). *The end of the world is just the beginning*. Harper Business.

Žižek, S. (2024a). Sudan: The latest battleground in the new scramble for Africa. *The Guardian*. https://www.theguardian.com/commentisfree/2024/04/19/sudan-the-latest-battleground-in-the-new-scramble-for-africa

Žižek, S. (2024b, October 25). Saving democracy from itself. *Project Syndicate*.

Zollmann, F. (2024). A war foretold: How Western mainstream news media omitted NATO eastward expansion as a contributing factor to Russia's 2022 invasion of the Ukraine. *Media, War & Conflict, 17*(3), 373–392.

Zuboff, S. (2015). Big other: Surveillance capitalism and the prospects of an information civilization. *Journal of Information Technology, 30*, 75–89.

Zuboff, S. (2019). *The age of surveillance capitalism: The fight for a human future at the new frontier of power*. Public Affairs Publishers.

Zubok, V. M. (2023). Myths and realities of Putinism and NATO expansion. In J. Goldgeier & J. R. I. Shifrinson (Eds.), *Evaluating NATO enlargement*. Palgrave Macmillan.

Zucman, G. (2024, May 3). It's time to tax the billionaires. *The New York Times*.

Index[1]

NUMBERS AND SYMBOLS
9/11 attacks, 130

A
ABCD companies, 71, 72
Achilles' Lance, 22
Advanced Research Projects Agency (ARPA), 79, 80
Afghanistan, 130, 140
Africa, 131, 133, 134
AI Doomerism, 49
Amazon, 61, 72, 74, 126, 161
American Dream, 29, 30
American Exceptionalism, 198
American South, 63
Amin, Samir, 196
Amnesty International, 140
Angolan Civil War/Angola's civil war, 121, 131
Anthropocene, 1, 5, 50
Anthropocene Traps, 30, 50–53
Apple, 61, 72
The Apprentice, 29
Archer-Daniels-Midland Company, 60, 71
Arrow, Kenneth, 84
Ars Moriendi, 174, 197–198
Artificial Intelligence, 13, 27, 49, 170
Attack of the Killer Clowns, 24, 39, 95

B
Bab al-Mandeb Strait, 144
Babbage, Charles, 86
BAE Systems, 153
Banana Wars, 128
The Bankers, 62, 67
Bardi, Ugo, 179
Belt and Road Initiative, 181, 186
Bezos, Jeff, 61, 75
Biden, Joseph, 116, 179, 190
Big Oil, 62, 115, 118, 143
Reparations due, 118

[1] Note: Page numbers followed by 'n' refer to notes.

Bik, Elisabeth, 91
BlackRock, 34, 42, 60, 61, 83
Blakeley, Grace, 73
Boeing, 73, 75, 153
Bolsonaro, Jair, 24, 95
Bombenomics, 149
Borrell, Josep, 154
Boxer Rebellion, 128
The Breakdown of Nations, 193
Bretton Woods institutions, 51
Brexit, 74
BRICS+, 142, 168, 185–187, 197
British Empire, 106, 185
Broligarchs, 162
Brown University, 131
Brzezinski, Zbigniew, 146
Bucharest Summit, 138
Buffet, Warren, 75
Bullshit Jobs, 48
Bunge, 60, 71
Bush, George W., 131
Business Plot, 129
Butler, Major General Smedley, 127, 128

C
The Campaign on Digital Ethics, 162
Cargill, 60, 71
Carter, Jimmy, 146
Carthage must be destroyed, 185
Cato Institute, 132
CBS, 62
Century of National Humiliation, 147
ChatGPT, 158, 159
China, 13, 130, 146, 157, 163, 168, 185, 186, 188
Chomsky, Noam, 148
Climate Activism, 76
Climate change, 35, 99, 174
Climate Rights International, 76
Climate tipping points, 111, 113, 182
Cliodynamics, 178
Club of Rome, 2, 179

Cold War, 129, 131, 146, 151, 167, 176, 186
Collapse
   definition of, 8
Collateralized Debt Obligations (CDOs), 67–68
Colonialism, 39, 41
Congressional Budget Office (CBO), 59, 184
Corbyn, Jeremy, 76
Cost of Living Crisis, 182
Cotton gin, 63
Covid-19, 91, 103
Credit Rating Agencies, 68
Crisis of early deaths, 7, 32
Crowded Safari, 186
Cultural Drift, 177, 194
Culture wars, 190
Currency of Life, 100

D
Dagalo, Mohamed Hamdan, 134
Dark Fleet, 165
Davos Man, 76
Deaths of despair, 7, 32, 194
Declinists, 195
Declinists vs. Optimists, 195
De-dollarization, 188
Defense Advanced Research Projects Agency (DARPA), 79, 80
Degrowth, 14, 27, 202, 203, 205, 208–210
Democratic Republic of Congo (DRC), 122
Demographic danger zone, 194
Derrida, Jacques, 88
Diamond, Jared, 5
Digital tokens, 38
Diverse Economies Approach, 202
Doomsday, 192
Doughnut Economy, 202
Duterte, Rodrigo Roa, 95

E

Earth Overshoot Day, 37
Earth System Boundaries (ESB), 35
Earth Systems, 174
East Germany, 93
Ecological Overshoot, 35, 42
The Economist Magazine, 41, 66
Egypt, 132
Eisenhower Doctrine, 144
Eisenhower, Dwight D., 9, 149
Elite Overproduction, 178
Energy Blindness, 100–101
Energy Cannibalism, 114, 181
Energy-Conflict Nexus, 98, 119–122
Energy Decent, 106
Energy-Economy Nexus, 98
Energy-Environment Nexus, 98
Energy Return to Energy Invested, 49
Energy Trap, 98
Enlightenment, The, 10
Enshittification, 48
Entrepreneurial Ecosystems, 32, 206–209
Entrepreneurs, 32
Entrepreneurship, 6, 43, 83, 106, 204
the West's obsession with, 24
Epistemic relativism, 88
Erdogan, Recep Tayip, 95
EU Roadmap on Climate and Defence, 155
Euroasia, 146, 147
European Parliament, 57, 89
ExxonMobil, 89, 116

F

Ferguson, Niall, 184
Fiat banking, 25
Financial crises, 208
Fink, Larry, 42
First Law of Venture Capital, 25
Fischer, Joschka, 145
The Food Barons, 60, 62, 71
Foucault, Michel, 88
Fox, 62

G

Gandhi, Mohandas, 6n2
Gangsters of Capitalism, 127
Gaza, 145, 160, 166, 191
General Dynamics, 75, 153
General Electric, 66
General Motors, 70
Genocide Convention, 160
Gerontocracy, 190
Gilded Age, 58
Global Financial Crisis (GFC), 24, 66–68, 87, 103
Global Mean Surface Temperature (GMST), 110
Global Positioning System (GPS), 80
Global South, 14, 39, 64, 164, 186, 204
Google, 48, 61, 85, 126, 161
Gorz, André, 203
The Grand Chessboard, 146
Great Acceleration, 5, 11, 12
Great Compression, 58
Great Depression, 58, 68
Great Divergence, 10, 39
Great Neoliberal Experiment, 64
Great Stagnation, 2, 10, 24, 43, 47, 80, 87, 102, 176, 184
Great Take-Off, 2, 12
Green growth, 35
Green Imperialism, 121
Greenland Ice Sheet (GIS), 111, 112
Grow-or-Die (Rule), 21, 25–27
Growth Spiral, 24, 25, 27
Growth Trap, 10
Gulf War, 121
Guns, Germs and Steel, 5
Guns-Oil-Oligarchy nexus, 2, 17
Guns Oligarchs, 61

H
Hanson, Robin, 177
Heartland Theory, 146, 147
Heinberg, Richard, 181
Hezbollah, 121
High-growth firms (HGFs), 23, 28
 misplaced obsession with, 33
Holocene, 111, 112
Horizon Europe, 80
Hotez, Peter, 88
House Budget Committee, 104
Houthi Rebels, 144
Hydrocarbon Age, 101–107

I
IBM, 61
Ibn Saud, Abd al-Aziz, 119
IMF, 40
Imperialism, 26, 39, 208
Individual Material Power Index, 57, 60
Industrial Revolution, 1, 10, 44, 100, 108
Infrastructure Lock-In, 182
In-Q-Tel, 160
Institute for Economics and Peace (IEP), 167
Institute for Policy Studies, 59
Intergovernmental Panel on Climate Change (IPCC), 110
International Court of Justice (ICJ), 191
International Criminal Court (ICC), 138
International Union of Geological Sciences, 5n1
iPhone, 14
Iran, 147
Iraq, 130
Israel, 40, 143, 146, 147, 160

J
Jevons Paradox, 39, 205
Johnson, Boris, 24, 141, 156
JPMorgan Chase, 61

K
Karp, Alex, 157
Katz, Jonathan M., 127, 128
Kazan Declaration, 186
Kennedy, John F., 79, 86
Kennedy, Paul, 176
Kingsnorth, Paul, 190
Koch Industries, 61
Korean War, 167
Kotkin, Joel, 185
Kübler-Ross Grief Cycle, 179

L
La Défaite de l'Occident, 178
Lehman Brothers, 68, 72
Leonardo, 153
Lenin, Vladimir, 26, 187
Limits to Growth (LtG) study, 2, 22, 180
Lincoln, Abraham, 63
Local Currency Settlements (LCS), 188
Lockheed Martin, 153
Louis Dreyfus, 60, 71
Lumumba, Patrice, 122
Luxemburg, Rosa, 26, 211
Luxemburg thesis
 of Rosa Luxemburg, 26
Lyotard, Jean-François, 88

M
MacCormack-Dickstein Committee, 129
Mackinder, Halford, 146

Machine Learning, 48
Mad Max, 22
Maduro, Nicolás, 164
Malthus, Thomas, 177n2, 192
Marshall Plan, 129
Marx, Karl, 4–6, 26, 41, 203
Mass Extinction Events, 113
Material Footprint, 35
Mauna Loa Observatory, 109
Maximum Power Principle, 104, 115
McCoy, Alfred W., 188
Mearsheimer, John J., 139, 141
The Media Moguls, 62
Meloni, Giorgia, 95
Meta, 61
Microsoft, 61, 126, 161
Middle East, 142
Middle Eastern Oil, 133
Militarisation of Africa, 131–134
Military-Digital Complex, 80, 85
Military Industrial Complex, 9, 61, 63, 126, 127, 153, 173
Military Intervention Project, 130
Military Trap, 150
Mobutu Sese Seko, 131
Modern Monetary Theory, 208
Modi, Narendra, 95
Moonshot, 79, 80, 86
Musk, Elon, 61, 75

N
NASA, 79, 80, 86
Nasser, Gamal Abdel, 143
National Defense Industrial Strategy, 149
National Health Service, 74
NATO, 130, 135, 139, 142, 150, 154, 161, 168, 191
Neoliberal capitalism, 3, 6, 32, 55, 183, 187, 201
Neoliberal global capitalism, 3

Neoliberalism, 24, 29
Neoliberalism capitalism, 23
New Development Bank, 186, 187
New Genomic Techniques, 89
New Seven Sisters, 116
Netanyahu, Benjamin, 24, 95
Niger, 133, 134
North Korea, 147
Northrop Grumman, 153
Nye, Bill, 88

O
Oakes, Walter, 129
Obama, Barack, 138
Odysseus, 86
Offensive Realism, 139
Oil, 99, 105
Oligarchs, 61, 94, 178
Oligarchy, 8, 56, 58, 153, 174
Olson, Mancur, 6
OpenAI, 158, 159
Orbán, Viktor, 24, 95
Ossified Economy, 21, 87

P
Palantir, 126, 157, 161
Paris Agreement, 111
Peak Oil, 2, 97, 104, 106, 108, 173
Peloponnesian War, 168
Pentagon, 165
Permanent War Economy, 55, 126, 127, 129, 130, 148, 160, 163, 167, 173, 174, 188
Permanent Warfare Economy, 162–163
Permian-Triassic extinction, 108
Permissionless innovation, 78
Petro-Aggression, 120
Petrostates, 104, 105, 125
Philippine-American War, 128
Piketty, Thomas, 6

Plutocracy, 8, 57, 62
Polanyi, Karl, 42
Politics of Exhaustion, 189
Polycrisis, 3, 42
Population growth
  and societal collapse, 177
Populism, 191
Post-growth, 27
  economics, 202
  moral-cultural system, 210
Postmodernism, 88
Powell, Lewis (Jr.), 74
Power Elite, 8
Princeton University, 63
Putin, Vladimir, 95, 136, 138

R
Reform environmentalism, 37
Republican Party, 65, 169
Resource Nationalism, 122
Responsible AI in the Military
  Domain, 161
Revolving door, 57, 69, 204
Rheinmetall AG, 153
Rich, Jeff, 168
Rockefeller, David, 65
Rolling Stone Magazine, 70
Roman Empire, 1, 5, 168, 176, 179
Reagan, Ronald, 40, 64, 67
Roosevelt, Franklin D., 119, 129
Roosevelt, Theodore, 128
Royal Dutch Shell, 115
Russell, Bertrand, 162
Russia, 135, 136, 138, 141, 147, 185, 186
Rutte, Mark, 138n13

S
Sachs, Jeffrey D., 139, 141, 141n16
Second Stone Age, 210, 211

Seneca Cliff, 180
Seneca Effect, 179
Seneca, Lucius, 179
Seneca Oil Company, 108
Seven Sisters, 115
Shale gas, 105
Siberian Traps, 108
Silicon Valley, 29, 157
Silicon Valley Hawks, 156–157, 161
Silicon Valley Mindset, 29
Sixth mass extinction, 113
Societal collapse
  definition of, 175
Soviet Union, 4, 16, 70, 78, 82, 84, 86, 87, 91, 92, 126, 184
SpaceX, 61
Spanish-American War, 128
Spengler, Oswald, 176
Sputnik, 78–80, 82, 85
Stalin, Josef, 88
Standard Oil, 115
Starbucks, 61
Starlink, 126, 161
State Street, 34, 60, 61, 83
Steady-State Economy, 202
Stockholm International Peace
  Research Institute (SIPRI), 152
Stoltenberg, Jens, 142
Suez Canal, 143
Surveillance Capitalism, 93
Sustainable Development Goals
  (SDGs), 14

T
Tactical nuclear weapons, 125
Tainter, Joseph, 176
Taiwan, 147, 191
Taliban, 179
Tech Bros, 72
Technofeudalism, 49, 72
The Technofeudalists, 62, 72

Technological solutionism, 201
Tesla, 61
Thatcher, Margaret, 40, 64, 67
Thermo-nuclear conflagration, 174
Thiel, Peter, 61
Thucydides Trap, 127, 167, 168
Time Warner, 62
Todd, Emmanuel, 178
Tony Blair, 57
Tooth Fairy Syndrome, 100
Tooze, Adam, 139
Tragedy of the Commons, 52
Tricontinental, 132, 186, 196
Trilateral Commission, 65, 74
Trump, Donald, 24, 29, 61, 74, 95, 162, 190
Tuft University, 130
Türk, Volker, 89
Tyson, Neil deGrasse, 88

U
Ukraine, 16, 136, 138, 139, 141, 149, 152, 169, 178, 191
Ukrainian Oligarchs, 76
US-AFRICOM, 131–133
US Civil War, 63
US Congress, 164
US Federal Reserve, 103
US Library of Congress, 115
US sanctions, 164
US Supreme Court, 74
US Treasury, 127
US War in Afghanistan, 130

V
Vanguard, 34, 60, 61, 83
Varoufakis, Yanis, 72, 139, 141, 198
Venture Capital, 159

Viacom, 62
Vietnam War, 167

W
Wagner Group, 134
Walmart, 61
War Economy, 56, 126, 129
  definition of, 9
Warfare Economy, 152
War in Gaza, 144
War on Terror, 130, 131
Washington Consensus, 40
Washington Post, 163
Weapons of Mass Destruction, 130
Welfare State, 31
Wells Fargo, 61
Western Offshoots, 5, 10, 176
Wilders, Geert, 24
Wolff, Richard D., 185
World Bank, 40, 44
World Economic Forum, 76
World War I, 184
World War II, 1, 27, 64, 107, 126, 129, 150, 164, 167, 191
Wright, Robert, 157

X
X, 61

Y
Yemen, 144, 146

Z
Zeihan, Peter, 196
Zero-Sum Economy, 12, 45, 46
Zuckerberg, Mark, 61